D0525453

LIFE STYLE

An account of the genesis and aims of the Life Style
Movement and what each one of us can do to 'live
more simply that all of us may simply live'.

LIFE STYLE

A Parable of Sharing

by

A. H. Dammers

TURNSTONE PRESS LIMITED
Wellingborough, Northamptonshire

First published in 1982

British Library Cataloguing in Publication Data

Dammers, A. H.
  Life style.
  1. Christian life
  I. Title
  248.4   BV4501.2

  ISBN 0-85500-159-3
  ISBN 0-85500-160-7 Pbk.

Typeset by Harper Phototypesetters, Northampton.
Printed in Great Britain by Nene Litho,
Earls Barton, Northamptonshire, and bound by
Weatherby Woolnough, Wellingborough,
Northamptonshire.

CONTENTS

CHAPTER ONE

LIVE MORE SIMPLY THAT ALL OF US MAY SIMPLY LIVE

The Corrymeela Children

After the destruction of the old Coventry Cathedral by fire bombs in 1940 a young serviceman visiting the ruins picked up three of the great nails which had fastened together the roof beams. He formed them into a cross. This original Cross of Nails became a sign of the ecumenical ministry of reconcilation and renewal which Coventry Cathedral shares with a network of Christian centres all over the world.

Some years ago I took one of these Crosses of Nails to the Corrymeela Community in Northern Ireland. Its members, both Protestant and Roman Catholic, 'are called together as a Community to be an instrument of God's peace, to serve our society and to share in the life of the Church.'[1]

Despite the remoteness of Corrymeela on the beautiful North Antrim coast some five hundred people assembled there for the open-air service at which the Cross of Nails was presented. We ended the brief and simple service by shaking hands with those around us. Afterwards a Presbyterian minister remarked with tears in his eyes, 'I have been a minister for over thirty years, but this is the first time I have ever shaken hands with a Roman Catholic priest.'

That handshake was 'a parable of sharing'[2] a sign of the cultural and spiritual sharing to which the Corrymeela Community is so effectively committed. Later I took part in the first residential course for school pupils ever to be held at Corrymeela. Some forty thirteen- and fourteen-year-olds from areas of special need in Belfast assembled with their teachers to study the geography of the coastal area. Half of them were from two Roman Catholic schools and the other half Protestants from two maintained schools. One Roman Catholic girl told me that she had been punched in the face by a member of a street gang of Protestant youths. A boy told me that he had on several occasions been paid fifty pence a time by IRA agents to throw stones at the soldiers. Another wrote afterwards about Corrymeela: 'At first I was afraid to go, as I thought there would be fighting. But it wasn't like that at all. We found out that they are just like us.'

Like everyone else, I was given a job to do—leading an Epilogue each evening. For one I had brought an Easter Egg with me, the season being appropriate. An egg makes an excellent teaching aid on the theme of new life and I proposed, as the climax of my epilogue, to break it open and share it around. But it looked to me a very small egg when I called for a plate, peeled off the silver paper and broke the hollow egg in two. With a silent prayer I handed the plate to the front row, inviting everyone to break off a piece and pass it on. At the end about a third was left and we voted unanimously to give it to Anna, the Corrymeela cook. It was like a celebration of the Holy Communion. I shall never forget the simple lesson those children were teaching me that evening; that when resources are limited there is enough for everyone's need, but not enough for anyone's greed.

I have begun as from time to time I mean to go on, with a personal experience. For this has to be a personal book. Within the limits imposed by a one-way means of communication I shall try to establish a relationship with you, the reader, sufficiently personal to enable me to invite you either to undertake or to reaffirm a personal commitment 'to live more simply that all of us may simply live'. My own comfortable life style ill equips me for the task. Yet, as André Frossard wrote: 'In the end I became convinced that a witness, however unworthy, who happens to know the truth, owes it to himself to speak out, hoping that the evidence, because of its intrinsic merit, will gain a credence which the witness himself would not deserve on his own account.'[3]

Frossard's book is about himself and God. Mine is about you and me, members together of the one Human Family. Yet since I too am a believer, I would not have been able wholly to exclude God, even if I had wished to do so. But He comes into the story courteously enough, I trust, as is His custom, in no way over-ruling the liberty of those who do not accept that He exists.

The personal commitment to which I am inviting you is first

and foremost a commitment to a truth, to an idea whose time has come and which therefore nothing can stop. Using the social categories of his day, Lord Rutherford once observed that 'a theory is only good if it is simple enough to be understood by a barmaid'. Thirteen years earlier Albert Einstein had written: 'A theory is the more impressive the greater the simplicity of its premises, the more kinds of things it relates together, and the more extended the areas of its applicability.'[4]

The simple yet profound truth which the Corrymeela children so generously and so sensibly enacted is that wherever and whenever resources are limited they have to be shared. The scope of this truth—it is more than a theory—extends to the development and even to the survival of the whole human family. Without, I hope, losing its compelling simplicity, this truth may be restated in global terms as follows:

1. The resources of the Earth for sustaining the development of the growing Human Family are not inexhaustible and therefore have to be conserved for our own and for future generations.
2. The distribution of these resources among the members of the Human Family is grossly inequitable. They have to be distributed more fairly.
3. To enable a more equitable distribution of these resources and their necessary conservation, those who are at present consuming inordinately or even substantially more than their share have to consume less; in other words, 'to live more simply that all of us may simply live'.
4. As commitment to such a voluntary simplicity of life runs counter to very powerful human instincts and inclinations, we must nourish it by at least an equal motivation in its favour.

The Life Style Commitment

To nourish the commitment of those who accept this fourfold proposition as both self-evident and urgently significant, the Life Style Movement has produced the Life Style Commitment which I am inviting you, but only when you have read this book, to make your own. This Commitment is prefaced by two paragraphs under the heading 'Life Style':

The Life Style Movement offers a Voluntary Common Discipline to those who are committed to a more equitable distribution of the Earth's resources among the members of the Human Family and to the conservation and development of those resources for our own and future generations.

Life Style offers guidelines rather than rules. Those who accept in principle the Commitment inside this leaflet are invited to join the Community of the Life Style Commitment by sending the return card to the Movement's Central Correspondent, the Dean of Bristol, Bristol Cathedral, Bristol BS1 5TJ.

The Commitment itself has seven points:

1. I recognize that the peaceful development and perhaps the survival of the Human Family are threatened by:
   The injustice of extremes of poverty and wealth.
   The excessive growth of population.
   The widespread pollution of natural resources.
   The profligate consumption of these resources by a substantial minority.
2. I therefore propose to:
   Live more simply that all of us may simply live, understanding that my greed may already be denying another's need.
   Change my own life style as may be necessary, before demanding that others change theirs. Give more freely that all of us may be free to give.
   Accept that those who are poorer than I can teach me a style of life which offers a practical alternative to the values and assumptions of a competitive, alienated and narrowly materialistic society.
   Enjoy to the full such material goods and available services as are compatible with this commitment. Enjoy also the consequent freedom from the tyranny of possessions.
3. I pledge my active support to such political and social action and to such economic policies as tend to conserve, develop and redistribute the Earth's resources for the benefit of the whole Human Family.
4. I intend to:
   Make my decisions on what to buy, how much to spend and what to do without as one who wants fair shares for all.
   Resist the pressures of advertising to buy what in fact I do not need or want.

Where possible, challenge wasteful packaging, built-in obsolescence and bad workmanship. Encourage the repair, renovation, re-use or recycling of materials and products as may be appropriate.

5. I shall decide (or have decided) what percentage of my net disposable income to give away for the benefit of those in need, especially in the developing continents. I shall review this decision regularly and intend to make this amount a first charge on the way I spend the money at my disposal. As an effective sign of this intention I shall decide (or have decided) whether regularly to do without a meal and gladly to give to the hungry the money so saved.

6. I intend:

To be generous without ostentation and hospitable without extravagance. Neither to eat nor to drink to excess, nor to consume what in my judgement depends for its production on the deprivation or the exploitation of the poor.

To make time in my life for reflection; for the deepening of my understanding of the world in which I live and of the people in it; for recreation and for the sharing of simple pleasures with others; and for sufficient sleep for good health and good temper.

In my proper concern for the whole Human Family not to neglect those near and dear to me or any others towards whom I have particular obligations.

7. As opportunity arises, I undertake to:

Commend this Commitment to others and invite them to join the Community of the Life Style Commitment by sending a card to the Central Correspondent.

Join a 'Life Style Cell' or with others form a new one, to meet regularly for mutual support, study and action.

Alternatively invite a friend to support and advise me from time to time in the working out of this Commitment.

'A Postscript for Christian Believers' follows:

The Life Style Movement is for all members of the Human Family without any reservation, whatever their creed or lack of it.

It so happens, however, that many of those who accept the Life Style Commitment are committed also to the Christian Faith.

The supplementary Commitment which follows may be found useful to them.

1. I intend to nourish God's gift of faith in me and the practice of the Life Style Commitment within it:

   by regular prayer, faithful witness, study of the Scriptures and participation in public worship. For most Christians this means regular and joyful sharing in the Eucharist.

2. As a sign of this intention I propose regularly to pray 'Give us this day our daily bread' as an intercession for the whole Human Family; and to do what I can towards the fulfilment of this prayer.

3. I commit myself also to work and pray for such changes within the Church as will promote an inner renewal of the Spirit; the mission of Christ in and for the world; the visible and effectual unity of God's People; and social justice, human dignity and freedom from oppression for all.

Three Basic Questions

In his seminal work, *The Critique of Pure Reason*, Emmanuel Kant proposes three basic questions: 'What can I know? What ought I to do? What may I hope?' Kant no doubt was concerned with theories of knowledge and truth (epistemology), moral imperatives, ultimate values and similarly high philosophical matters. Yet, as Hans Kung points out, these 'ultimate questions which—according to Kant—combine all the interests of human reason, are also the first questions, the commonplace questions.'[6] They serve our present purpose to perfection as we seek to verify the idea whose time I believe has come and which therefore nothing can stop. What can I know? What ought I to do? What may I hope?

CHAPTER TWO

WHAT CAN I KNOW?

I cannot escape the knowledge that the peaceful development and perhaps even the survival of the Human Family are threatened by:

The injustice of extremes of poverty and wealth

The excessive growth of population

The widespread pollution of natural resources

The profligate consumption of these resources by a substantial minority

Poverty, Population, Pollution and Profligacy are the Four Horsemen of the contemporary Apocalypse. In the increasing thunder of their hoofbeats a still, small voice reminds me also that 'washing one's hands of the conflict between the powerful and the powerless means to side with the powerful, not to be neutral.'[1]

Poverty. The First Threat
In India once, a poor man came to our door. He was obviously not accustomed to begging and, just as obviously, hungry and thirsty. A dignified man with strong hands, he told me that he had walked twenty-five miles to the town as the two wells in his village had both run dry and there was nothing to eat. We gave him a meal and a little money and sent him on his way. What less could we have done? On the other hand what more could we have done?

Whether or not we have experienced such face-to-face encounters with poverty, we can at once grasp something of the implications of a report in *The Guardian* of

the vice-like grip of feudal forces in the villages [of Bihar].

Money-lenders and rich farmers rule the roost. A missionary who conducted a sociological survey of some villages found to his horror that in one a landless labourer had been working for twenty years to repay a loan of £5.

The tragedy is that Bihar is by no means poor in resources. It has vast supplies of minerals and is blessed with perennially flowing rivers.[2]

We can only admire the resilience of so many of the very poor. For Abid in Bangladesh,

it is a constant battle to keep up. Even Abid's tiny land-holding is split into three pieces half a mile apart. He will have to spend time this year shoring up his house. If he has money left over it will buy a cheap cotton sari for his wife, perhaps a treat of sweets for the children, or a new loin-cloth for himself. He has not had a new one for a year and day in, day out wears the same vest and loin-cloth, grey with washing and held together by darns. But, says Abid, 'Allah is good, I have my land, my son, and I stay alive.'[3]

Abid's gratitude to Allah is a sign not of mere acquiescence but of a serenity which has to accept what he cannot change but what nevertheless has to be changed. Looking for change, taking an initiative which denies the cruel slander of work-shy fecklessness, were the men in this story:

A little time ago the Fire Brigade in Calcutta needed two men to complete its strength. So it advertised, asking for candidates to bring their credentials at a certain time. As the hour approached a *huge* queue formed which eventually comprised *ten thousand men* stretching all down the street and into another—unemployed men hoping, longing, yearning for work. The authorities hastily fetched a loud-speaker and asked the applicants to go home and apply by letter, as it would be impossible to interview each person separately. If two at the top of the queue had been accepted there would have been a riot. The queue dispersed.[4]

That queue constitutes the vanguard of an immense army.

If you lined up in a queue all the hungry people in the world and if the queue started at your front door, it would stretch out over the horizon. And if we could ignore the oceans and mountains, it would go round the world for twenty-five thousand miles and the queue would appear at your back door as well. Then that queue would go round the world again, not twice, or ten or twenty times, but twenty-five times, so that if you took your car and drove for five hundred miles a day it would take you three and a half years to get to the end of the line, passing a hungry man every two feet.[5]

Can this be true? It depends, I suppose, on your definition of 'hungry'. In 1978 Altaf Gauhar wrote: 'The real truth is . . . that today there are eight hundred million people living in absolute poverty (an income of less than two hundred and fifty US dollars a year). Twenty-five years ago their number was less than five hundred million. There are today more hungry people, more ignorant people, more people living in conditions of indescribable misery than the world has ever known.'[6]

In a reference to Abid's homeland, Bangladesh, Simon Winchester further defines the worsening crisis:

The numbers of what are called the 'absolutely poor' and the 'extremely poor' are getting steadily larger. In 1963 just 40 per cent of the population was regarded as 'absolutely poor', having a daily calorific intake of 1,935 or less (a rickshaw puller needs more than 4,000 calories daily to prevent him wasting away). Today 62 per cent is in the category. In 1963 only 5 per cent were so impoverished as to take in only 1,720 calories daily, and thus justify a rock-bottom classification as 'extremely poor'. Today that figure is 41 per cent—a shocking fact and more so when it is remembered that this is a country with more than 80 million people. 35 million of them eat less than is necessary to keep a Western body lazing in an armchair all day—small wonder productivity is low, and that a Bangladeshi baby born today can expect to be dead in 45 years.[7]

What do these figures mean in terms of personal suffering?

'I had imagined, in my unforgiveable ignorance,' writes Jill Tweedie,

that starvation like great cold, after the first agonizing pains, lulled you to a death disguised as apathy and sleep. Horribly, this is not so. Pain takes its toll to the last, starvation is torture. Keratomalacia turns children's eyes to blank marbles. B2 deficiencies strip the tongue of its surface, burn the lips, ulcer the mouth and, with hideous irony, make swallowing difficult. C deficiencies cause bleeding gums, loosening teeth, multiple haemorrhages. Children without vitamin D have gross deformations of the bones, without vitamin K bleed with no coagulation. Lack of nicotinic acid produces pellagra, a redness like sunburn that ends in great purple eruptions. Kwashiorkor blows up children's stomachs to grotesque balloons, dwindles their limbs to sticks. In all undernourishment infection is a constant threat and, eventually, the body ceases to function and death ensures— but only after prolonged vomiting and diarrhoea.[8]

Lack of commitment to 'a more equitable distribution of the Earth's resources among the members of the Human Family and to the conservation and development of those resources for our own and future generations' use, amounts to condonation of, if not participation in mass murder on an appalling scale: 'Washing one's hands of the conflict between the powerful and the powerless means to side with the powerful, not to be neutral.'[9]

'Women hold up half the sky'[10]

One of the saddest consequences of extreme poverty is the miserably frequent death of babies and small children. According to figures supplied by Population Reference Bureau Inc USA[11] eighteen infants out of every thousand die during their first year in Australia and the United Kingdom, nineteen in Eire and the United States, twenty-four in the Soviet Union and the Federal Republic of Germany and only twelve in Sweden, thirteen in Japan and fifteen in France. Each one is a personal tragedy. But in five African countries the figures are: Tanzania 162; Central African Republic 163; Swaziland 169; Upper Volta 182; Somalia 190. For India and Pakistan they are respectively 139 and 142. No study of poverty, even so brief a one as this, can be complete without reference to the particular hardship of women in general and mothers in particular. How wretchedly in practice do we treat the mothers of the Human Family, those whom it is less than human to treat otherwise than with honour, solicitude and love. For Christians in particular nothing should be too good for the countless mothers of the poor who live and die in Asian and African villages. Our Lord himself had such a one.

In Britain in 1974, according to information supplied by

Pauline Webb,[12] in manual work in which the majority of women were employed the average earnings per hour were: men 107.8p; women 72.2p. The teaching profession was the only profession in which women outnumbered men, with 66 per cent of the women employed in primary schools. Of 3,675 university professors only 104 were women. The then newly passed Equal Pay Act did not apply to 95 per cent of women workers who worked in jobs done only by women. A wife had no right to know her husband's income but he had a legal right to know hers. Of 1,400 Trades Union Congress officials, only 25 were women. On the Select Committee for the Abortion Bill, a matter in which it might be supposed that women have a particular interest and responsibility, there were fifteen men and four women, three of whom subsequently resigned.

To this information supplied by Pauline Webb I feel bound to add that, as far as I know at the time of writing, only two Cathedral Chapters of the Churches of England and of Wales admit girls to their Cathedral choirs on equal terms with boys; and that, I am told, not on principle but because of difficulties in recruitment. Moreover because the Church of England does not admit women to the priesthood, we have suffered the humiliation of having to ask for and obtain a special exemption from the provisions of the Equal Opportunities Act.

Such discriminations against women as these may, however, appear trivial in the context of the plight of women worldwide. In the developing countries women are generally to be found, with of course many exceptions today, in four main categories. The top social group generally live in seclusion, often behind the veil, doing little work and living comfortable if aimless lives. Many of these are found in Arab countries. The second group confine themselves largely to domestic duties, helping their husbands in the fields at harvest time, perhaps also keeping poultry. There are many such women in South America. In many parts of Asia and Africa a larger number fall into the third category, doing all the domestic work but also helping their men very substantially in the fields. In South India for example village women work an average of twenty hours a week on the land while the men work thirty hours. In the Philippines the equivalent figures are thirty hours and forty-three.

The fourth and largest category includes most Harijan or casteless women in India and very many African women. Many of them are more or less supporting themselves and their children independently of their men. Such Indian women work as landless labourers (for less pay of course than the men) while many African women acquire on their marriage the dubious yet essential privilege of the right to work a piece of land. In Gambia for example the women work an average of twenty hours a week on the land while the men work only nine hours.

Women of course are the universal water carriers, in many places spending between one and four hours a day collecting it, usually in heavy buckets or jars which they carry on their heads. They start this work as young girls and at least it provides many of them with a vigorous social life outside their homes; unless of course, like the woman whom Jesus met at the well of Samaria at the unfashionable hour of noon,[13] they are ostracized from it. In the cities about a quarter of the people have reasonably clean water in their house or courtyard and another quarter have fairly easy access to standpipes in the streets. What the other half do for water only they can tell. In the developing countries as a whole, urban and rural taken together, less than 10 per cent are said to have easy access to a hygienic water supply.

Living as they do such harsh lives, Third World women find that their life expectation is reduced. Whereas in the United States the life expectation for men is 68 years and that for women is 76, in Pakistan (for example) the position is reversed. Men can expect to live to 54 years and women only to 49. Mortality in or as a result of childbirth is a particularly tragic feature of the extreme poverty of so many of the world's women. In the Netherlands there are nearly eleven maternal deaths from deliveries, complications in pregnancy and diseases related to childbirth per thousand live births, and in Spain approximately twenty-four; but the figure for the Philippines is nearly 138 and for Sri Lanka over 179. Two thirds of the world's illiterates are women. Parity between boys and girls in enrolment in primary schools has been attained in only fourteen of the ninety-nine countries for which UNICEF has comparative statistics.

The Global Village
So,

Let us look at the world as if it were a village—a village with a population of one thousand. In this village there would be one hundred and forty North and South Americans (sixty of them representing the United States); two hundred and ten

Europeans; eighty-six Africans; five hundred and sixty-five Asians. There would be three hundred white people, seven hundred non-white people; three hundred of the thousand would be Christians. Half of the total income of the village would be in the hands of the sixty people representing the USA. Almost all the affluent part of the village would be composed of Christians from Europe and North America. Over seven hundred of the thousand villagers would be unable to read. Over five hundred would be suffering from malnutrition. Over eight hundred would live in what we call sub-standard housing. No more than ten would have a university education.[14]

In the global village everybody knows everybody else's business. So you and I can and do know that we have a responsibility towards our fellow members of the Human Family which we are hardly beginning to discharge. 'Thought for Food'[15] is a string of eight quotations assembled to point up that responsibility:

One third of all mankind is ill with chronic hunger. Five hundred million of these are starving children. An alarmingly high figure when you consider that there are 1.2 billion children in the world under the age of fifteen.
    —Willy Brandt speaking to a UNICEF meeting in Geneva 12 December 1974.

In the Sahelian region of Africa, where drought and famine are rampant, thousands of the best acres and a large share of the scarce water resources are assigned by multi-national agribusiness corporations to the production not of foodstuffs for the native population but of raw materials and other products for marketing in the developed world.
    —Geoffrey Barraclough, reporting the findings of the Transnational Institute, *New Yorker Review*, January 1975.

In Mali, production of food for domestic consumption has declined steadily from 60,000 tonnes handled by official marketing channels in 1967 to a current 15,000 tonnes. But export crops—notably peanuts—have increased during the same period, despite the ravages of the recent drought.
    —World Bank.

The US is buying 700,000 tonnes of protein-rich fish meal from Peru and Chile to enrich cattle and pig feed. This would

supply enough protein to satisfy the needs of fifteen million people per year.
      —Peter Collier in *Ramparts*, 1975.

The rich world imports more protein from the poor world than we export to it. Europe for example imports one third of the African peanut crop to feed its livestock.
      —Frances Moore Lappe, 'Fantasies of Famine', *Harpers*, February 1975.

US Food Aid shipments were eighteen million tonnes in 1964/65 and seven million tonnes in 1973/74 . . . The thirty-two developing countries that the UN lists as 'most seriously affected' by the economic crisis—receive less than a third of the wheat that the United States sold on concessional terms in 1973.
      —Emma Rothschild, *New Yorker* magazine, May 26 1975.

The market, playing freely, will always feed the rich. You cannot expect the trade to arrive at a fair distribution of goods in the world. The trade is to make money.
      —Dr Ardeke Boema, Director General, Food and Agricultural Organization, Rome.

Affluence is also affecting the environment's capacity to feed the population. Almost a quarter of the food consumed last year is attributable to this new factor. Affluence is not only changing patterns of food consumption but reshaping world trade. The major food importers are thus no longer the developing regions alone.
      —Maurice Strong, United Nations Environment Programme.

As I read through these eight short statements, considering their implications, I cannot help knowing with a fresh and piercing relevance the poetic truth of perhaps the best-known statement ever made by an English Dean: 'No man is an Island, entire of itself . . . Any man's death diminishes me because I am involved in Mankind.'[16]

Population. The Second Threat

Ritchie Calder has likened the world's Population growth to the performance of an aeroplane:

The curve of population from the days of our primitive

ancestors climbed steadily like a plane from take-off, soared pretty steeply from 1600 until today and is now rising vertically like a rocket off a launching pad.'

... It has taken the whole of man's history on this planet—some two hundred thousand years—to reach the present population figure; it will take less than forty years to double it and more.[17]

The inclusion of population at this point may raise the alarm in two camps. Those Roman Catholics who feel bound in loyalty to papal pronouncements may be fearing a passionate advocacy of contraception to follow. So may some Marxists and others for opposite reasons. They know that the checking of the inordinate growth of population depends not on birth control campaigns but on the removal of the causes of extreme poverty. Yet the facts are inexorable. The world's population reached one billion around 1600, the second billion around 1900 and the third billion by 1950. Today it is around four billion and it appears that nothing but catastrophe can prevent it reaching seven billion by the year 2000. A 1 per cent growth rate doubles a population in seventy years, a 2 per cent growth rate in thirty-five years and a 3 per cent growth rate in twenty-three years.

The first point to be made about the apparently inevitable strain on our Earth's resources represented by these figures is its inextricable linkage with the previous issue of poverty. In 'The Economic Importance of Children in a Javanese Village'[18] Ben White points out that 'by the age of eight, children in Java have begun to join in all the subsistence activities and daily work of their parents'. Ploughing apart, small boys can perform many agricultural tasks with as much skill as adults. Little girls can prepare and cook food, look after babies, clean pots and pans and take part in home industries. Boys and girls alike can collect wood and water, releasing adults from time-consuming jobs. They can also look after ducks and goats, sheep, cows and water buffalo and cut fodder for them. Remembering also the high infant mortality rate among the very poor, to which I have already referred, and the importance of ensuring the survival of enough sons to nourish their old age, it is hardly surprising that it becomes socially and economically advantageous to the very poor to have very large families. Nor must we forget the love and joy and delight which young children bring into the homes of rich and poor alike.

By contrast in the Western world, larger families may mean moving into a larger house with a larger mortgage, higher rates and more life insurance. Food and clothing bills mount up and wear-and-tear increases costs further. School brings further heavy expenditure. Those who enjoy higher or further education may start their own homes and families before ever they directly benefit their parents in any economic sense. James Kocher has stated bluntly that 'the essential change which must take place before people in low-income countries want smaller families is that children must become economic liabilities rather than economic assets.' Only as that change takes place, it seems will contraceptive campaigns make any major impact. So the assertion made in a 1976 report *Future World Trends*, issued by the Cabinet Office, that 'only the improvement and widespread use of contraceptive methods can prevent mass starvation', is dangerously naive. Birth Control Campaigns have their value. In particular they bring liberation to thousands of women. But Richard Norton Taylor is nearer the mark when he writes:

> The real problem now is political and social, in Europe as well as in Latin America or Asia with trade in food increasingly dominated by multinational agribusiness companies, and with a mere 2.5 per cent of landowners with holdings of more than two hundred and fifty acres controlling nearly three quarters of all the land in the world, and with the top 0.23 per cent controlling more than half.[19]

To think otherwise is to attempt with cruel injustice to project the population problem onto the narrow shoulders of the countless poor. There is a sense in which increases in population in the Western world are a far greater burden on the Earth's resources, because we consume inordinately more, as Barbara Ward makes clear:

> An American baby (on 1968 figures) who will require a million calories of food and thirteen tons of coal (or 2,700 gallons of oil) a year during an average lifetime of sixty-five years is going to run through the biosphere's available supplies at least five hundred times faster than an Indian baby looking forward to fifty years with an annual consumption of perhaps half a million calories and almost no energy save what he will himself produce from those calories.[20]

Edward Goldsmith draws our attention to another

consequence of increases in the population of the West:

> In the United Kingdom today, the world population explosion is seen as a Third World problem. It may affect India and Bangladesh, but not us—a very dangerous illusion.

> Britain, at the moment, must import 50 per cent of the food needed to feed its massive population. Some of this comes from Third World countries that can ill afford to sell it to us.

> To do so, vast areas (25 per cent of the arable land of Santo Domingo for instance and 55 per cent of that of the Philippines) which should be producing food for the chronically undernourished local population, are used to produce cash crops for export.[21]

The Urban Pioneers

A striking feature of the population explosion is rapid urban growth, a development that has both positive and negative aspects. In 1950 there were sixteen towns or cities in the developing world with more than one million inhabitants, in 1975 there were more than sixty and by the year 2000 there will be two hundred. In 1900 less than one eighth of the Human Family lived in towns of over 20,000 people, by 1960 the proportion was a quarter and by the year 2000 more than half of us will be urban dwellers. In 1940 there were twice as many town dwellers in the developed as in the developing countries. A recent survey showed that, on the whole, developed countries are still more urbanized than the undeveloped. Apart from Malta and Macao, which are nearly 100 per cent urban, Belgium, Australia, Israel, Sweden and Uruguay are the countries with more than 80 per cent urban dwellers. The United States has 73.5 per cent and South Africa with 47.9 per cent records the highest figure for Africa.

This pattern is, however, being reversed. Three of the four largest cities in the world are in Asia with Shanghai (10,820,000) well in the lead. There follow Tokyo (8,841,000), New York (7,895,000), Peking (7,570,000), London (7,379,000) and Moscow (7,050,000). A brief table may serve to sum up the situation:[22]

	1900	1950	1980	2000(?)
Total World Population (Millions)	2000	3000	4000	7000
World Urban Population	25	750	1750	3500
Urban Population, Developing World	5	250	1000	2250

The effects of this rapid change are daunting. In Calcutta 79 per cent of families live in one room. In Brazil only 45 per cent of towns have reliable water supplies and only 34 per cent have sewerage systems. In Chile only 29 per cent have sewerage We can only admire the resilience with which this vast new challenge is being met.

China's biggest city (Shanghai) now has ten satellite towns, some of them newly built, a mere 1,700 per square kilometre here, most with gas and electricity and even lavatories. Food for the entire 10.7 million population is pedalled in each day from nearby rural areas whose crops the city fertilizes with 2,500 tons of organic garbage and 9,000 tons of human manure a day.[23]

The urban pioneers, then, constitute a vital human resource for the development of the Human Family. Professor Koenigsberger has reminded us that, faced with the choice between marginal existence in the village and movement to the city,

The best of them, the most enterprising and ambitious among them, choose the second alternative. Rural-urban migration is a phenomenon of our time. It is essential that its nature be clearly understood. Emotionally-coloured terminology can do a great deal of harm. What we are witnessing is neither a 'drift' nor a 'flood'. The migrants are not 'drifting aimlessly towards the attraction of city lights', nor are they 'refugees from a sudden disaster who flood into the unfortunate city'. They are a self-selected group of men and women at the peak of their working power who have taken a deliberate decision about their own future. If an emotion-charged term was needed to describe the city-bound migrants, I would suggest 'urban pioneers'. Like the pioneers who developed the American West, they have broken with a past that holds no hope. They are moving to seek a better future—if not for themselves then for their children and grandchildren. They do not expect an early success and an easy life. On the contrary, they are prepared to rough it, to work hard for low wages and to save patiently for a better future.[24]

I have seen this generalization to be true in Calcutta which, despite all its horrors, remains a hotbed of hope. In one of the 'bustees', the local name for areas of temporary housing, we observed men at work in the doorways of their tiny dwellings, making pencils, shoes and other goods for well-known international companies; or rubber buckets out of worn tyres. The one-room school, the result of a local initiative, was spotless if desperately overcrowded. Not a single person asked for alms. A bright little girl did, however, accompany us for a while, telling our guide how much she longed to go to school. Her parents could not afford the fees of about 10p a month.

Please God this wonderfully courageous quality of life may continue among the powerless, whatever the powerful may do or not do about it. The urgent need to develop the comparatively new study of Ekistics, or Human Settlements, has high priority. In his introduction to a Habitat Forum organized by the School of the Environment at the Central London Polytechnic, Professor Thomas Blair states the case in these words:

The ills of our time—the drab sprawling cities, the tense people, the reeking waste tips, the poisoned biosphere—are interconnected with the life-force and life-span of our Spaceship Earth. They reveal a deep-seated flaw in modern society which is a threat to ourselves. They are products of our so-called virtues—technology, mastery over Nature, productivity, progress and prosperity. But accelerating growth based on the rape of the Earth and its resources cannot go on forever. The challenge is to change the very structures, attitudes and technologies by which we have prospered. Action is now needed to create an ethic that will influence all human affairs by demanding effective solutions for environmental conservation, and against environmental degradation. A degraded environment is one that degrades its inhabitants by depriving them of the opportunity to develop and use their cultural and spiritual needs for repose, beauty and contact with Nature.

Professor Blair's words provide a bridge to our next challenge or threat, that of Pollution, and summon us to radical change. So do Barbara Ward's:[25]

> Some changes in our patterns of claims and consumption are inevitable. Under no conditions can unlimited growth and 'trickle-down' economics postpone the problems of justice and solidarity for more than a decade or so. Under no conditions can we bolster our consumption by simply continuing not to pay for the pollution and waste it causes. Under no conditions can a world fully inhabited and carrying seven to ten billion people offer still rising standards to a minority and, at best, stagnation to everyone else.

So what can I know about the population explosion? I cannot escape a knowledge of the main facts and figures, of the terrifying urgency of the issue, of the signs of hope, of the controversies about how to deal with it, of the high degree of unpredictability about it, of its great complexity and of its inextricable connection with the previously-discussed issue of poverty.

Pollution. The Third Threat

> Happy the man whose lot it is to know
> The secrets of the earth. He hastens not
> To work his fellows hurt by unjust deeds,
> But with rapt admiration contemplates
> Immortal nature's ageless harmony
> And how and when her order came to be.

Witty critic of the conventional religion of his day though he was, Euripides was also sensitive enough to the 'ageless harmony' of Nature and the incompatibility of our contemplation of its secrets with the practice of 'unjust deeds'. We may place alongside his humanist beatitude St Augustine's impassioned yet keenly observant tribute to the beauty of creation:

> How can the tongue describe all the beauty and use of the creation which the divine bounty has poured out for men to see and take, although he is condemned to such toils and miseries? The diverse and varied beauty of sky, earth and sea, the abundance and loveliness of light in sun and moon and stars, the shady woods, the colours and perfumes of flowers,

the many species of bright and chattering birds, the vast variety of living creatures, the smallest of which move us to the greater wonder (for we are more surprised by the accomplishments of ants and bees than by the size of whales).

Let a contemporary theologian, John Austin Baker, round off the picture:

> When we consider the simplicity of some basic unit of the universe such as the hydrogen atom, and the fact that its potential for change is apparently limited to the rise and fall of its energy level, to the greater or lesser excitation of its components, and reflect that with this were made the humming bird and the whale, the mind of an Aristotle . . . the music of Handel and the utterance of Shakespeare, the Wiltshire Downs and the green mountains of Vermont . . . and the courage of good men, no miracle, no portent can ever arouse more wonder than the fact of the natural order and the mystery of the human soul.

Much of this is now at risk as never before. I remember being driven by a friend along the shore of a lake in the United States, several miles long and possibly half a mile wide at most; completely devoid, so my friend told me, of all animal and plant life because of the effluent from the potash works on its shores. However, further toxic discharges had recently been forbidden. And it was hoped that in about thirty years' time the lake would have regained its vigorous flora and fauna. There is in fact a whole battery of weapons with which the Human Family can fight pollution. A four-State anti-pollution programme for Lake Michigan in 1969 included no less than twenty-five specific and effective recommendations, although doubt was expressed at the time whether the necessary finance would be forthcoming.[26] The United States does appear to be the most effectively pollution-conscious nation in the world. One particularly neat piece of State legislation for example ensures that any industrial enterprise which discharges waste products into any river must extract its water from a point within a specified distance below the point of discharge. I am reminded of the fact (or at least so I was informed at Whalley Abbey near Blackburn) that mediaeval Abbeys were not normally built within nine miles upstream or downstream of an existing community.

Of course what was considered safe then would not be so

regarded today. Some years ago the Manchester Ship Canal
actually caught fire when someone dropped a match in it—so
thick was the oil and petrol pollution. At about the same time
forty million fish were reported to have died within five days in
the river Rhine. It was even alleged that a photographer was able
to develop his film in chemicals extracted from a backwater of
that mighty stream. By 1975, however,[27] the three big German
chemical producers were spending such huge sums on protecting the Rhine and other rivers from pollution that they
believed themselves to be at a considerable disadvantage unless
competitors in other countries were compelled to follow their
example. It is said that even the fish in the Rhine have become
Social Democrats, left wingers, swimming upstream on the port
or German side, a statement vigorously opposed by the French-
men present when I told the story at an international gathering!
Meanwhile, Britain was opposing EEC legislation which would
make such a degree of control of pollution mandatory.

Few areas of Britain are more at risk than my own beloved
homeland of the Norfolk Broads. Under the heading, 'Wildlife
Paradise May Become a Desert', Anthony Tucker reported:

> The Norfolk Broads are in danger of turning into a wild-life
> desert unless drastic steps are taken to halt the existing
> massive declines in plant life and fisheries. In only a few
> Broads isolated from rivers do clean and healthy conditions
> still exist. Eleven out of twenty-eight Broads appear to be
> completely devoid of aquatic plants and growth is poor in
> others. As the plants provide the environment for the
> organisms on which fish feed, the fish stocks are also
> declining. With the decline in fish comes a drop in bird
> population.

The same writer, however, has been able to report the signing
of an important 'Convention on Wetlands of International
Importance, Especially as Waterfowl Habitat', which is
intended to protect from further pollution and development a
number of areas throughout Britain, including in England
Bridgewater Bay, Bure Marshes, Hickling Broad and Horsey
Mere, Lindisfarne, Minsmere and Walberswick, the North
Norfolk coast, and the Ouse Washes in Norfolk and
Cambridgeshire. All the same he has to return to the same
charge[28] to expose the extinction which still threatens parts of
the Somerset Levels, while on the same page of *The Guardian* Dr

N. W. Moore discusses the urgent need to reconcile the conflict between farmer and conservationist.

Pollution Kills People

I love the Pinkfeet and the Sheldrakes, the Bitterns and the Bearded Tits, the Swallowtails, the Marsh Marigolds and the Bulrush heads. But lest this section be concerned overmuch with them rather than with people, let us now take wings to the other side of the globe.

In Japan[29] fish forms a main part of the national diet. Fish from polluted seas and rivers have made people ill. The long term effects are unknown and the fishing industry has suffered severely. Air pollution brings bronchial illness and photochemical smog from car exhausts in particular causes eye and throat complaints. In the cities a public warning system informs schools when it is necessary to keep all the pupils inside with the windows closed. Also from Japan comes a report of cruelly irresponsible industrial pollution:[30]

> 'The first sign of the horror that came to Minamata was when the local cats began to go berserk. Some even killed themselves by plunging into the sea. Soon after this people began appearing in the streets slavering and twitching, with paralysed hands and grotesquely dilated pupils.'

What then can I know about Pollution, the third Horseman of the contemporary Apocalypse? Not only are sufficient facts at my disposal. I cannot help experiencing their effects. From my urban home I often cannot see the stars at night. There is a relevant if somewhat opaque parable to hand about that too, from the distinguished pen of Soren Kierkegaard.

> When the prosperous man on a dark but starlit night drives comfortably in his carriage and has the lanterns lighted, aye, then he is safe, he fears no difficulty, he carries his light with him, and it is not dark close around him; but precisely because he has the lanterns lighted, and has a strong light close to him, precisely for this reason he cannot see the stars, for his lights obscure the stars, which the poor peasant driving without lights can see gloriously in the dark but starry night. So those deceived ones live in the temporal existence; either, occupied with the necessities of life, they are too busy to avail themselves of the view, or in their prosperity and good days they

have, as it were, lanterns lighted, and close about them everything is so satisfactory, so pleasant, so comfortable—but the
view is lacking, the prospect, the view of the stars.[31]

A famous painting, painted by R. Wenig in 1880, depicts King
Ludwig of Bavaria sleighing at night from Neuschwanstein to
Linderhof. The pale king bears a haunted look, despite the
warmth of his ermine rug, the splendour of his gilded sleigh, the
brilliance of his lantern. The notorious profligacy of his life style
has isolated him from his fellow citizens of our planet Earth and
driven him into a deep and lasting melancholy.

But let Barbara Ward again sum up:

> Our sudden vast accelerations—in numbers, in the use of
> energy and new materials, in urbanizing, in consumptive
> ideals, in consequent pollution—have set technological man
> on a course which would alter dangerously, and perhaps
> irreversibly, the natural systems of his planet upon which his
> biological survival depends. Today when only a third of
> humanity has entered the technological age, the pressures are
> already apparent.
>
> Rivers have caught fire and burned their bridges. Lakes and
> inland seas—the Baltic, the Mediterranean—are under threat
> from untreated wastes, many of which feed bacteria and
> algae; these in turn exhaust the water's oxygen and threaten
> other forms of marine life. The burning of fossil fuels is
> increasing, with unforeseeable consequences for the Earth's
> climates and atmosphere.
>
> Dust particles in the atmosphere may also alter the earth's
> temperature in unpredictable ways. Even the vast oceans,
> covering 70 per cent of the globe and providing an apparently
> inexhaustible reserve of moisture, an endless dump for wastes
> and a perpetual source of freshening winds and currents, are
> far more vulnerable to man's polluting activities than had
> been assumed. Run off into them too many poisons, in-
> secticides and fertilisers, void too many bilges, choke too
> many of the estuarine waters where the fish spawn and
> multiply and even the oceans may cease to serve man's
> purpose as effortlessly and reliably as he now seems to
> suppose.[32]

Profligacy. The Fourth Threat
I suppose that this word, the fourth of our P's, is slightly less

familiar to common usage than Poverty, Population and Pollution. But it precisely describes the inordinate consumption of the Earth's resources by the substantial minority of the Human Family who have the opportunity of such indulgence. This minority includes me and very probably you also.

Such mindless exploitation is as old, if not as the hills, at least as human experience: 'Using a Stone-Age flint axe which had not been sharpened for four thousand years, three Danes recently cleared six hundred and sixty-eight square metres of birch forest in four hours, cutting down one hundred trees.'[33]

Today one issue of one daily newspaper may consume the wood from one hundred acres of trees. What I am calling 'profligacy', Aurelio Peccei, President of the Club of Rome, describes as 'rapacity':

> Something deep-rooted and far-reaching must happen . . . a revolution, which changes our individual and collective outlook and action . . . The Club of Rome has always represented the view that a serious change in the thoughts and feelings of the great mass of mankind is necessary . . . a cultural and social metamorphosis that must be grounded in a far-reaching conviction that a final change in direction has taken place.[34]

Such a deep-rooted change must match the deep-rooted character of this rapacity, this profligacy. According to John Hall's review of *Origins* by Richard Leakey and Roger Lewin: [35]

> Most of our ills stem from the point at which men stopped rummaging around for nuts, roots and piglets, and started planting corn. Up to that point, his existence depended very much on mutual co-operation—probably for at least three million years, the hominid hunter-gatherer needed the help of his fellows in stalking prey. The habit of meat-eating itself tends to be a co-operative business, in contrast with the solitary vegetarianism of leaf croppers. Then, about ten thousand years ago, agriculture was invented, and instead of hunters, parading around shared game areas, we had farmers protecting their crops, accumulating possessions, and lapsing into an awful 'psycho-materialism'. As more goods were acquired, and more land won, there grew a need to protect these little prehistoric Ponderosas, and for the first time it was possible to gain material well-being by beating up your

neighbour. Transition from the nomad, hunting way of life to the sedentary one of farmers and industrialists made war possible and potentially profitable.

Leakey and Lewin go on to say:

The important thing to remember now is that we are a single species. Racial differences are no more than regional adaptations. We are relatively new arrivals on earth, and unless we achieve an awareness of our place in the natural world, then no matter how special we are as animals, our species will become extinct. We are the first animals capable of controlling our environment to some degree, which puts us in a unique position of power—but it is a power which can operate either direction. If we can recognize that we are a single species, with a shared destiny, and we can operate in sympathy with our planet, then our potential is almost beyond imagination.

Leakey's interpretation receives unexpected support from a complementary account of these matters as ancient as his is modern:

At one level of interpretation the story of Adam and Eve and their expulsion from the Garden of Eden represents the movement of our anthropoid ancestors away from their arboreal, fruit-eating existence, out into the harsh toil of the most primitive forms of agriculture. The eating of the forbidden fruit is a symbol of their natural reluctance to abandon their old securities and launch out into the new world in which alone they could ensure their survival. In the end they were forced to go by environmental changes, a flaming sword which turned every way inexorably preventing their return. It is not a mere piece of male chauvinism, though it is partly that, that in the story it was the woman who tempted the man to taste the forbidden fruit. It remains natural enough for her to have a primary concern for the old certainties.[36]

Cain's murder of Abel which follows illustrates unforgettably the point made by Leakey and Lewin that 'transition from the nomadic, hunting way of life to the sedentary one of farmers and industrialists made war possible and potentially profitable.' This transition of course was our inevitable destiny as now it is our destiny to move out of the twelve-thousand-year-old era of the exploitation of the Earth's resources into a new era of conservation and sharing.

Profligacy, Private and Public

Now it is possible to replace the hundred trees cut down by those three Danish scholars with their little Stone-Age axes or even the hundred acres of trees that were felled to provide one edition of your favourite daily newspaper. Not that we should be complacent about the profligate consumption of so-called renewable resources; these can so easily reach the point of no effective renewal.[37] But what about our profligate use of non-renewable resources?

In his Fawley Lecture[38] in 1975 Lord Ashby gave the number of years the known global resources of the following minerals would last at the current exponential rate of utilization: aluminium 31 years; chromium 95; cobalt 60; manganese 46; mercury 13; nickel 53; platinum 47; tin 15; and tungsten 28 years. These figures are the more significant in that it was the lecturer's purpose to point out that in fact these resources were likely to last longer than the times stated. As any resource becomes scarcer the pressure increases to develop alternatives and therefore conserve the resource. Moreover, Governments and multi-national companies become alerted to the dangers of the exhaustion of the resource. This latter circumstance, however, is dangerous, leading to political conflict, possibly to war, in attempts to secure control of a scarce and valuable resource.

The precise future of any particular resource is therefore uncertain, and the experts may legitimately differ in their speculations about how long it may last, or how effectively its use may be superseded by technological developments as yet unachieved. The basic fact, however, cannot be avoided that sooner or later non-renewable resources come to an end. Equally basic is the fact that whether they run out sooner rather than later depends on the degree of profligacy with which they are exploited.

In the use of renewable and non-renewable resources we may distinguish but not disentangle two main forms of profligacy: public and private. The manufacture of those beautiful supersonic passenger aeroplanes is a good example of public profligacy. Even that absurdity would have been out of the question had there not been a small number of individual persons with the opportunity to fly in them: government servants, industrialists and others; for the most part at the expense not of their own pockets but of those who consume the goods they produce or the services they provide. On the other hand the manufacture of large fast cars satisfies a peculiarly personal and private taste. Here again most of these products are so-called 'company cars', paid for in the end not by those who own and drive them but by the consumers of 'company' goods or services. For there is no such thing as a free lunch.

Large Fast Cars

I turn now to the symbolic example of private profligacy already quoted, the large fast car. Let us look at the captions for a full-page colour advertisement of a British model in *The Guardian* newspaper.[39] The main caption reads in bold, black type: 'September 10 1975. A Black Day for Modena, Stuttgart and Turin.' These jingoistic, anti-European words are repeated underneath. Can they be a serious attack on the ideals and principles of the European Economic Community in which we are all supposed to be friends and brothers? Or is this some kind of a joke? The joke is developed: 'What's good news for Britain has to be bad news for our foreign competitors . . . the most luxurious, most expensive, most exclusive Jaguar ever produced.'

I suspect that this good news is short-lived. What are the statistics of obsolescence in this field? How long is it before the lucky owner of this luxurious, expensive and exclusive toy feels bound to part with it? 'Zero to sixty takes under seven seconds . . . the top speed, where permissible, is in the region of 150 miles per hour.' This latter, nerve-tingling information is of course in no way an invitation to murder or suicide, nor even to any minor breaking of the law. It gains a certain piquancy from its proximity to a following reference to 'the five-mile-per-hour no-impact bumpers . . . the first of their design in Europe.' This is the car, we are finally told, that 'everyone dreams of but very, very few can ever own.'

Needless to say, the little matter of the price is nowhere mentioned. I shall never know whether it was competitive with any similar products that may have come out of Modena, Stuttgart or Turin, Detroit or Tokyo. Nor shall I ever know whether its cost would have kept one hundred African or Asian families in food and clothing during the brief period of its first owner's enjoyment; or more, or fewer?

In the years since 1975 many writers[40] have denounced such cars as illustrations of what an Indian Christian woman has described as 'the values and assumptions of a competitive, alienated and materialistic society.'[41] The tone of the advertisements has certainly improved. My own serious objections to the manufacture of these status symbols in a small country such as Britain, and their import at the cost of scarce foreign currency into a country which still has to import about half of such a basic commodity as food, still remain however. They may be listed under six headings.

First, they consume inordinate amounts of non-renewable petroleum in their operation, and of steel, rubber, plastics and other materials in their manufacture; including, it is alleged, an astonishing average of one hundred thousand gallons of water in the production of a single car.

Secondly, they divert from the production of more socially useful goods, such as buses for example, massive resources of skilled and unskilled labour, of management and of sales personnel, of expensive plant and research facilities.

Thirdly, the dangerous speeds which are possible in the hands of determined and aggressive or strained and fatigued drivers contribute to a totally unacceptable number of killings and maimings. There is a very high social cost to pay for large fast cars in terms of scarce medical facilities, the diversion of police forces from the maintenance of law and order, massive insurance provision and so on. Compare the insurance premiums for these cars and for smaller, slower ones. The insurance companies know the risks. It is their business.

Fourthly, the need for generously engineered roads to contain all this fast traffic means a large-scale absorption of farmland and destruction of amenity. Noise pollution and lead poisoning follow from the crowding of too many cars and lorries on our roads. So do the ruination of our city centres and the general subjection of planning decisions about them to the interests of the motorist. Professor Doxiades, founder of the Ekistics Centre in Athens, tells the story of the American lady who found a skunk in her kitchen. She telephoned the authorities, who advised her on no account to disturb the intruder but to lay a trail of bread from her kitchen to the nearest wood. The skunk would quickly leave her in peace. The next day she indignantly telephoned the authorities again: 'I did what you told me. Now I have two skunks in my kitchen.' Here ends the parable of the urban motorway.

Fifthly, as already mentioned, a majority of the larger cars are 'company cars' whose cost is therefore ultimately and unjustly borne, not by the user, but by the consumers of the company's products.

Sixthly, the dehumanizing environment of the mass-production of these baubles leads to widespread personal dissatisfaction with daily work, many strikes and lay-offs, higher wages leading to inflation, consequent burdens on the national economy and frustration and anger for the unfortunate taxpayer who finally foots the bill.

I would not, however, go as far as those who have seriously proposed in affluent Sweden to abolish the private ownership of motor cars altogether. I have myself owned a motor car for many years and have valued the very great convenience of such ownership. But I would seriously propose that Britain would be a happier, healthier and ultimately a more prosperous country if the manufacture and import of private motor cars of more than, say, 1600cc capacity were phased out over the next five years. Within such a limit, experienced designers would still be able to design somewhat more expensive, high quality, durable cars for those who could afford them as well as sufficiently large, if by present standards somewhat underpowered, cars for large families. Even from the commercial point of view our concentration on the production of smaller cars might enable us to capture a bigger share of the Third World market and paradoxically of the North American market too, where the energy crisis is bringing an increasing number of people to their senses. Such a ban would also be an extraordinarily powerful signal of a change of direction and a change of heart.

I am not quite sure how appropriate it is for me to deploy that market argument. I do know that this somewhat radical proposal is surprisingly well received by a variety of audiences. I reserve the last word in this section for three small boys whose poems[42] collectively illustrate the deplorable values with which we are indoctrinating innocent children and vividly summarize the profligacy of which the large fast car is so offensive a symbol.

THE TRAFFIC JAM

There are hooting and yells as fumes rise rapidly
   and beads of sweat pour down my face.
The yells and hooting grow madder than ever.
But the queue of maddening cars is slowly
   but surely breaking up.
The speed of the cars is quickening now
   as they slowly move away.
Now the road is as busy as ever,
   with vehicles darting here and there.
The road is no longer a jam
   but a kaleidoscope of cars.
Now the cars are zooming along
   flashing like arrows in the sun.
The beads of sweat are now
   just an unpleasant dream.

E. B. Thompson (age 10)

AFTER THE PARTY

I slammed the car door and switched on—
Stupidly going into third gear—"Crunch".
The engine spluttered and went dead on me.
After a few good kicks on the accelerator
I got the engine running well.
Apart from narrowly avoiding a lamp post
   and killing two men
I reached home safely.

R. P. Vacher (age 10)

TRAVELLING IN COMFORT

People stop and stare admiringly,
As I glide along in my elegant Rolls.
As she purrs along the motorway, people let me by.
What supremeness a Rolls can bring.
At dusk I guide her to her resting place,
Until the next day's work begins.
In the morning light, when the wheels of the World
   begin to turn,

I reverse her out and off I set once more,
Smoothly gliding on my way.
On the road, at least, I am King.

N. S. Eyre (age 11)

Private Profligacy Postscript

'On the road, at least, I am King.' If the profligacy of the large fast car is so often the symbol of male virility, success and power, a symbolism effectively fired and fuelled by a sophisticated advertising industry, then fashionable clothes are as often a feminine equivalent. As long ago as 1972[43] I came across a notice in a newspaper of a 'sleeveless tabard with tie-belt, matching trousers and full sleeved shirt' on sale for a total of £110, a shirt-dress for £92 and a pair of dungarees for £60. Such is the rate of profligacy-induced inflation that at the time of writing these figures seem almost reasonable. But in 1972 it struck me forcibly that most of the world's families could feed and clothe themselves for a year at least for the price of a pair of dungarees!

Some years ago, and therefore before the more recent excesses of inflation, a well-known West End store sent me two copies (why two copies?) of their expensive and glossy catalogue. On the first page, under the title 'Beyond her wildest dreams . . .', I read of a baby crocodile handbag for £315, a nice silk scarf for £30, a one-ounce bottle of scent in a presentation case for £125, a 'rare and outstanding full-length natural Canadian Silver Fox coat' at £8,000 and a matching hat for £250.

Looking for something a little more reasonable in price I came across a 'fully stranded dark ranch mink coat of exceptional quality' for £3,750 with a matching mink umbrella cover for £149. 'And to prevent your dog from being jealous, a coat for him or her as modelled by Toby' for £195. It was towards the end of this fantasy-laden catalogue that the dreadful impact of all this in the light of the real needs of the Human Family became most powerful. The Christmas Hamper included a whole York ham, a brace of pheasants, a side of Best Scotch Smoked Salmon, brandy marmalade, mincemeat flavoured with Cognac and so on. It cost only £115 as compared with the £135 for the 'Perfect Christmas dinner for four to six people' also 'packed in a wicker basket'.[44]

Perhaps the extra cost of the Perfect Christmas Dinner was occasioned by the inclusion of a box of 'Romeo and Juliet' cigars.

According to Richard Norton-Taylor, 'multi-national companies are vigorously promoting the sale of high-tar cigarettes in Third World countries where there are no health warnings and almost total ignorance of the threats to health from smoking proved by scientists in the West.'[45] Taking his information from *Tomorrow's Epidemic? Tobacco and the Third World*,[46] Norton-Taylor reports that 'the facts of tobacco today are that the countries where consumption is growing fastest are the world's poorest and hungriest.'

The cynical sale of high-tar cigarettes may however be only a temporary expedient while production lines last, to be replaced by the disposal of rubbish to the unfortunate Third World consumers. A leading toilet paper manufacturer is perfecting a process of mixing tobacco stems and stalks, so-called 'tobacco offal', with cellulose sheet, pulping it, drying it and wrapping the mixture in paper for sale in developing countries as a popular cigarette.

Supersonic Transport

The party of Bristol churchmen with our guests from Hannover entered a large shop, one of several at British Aerospace, full of gleaming aero engines. At once all eyes were riveted on the one and only Concorde engine, four of which, as I am informed, could have driven the 'Queen Mary'. Tall and upright, it dominates the shop floor where it stands, like the altar to some unknown god. It is as beautiful as is the aeroplane which it powers. What admirable managerial, technological and manipulative skills have gone into its construction. It is a genuinely tragic story in which, as in most classical tragedies, hubris, the flaw of pride, has played a prominent part. In this technological triumph we find a symbol of Western profligacy, compounded of British imperial nostalgia and French notions of national glory.

When I took up my present job in Bristol I was anxious lest, if the local press were to call, I should be asked my opinion of Concorde. I knew that a great many Bristolians were employed on its manufacture at the time. I did not know much about it in terms of hard facts and figures. I need not have worried. The local press did call, but it did not occur to them that a clergyman might have an opinion to offer on so technological a subject.

The clergyman who has expressed himself most forcefully on this issue is Hugh Montefiore, now Bishop of Birmingham. As

Bishop of Kingston he was pastorally concerned for those who had to live underneath the Concorde's flight path from Heathrow Airport. According to Geoffrey Holmes, Chairman of the Local Authorities Aircraft Noise Council, the noise under the flight path of the inaugural flight was 'excruciating—above the level of pain'.[47] On the other hand, according to the pamphlet 'Concorde—the questions answered', issued by the British Aircraft Corporation, it has been established that 707's, DC8's and VC10's are more or less as noisy as Concorde. Whom are we to believe?

I understand that Bishop Montefiore was accused for his pastoral pains of being unpatriotic by the Duchess of Argyll. Of the inaugural flight to Bahrain she enthused: 'I absolutely loved it. I shall make a habit of it.'[48] She should not find it overcrowded. On its fourth service flight, thirty-nine of its hundred seats were occupied. Soon after that it actually flew to Bahrain without a single passenger on board.[49] The influential Crown Prince of Bahrain was to be on the return flight. All may yet be well, however, for no less a person than Mrs Thatcher is reported to have said: 'It will be of immense help to people like me.'[50]

Charles Gardner, author of the pamphlet already mentioned, 'Concorde—the questions answered', seems to me to deal more convincingly with the technical questions of sonic boom, smoke pollution, water vapour into the stratosphere and change in ozone layer than he does with the more immediately comprehensible issues of fuel consumption and economics. I understand that the development costs of Concorde amounted to more than a thousand million pounds, about half of which was contributed by the taxpayer. Moreover the sale of each plane had to be further subsidized. Some £300 million for the first sixteen was estimated.[51]

From the taxpayer's point of view it is therefore as well that so few have been sold. At the time of writing (July 1979) it has just been announced that British Airways, while making a substantial overall profit, made a loss over the last year of some £2 million in operating Concorde.

It is also clear that from the point of view of fuel consumption it is as well that so few Concordes are flying. In the heady early days it was calculated that:

Even by 1980 the planned fleet of supersonic transports—

three hundred Anglo-French Concordes and eighty American Boeings—will demand the production of about 320 million metric tons of crude oil each year.

This is nearly a third of the total planned oil consumption of Western Europe or the United States in the same year. It is more than one and a half times the forecast need of South East Asia, more than three times that of Africa . . . In 1985 the Boeing fleet will have swollen to two hundred and eighty-five, making a total of nearly six hundred supersonics . . . The British Aircraft Corporation says that one Concorde will consume 18,600 gallons on a three-and-a-half-hour London —New York flight. To justify investment in the aircraft, airlines will have to operate four transatlantic flights by each plane each day . . . This means that a single Concorde will consume 272 metric tons of kerosene each day, three times its own weight . . . If the manufacturers' target of three hundred Concordes is to be reached by 1980, subsequent planes will come off the production line at the rate of one a week. In 1980 these three hundred aircraft will burn thirty million tons of kerosene.[52]

Such projections are vulnerable to error. We can now be thankful that they were not fulfilled. Can even we have planned to devote three times as much oil in 1980 to supersonic travel as to the whole of the needs of Africa? There is a sense in which supersonic transport is already obsolete. The party of Bristolian and Hannoverian churchmen already mentioned watched a propaganda film on Concorde. One passenger in the film was a Dusseldorf businessman flying to Texas in a hurry to sign a contract. 'But,' said one of our Hannoverian guests, 'his journey was unnecessary.' Very soon if not already it will be possible to sign in Dusseldorf and have the signature transferred by satellite and without possibility of forgery to any part of the world. Meanwhile those involved in the political and financial decisions which launched the Concorde have a heavy responsibility for organizing alternative employment for the thousands of workers employed on this project. There are of course a number of possibilities.

On 16 February 1966 the British Minister of Aviation was reported to have flown to Paris to discuss the Anglo-French-German Airbus A300.[53] On 5 September 1967 he flew to Bonn to sign the agreement to build it. Further discussions were recorded or decisions forecast in the press in 1969, 1970, 1974 and 1976, yet on 13 December 1977 President Giscard referred to British participation as only a possibility. But then of course the European airbus, as its name implies, looks like a useful and popular aeroplane whose rapid development might even reduce some air fares to a level more appropriate to the pocket of the less exalted. To try to expose Concorde, as I have briefly done, as a symbol of public profligacy is not of course to decry sophisticated and advanced technology. I have already expressed my admiration for the managerial, design and engineering skills involved. The Human Family needs rapid advances in sophisticated technology in many fields for the foreseeable future. Nor, as the reference to the European airbus should be sufficient to make clear, am I attacking air travel in general. Commercial aircraft do make a great deal of noise, consume a great deal of petrol and use up a great deal of land, labour, capital and non-renewable resources in their manufacture and operation. Moreover, the immense prestige acquired by a developing nation in operating its own airline and running its own airport or airports may divert precious resources which would otherwise directly benefit the poorest of the poor. But commercial aircraft also enrich the lives of many thousands of people. Indirectly their use and development may well in the long run benefit the very poor.

The Arms Trade
The arms trade constitutes another major area of public profligacy with its own specific ethical problems. Only the wholehearted pacifist will object to the manufacture of arms for genuine self-defence in an uncertain world in which great destructive power still resides in sovereign nation states; or even to the sale of such arms to actual or potential allies for strategic or political reasons. Regrettably, commercial considerations often outweigh these factors. Long runs of arms production mean more competitive prices. Arms are often sold to both sides in a conflict, as well as to repressive regimes for use in internal security. This whole massive scandal is well documented both by voluntary pressure groups such as the Campaign against the Arms Trade, founded in Britain in January 1975, and by more official organizations such as the United Nations.

Following a UN General Assembly resolution on 16 December 1971 the Secretary General introduced a Report on the 'Economic and social consequences of the arms race and of military expenditures'.[54] The first conclusion of this report contains the words:

> The threat of ultimate disaster the arms race has generated is by far the most dangerous single peril the world faces today— far more dangerous than poverty or disease, far more dangerous than either the population explosion or pollution —and it far outweighs whatever short-term advantage armaments may have achieved in providing peoples with a sense of national security.[55]

A later Report entitled with great urgency 'Economic and Social Consequences of the Armaments Race and its Extremely Harmful Effects on World Peace and Security'[56] brings the issue more up to date. By 1976 the Arms Race cost about 350,000 million dollars a year. Military activities absorbed a labour force of sixty million people and financial resources equivalent to some two thirds of the gross national products of all those countries whose populations comprise the poorer half of the Human Family. The arms race hinders national development by the resources it pre-empts and undermines national security by the fears it creates. Disarmament would release resources for development on a huge scale.

The major Powers are the chief culprits. The United States, the Soviet Union, China, France, the United Kingdom and the Federal Republic of Germany together account for three-quarters of the total world expenditure on arms. These countries are both the major arms exporters and the initiators of nearly all expensive and sophisticated innovations. In particular, nuclear arms technology is proliferating. Twenty countries had nuclear power plants in 1976 and another eight were expected to acquire them before 1980. The arms trade has both a direct and an indirect bad effect on development. Thus the World Health Organization spent some eighty-five million dollars over ten years to eradicate smallpox throughout the world; an amount that would not buy a single strategic bomber. The WHO programme to eliminate malaria at an estimated cost of about 540 million dollars was flagging for want of funds. Yet this total cost was less than half of what is spent on armaments *in a single day*. Malaria, in fact, was regaining lost ground in some areas. In Calcutta for example, because of the rapid rise in the cost of oil, the authorities were no longer able to afford to spray the large

areas of stagnant water in and around the city with paraffin and
so destroy the malarial mosquitoes. For a rickshaw puller or
heavy manual labourer the debilitating effects of malaria can
make it a killer.

Developing countries in general spend at least as much on
military activities as they do on agricultural investment. Insofar
as they require development assistance in agriculture from the
industrialized nations, an amount equivalent to 1 per cent of our
military budgets would appear to be sufficient. Then again the
very great resources of scientific skills and energies that are
devoted to arms research and production could be released to
great advantage in order to develop the food and minerals in and
under the oceans, to discover new sources of energy, to survey
natural resources and to forecast natural disasters. Let that old
campaigner, Bertrand Russell, have the last word on this
uniquely dangerous form of public profligacy:

> The hatred, the expenditure of time and money and intel-
> lectual ability upon weapons of destruction, the fear of what
> we may do to each other, and the imminent daily and hourly
> risk of an end to all that man has achieved is a product of
> human folly. It is not a decree of Fate. It is not something
> imposed by natural conditions. It is in our hearts that the evil
> lies, and it is from our hearts that it must be plucked out.[57]

Greed Versus Need
That such public and private profligacy is as dangerous and
immoral as it is characteristic of our Western society can hardly
be denied. How sad that as sparkling a stroke-maker as Greg
Chappell was compelled to observe: 'My long-term future lies
with Coca Cola, not cricket.' Under the heading 'The dangers in
making greed a respectable philosophy of life', Philippa Pullar
observes:

> Most industry invades the lives of millions of people. In the
> name of profit, it confines and mutilates animals, poisons,
> creates shoddiness, ugliness and excruciating noise. Thou-
> sands of people have their nights disrupted by aeroplanes
> howling through their bedrooms, their days shattered—no
> matter that their profitability is reduced. Our modern
> architecture is mainly a heartbreak; our architects, controlled
> as they are by the developers, have filled our cities with
> buildings of meanness and unexampled ugliness. Our health,

our bowels and our teeth are rotten as a result of our modern diet of confectionery and refined carbohydrates pressed upon us by the food industry.[58]

This latter point is taken up by the Politics of Health Group, a team of doctors, nurses and social scientists. In their pamphlet,[59] 'Food and profit—it makes you sick', they invite us to think of ill health in terms of social conditions—the food we eat, for example. As food is produced primarily for profit, our diet comes to be dominated by highly profitable sugar, fats and refined flour, although together these cause much ill health. Moreover research shows that from 1964 to 1974 weekly wage earners and their families ate 55 per cent less fruit, 20 per cent less fresh green vegetables but 32 per cent more sugar than middle-class families. We are not surprised to learn that unskilled workers are twice as likely to suffer from chronic illness as professional people.

When Philippa Pullar added that 'commercial greed is the prime obscenity of the 1970s', she was right. But we individual consumers, taxpayers and voters cannot evade our personal responsibility. Edmund Burke, too, was right when he pointed out that 'men are qualified for civil liberty in exact proportion to their disposition to put moral chains upon their own appetites'. As Gandhiji said, there is enough in the world for everybody's need but not enough for everybody's greed.

The Energy Crunch
The readiest and most effective way of measuring and assessing all this profligacy is in terms of the consumption of energy. Colin Pritchard, who works for the Society, Religion and Technology Project of the Church of Scotland, sets the scene for his article on 'The Energy Crunch'[60] with these three quotations:

British Industry is going to miss the boat in the fastest growing and potentially the largest export energy industry (wave, tide and wind energy equipment) because of an insular obsession with North Sea oil and nuclear energy.

—Dr Albert Strub, Chairman of the EEC Committee on energy policy.

We have before us the choice of a fast breeder programme which would enable us to carry on for a few more years the exponential growth which will in any case soon be halted by shortage of raw materials, or the early recognition that our generation has neither the right to continue to squander these resources, nor to impose on succeeding generations a legacy of radioactive waste which may have long-term biological effects.

   —Sir Martin Ryle, Astronomer Royal.

The whole experience of nuclear power has been that of a clean and safe way of providing the energy we require. I see no reason why, with an expanded programme, we shouldn't continue to have this safe and clean form of energy.

   —Sir John Hill, Chairman of UK Atomic Energy Authority.

I have used these three quotations as a basis for group discussion, adding the questions: 'With whom do you agree? Does your opinion matter? What can I know about these matters? I can at least know that the nuclear option is fraught with uncertainties.

At least six obstacles or problems beset nuclear power; the risk of a reactor meltdown or other accident; the dangers of nuclear materials falling into the hands of terrorists; the lack of a satisfactory technique for disposing of nuclear waste; the possibility that nuclear weapons will proliferate; the long-term inadequacy of fuel supplies; and the cost of nuclear power, including the cost of waste disposal and of decommissioning worn-out plants.[61]

To this succinct summary, Lester Brown adds the comment: 'The difficulties inherent in dealing effectively with any one of these obstacles, much less with all of them collectively, help to explain why the nuclear dream is fading.'

I can also know that this great pressure is on us with the consequent danger of disastrous decisions just because of that voracious profligacy which demands more and more energy. If only we could reduce that pressure by a widespread adoption of simpler life styles, we might have time to solve the technological problems that haunt the development of nuclear energy; at the same time stepping up our exploration of solar energy, a development that would be bound particularly to benefit the poorer, tropical peoples. The trioiology of wind, wave and water power could also be developed.

Meanwhile the developed countries with 30 per cent of the world's population consume 80 per cent of the world's energy.

With only 6 per cent of the world's population, the United States consumes 30 per cent of the energy. Britain's figures are just over $1\frac{1}{2}$ per cent and 3 per cent respectively. If there were ever to be a roughly equal use of energy within the Human Family, North America would make do with about one fifth of its present consumption and Britain and many other European countries with about a half. On the other hand it has been estimated that an overall reduction in energy consumption of only 5 per cent would close the fatal gap between the demand and the supply of energy. In the light of such facts the former President Carter called largely in vain for 'the moral equivalent of war' against the profligate use of energy. President Reagan does not appear to share these anxieties.

Once more it is the very poor who suffer most as a consequence of this our energy crunch. The seventy-two thousand inhabitants of the Janata Colony near Bombay are reported to have received assurances of secure tenancies there when many of them moved from their previous homes, which were destroyed up to twenty-five years ago in a slum clearance programme. They have houses, shops, mosques, temples, churches, schools, markets and so on. Now they are threatened with dispossession because the Government Department of Atomic Energy wants the land for housing its officials and professional workers.[62]

Under the heading 'Uranium and a Nuclear Society', the Australian Council of Churches has usefully brought together the facts in favour of 'at least a delay in uranium mining in Australia and extensive public discussion of the issue.'[63] In 'From Massacres to Mining'[64] Jan Roberts develops the theme in more detail. She points out that it is the Aboriginals who suffer most extensively from these depredations. As fellow members of the Human Family have we not all a responsibility to try to take some of the pressure off by a less conspicuous style of energy consumption? 'If we do not have the energy supplies,' writes Harford Thomas in an article entitled 'Closing the World Energy Gap', 'to sustain the kind of industrial economy we are struggling, not too successfully, to manage now, then ought we to be looking for an alternative and perhaps more satisfactory, if simpler lifestyle!'[65]

So What Can I Know?

There are some signs of hope, not only in the international field but also at the personal level. At the London exhibition on the 'British Genius' I noted down the numbers of visitors who by 5.00pm on 21 September 1977 had indicated the choices presented to them by means of an electronic machine as follows:

1a You think that present living standards are more important than protecting the future.   24,182
b   You would accept less pay now to leave a richer, cleaner country for your children.   39,448
2a You think we should retain the ideal of a car for everyone but should improve them.   48,332
b   You think cars should be discouraged and public transport should be given priority.   50,850
3a You would accept £5 a week less pay for a more satisfying job.   52,581
b   You would take a less satisfying job for £5 a week more.
                                                            34,280

In each case there is a majority, in some a very substantial majority, in favour of the less profligate life style. But are those who pay to go to such an exhibition typical of the country at large? The political managers of our two largest parties clearly thought not, judging by the cynical appeals to consumerist values which characterized the 1978 General Election Campaign.

So what can I know? As must be obvious, I make no claim to be an expert on the politics or the economics of development. Most of my sources of information are secondary, culled from a daily newspaper, some occasional literature, a handful of popular books. I have not been able to present more than a personal view of a vast subject. But this means that what I can know, you too can know, simply by keeping a file on the newspaper you read, aided by a discreet choice of periodicals and paperbacks, with some selective attention to radio and television. The facts that I have assembled are basically common knowledge. You and I have no excuse for not knowing them.

According to an old Chinese proverb, 'What we hear we may forget; what we see we may remember; but what we do we shall understand.'

What then ought I to do?

CHAPTER THREE

WHAT OUGHT I TO DO?

Four Lines of Action

I understand that Goethe expressed the wish that instead of 'In the beginning was the Word' at the opening of the Fourth Gospel we could read 'In the beginning was the Act'. No doubt there were existential reasons for this preference which any professional student of philosophy could supply. But for me it characterizes our distinctively European approach. An Indian philosopher might well have preferred 'In the beginning was the Thought'—an image of God in undifferentiated bliss, brooding over that which is and that which is not. In fact 'In the beginning was the Word' enshrines the Judaeo-Christian insight. God does not just think about us nor does He just act upon us, pushing us around. He speaks to us, an I-Thou, not an I-it relationship.

However that may be, we Europeans, and in particular those of us who are heirs to the Protestant ethical tradition, lay great emphasis, in theory at least, on personal action, on 'doing the truth'.[1]

In front of me as I work at my desk I have placed a quotation from that eminent Victorian, Thomas Huxley:

> Perhaps the most valuable result of all education is the ability to make yourself do the thing you have to do, when it ought to be done, whether you like it or not; it is the first lesson that ought to be learned; and however early a man's training begins, it is probably the last lesson that he learns thoroughly.

Now this our need for personal action is in particular danger of frustration and paralysis in the face of the great issues which occupied the previous chapter. What can I know? What ought I to do? Well, I also know that there are at least four lines of action, another four P's, which I can pursue and ought to pursue. They are Prayer, Prophecy, Political Action and Personal Moderation. Since it is a question of what I personally ought to do, I make no apology to atheist and agnostic readers for the unashamedly religious character of the first two categories. But I do invite you to transpose these terms into your own milieu of thought and action. For Prayer, please substitute whatever communication you would wish to maintain with whatever truths, values, ideology or philosophy of life make you tick. For Prophecy, which for believers is the declaration of the will and the word of God, please substitute whatever means of communication of your own truths and values you may wish to employ.

Prayer. The First Response

O God (if there be a God), on the strength of Thy word (if Thou didst speak it), I pray Thee (if Thou canst hear), forgive my sin, be with me in my fears, comfort me in loneliness, show me my neighbour, make my heart burn with love; and in every time, good or bad, the high points and the bitter, empty places in my life, let me feel Thy hand, reaching out for me and guiding me, lifting and carrying my burdens, stroking away the care that marks my brow, and making death itself easy to die, because my heart can rest in Thee.

Tomorrow I shall rise . . . and serve my neighbour as if Thou didst exist. Then shalt Thou break the silence and suddenly be near to me. Then shalt Thou say: Well done, good and faithful servant; enter into the joy of your Lord?

I once began a sermon on prayer with the true statement: 'I am not a religious man.' I went on to quote the above 'Prayer for use by those in doubt'. Many Christians do not find it easy or natural to pray or indeed to think about God at all. But I know that I am right to put Prayer first among the four P's.

I also know that if and when I pray for the Human Family I am doing at least three essential things. First, I am simply crying for help to the only One, who, as I believe, can save us from our sins and follies and their devastating consequences. The global consequences of Poverty, Population, Pollution and Profligacy are so vast and so complex that only the love of God can redeem us from them.

Such a cry for help, however, is emphatically not an abandonment of responsibility; so, secondly, by Prayer I am identifying myself with that sovereign power of Love, committing myself firmly to His cause. Thirdly, therefore, I am also committing myself to appropriate action. Jesus of Nazareth reserved his severest condemnation for hypocrites—in this context, those who pray and then do nothing. We incur that condemnation if, for example, we pray 'Give us this day our daily bread', and then do nothing to ensure that as many of our fellow members of the Human Family as possible actually get what we have just prayed for on their behalf.

But how am I to pray? I propose and shall briefly illustrate four recommendations. First, and I believe most important, I must do my best to get my theology right; that is, pray to the One Who is What He is, rather than to some false image derived from my own cultural background. Secondly—and this is inextricably linked for Christians with the first point—I must try to discern and follow the practice and teaching of Jesus Himself on prayer. Thirdly, I should humbly and sensitively make use of the immensely rich treasury of the prayers of others, in this context particularly the prayers of the poor and of those who directly minister to them. Fourthly, I should try to make my prayers up-to-date and well informed.

This looks like hard work; to be done in the morning when my heart and mind are fresh.

To enable us to get our theology right, stories about God on the one hand and authentic credal statements on the other may be helpful, particularly if they come from a cultural milieu other than our own. Here is an anonymous 'Creed for Calcutta':

Glory to God, I believe in You.

I believe that You are Holy and One and Just.

I believe that You are the Creator of all things and that You have given man dominion over all your created world.

I believe in one world, full of riches meant for everyone to enjoy.

I believe in one race, the family of Man; and I affirm that each man is my brother and that we are responsible for each other.

I believe that we must seek to build a society where there is social, economic, political and religious freedom.

I believe in Jesus and the Bible's evidence about Him, whose life, death and resurrection prove God's permanent love for the world.

I believe in the purpose of God to unite in Christ everything, spiritual and secular.

And because I believe in this, I commit myself to working with all men of good will to bring about God's revolution of Love in Calcutta.

Professional theologians might rightly wish to qualify or more closely define the admittedly biblical notion of man's 'dominion over all your created world'. This concept can be troublesome unless carefully defined. They might have preferred 'the Human Family' for the 'family of Man' and 'We are all brothers and sisters' for 'Each man is my brother'. There are also theological difficulties about associating the word 'prove' with 'the Bible's evidence'. Despite these difficulties this Creed does speak to me powerfully about 'Jesus and the Bible's evidence about Him'. This brings me to my second criterion as a Christian for true prayer: to discern and follow the practice and teaching of Jesus.

It is a curious fact that in St Mark's Gospel, the earliest to be written, there are only three references to Jesus at prayer, each one at a point of particular crisis in His life. This is not to suggest that He was not a man of prayer but rather that He practised what He preached, and attendance at public worship apart, mainly prayed in secret. Traditional teaching has distinguished five main types of prayer, Petition, Intercession, Confession, Thanksgiving and Adoration. Intercession was felt to be less self-regarding than Petition and therefore spiritually superior. Confession was necessary as was Thanksgiving. But Adoration was less self-regarding than either, and therefore the Crown of Prayer. But by contrast the Lord's Prayer is in fact a string of petitions. Most of Jesus' own parables and other teaching on prayer seem to concentrate on the straightforward asking for the good things, material and spiritual without distinction, which our Heavenly Father will not fail to give us. So we come back, relieved and deeply thankful, to that straightforward, if agonized, cry for help, a *cri de coeur* if ever there was one, 'Give us this day our daily bread.' As we have seen together, 'Us' means the whole Human Family, for some eight hundred million of whom this prayer is the most meaningful of all prayers. If we really mean it, too, God will use us to secure its fulfilment. Of course it is a fundamental truth that 'Man shall not live by bread alone, but by every word that proceedeth out of the mouth of

God.'³ It is also true that without bread to eat no man has ears to hear that word of life.

To illustrate my third point about how to pray, the use of the rich treasury of the prayers of others, I quote from 'A Litany of the Disciples of the Servant'⁴ as used in the Andhra Theological College at Hyderabad. The response to each petition is: 'Help us to follow You, Christ the servant.'

Servant-Christ, help us to follow you deep into the waters of Baptism, to link our lives with all those grieved about man's unjust way of life; to break free from the chain of past wrongs; to become fit to face your coming new age; to be renewed by your Spirit, anointed to preach good news to the poor, the oppressed and the prisoner:

Help us to follow you far into the desert, with you to fast, denying false luxury, refusing the tempting ways of personal satisfaction and unscrupulous persuasion:

Help us to follow you in untiring ministry to town and village, to heal and restore the broken body of humanity, to cast out the demonic forces of greed, resentment, communal hatred and self-destructive fear:

Help us to follow you into the place of quiet retreat, to intercede for the confused, the despairing, the anxiety-driven, to prepare ourselves for costly service with you:

Help us to follow you on the road to Jerusalem, to set our faces firmly against friendly suggestions for a safe, expedient life, to embrace boldly the way of self-offering, of life given for others' gain:

Help us to follow you into the city, to claim its whole life for God whose image man bears, to confront the ambitions of the power-hungry, the inhuman orthodoxy of the legalist, with the startling message of your present action, your living power:

Help us to follow you into the temple of your chosen people, to erase from the worship of your Church all that hinders the sense of your presence, the free flow of your Word; to open up your house so that it may be a house of prayer for all people . . .

The remaining petitions follow Christ through His passion and death to His resurrection.

Another powerful Litany, more than worthy to be placed alongside the Litany of the Disciples of Christ the Servant, need not be quoted here in full, being both well known and readily obtainable from Coventry Cathedral. I was glad to see this Litany of Reconciliation included in 'A giant upon the earth', an order of service full of good things published by the World Development Movement for their 'Europe 73 Programme', subtitled 'Europe for the Third World'. I vividly recall the visit to Coventry Cathedral of the former Evangelical Bishop of Dresden, not long before his death. He attended the Friday Litany of Reconciliation in the Cathedral Ruins at 12 noon. As he stood there in the drizzle, the tears streamed down his face. Whereas when Coventry was indiscriminately bombed some five hundred people were killed, when Dresden, no longer a target of any great military significance, was also bombed towards the end of the Second World War, between thirty-five thousand and one hundred and ninety-eight thousand people were burned to death or otherwise killed. The great discrepancy between the smaller and the larger estimates represents the appalling impersonality of the event. A dear friend, a native of Lubeck, once told me that when Lubeck was bombed, the bombs were accompanied by leaflets inscribed 'In revenge for Coventry'.

On another occasion a party of students from the Soviet Union visited the Cathedral. Completing the tour in the Ruins, they were told that 'Father forgive', inscribed in gold behind the altar, meant 'Father forgive us all' for, in St Paul's words, 'all have sinned and fallen short of the glory of God'.

One of the students, a beautiful girl of Tartar origin, made a short speech. 'We shall remember about forgiveness,' she concluded. 'It has no place in our Socialist thought and indeed it is hard for us to forgive the former enemies who so terribly laid waste our country. But it is a noble idea and we shall take it home with us and try to practise it in our daily lives.'

Father, forgive the Greed which exploits the labours of men, and lays waste the earth; our Envy of the welfare and happiness of others; our Indifference to the plight of the homeless and the refugee . . .[5]

These reminiscences of Coventry emphasize the point that forgiveness for ourselves and reconciliation with others are essential themes of our common prayer for the Human Family.

Whether or not that girl was correct in saying that they have no place in Socialist thinking, they can certainly not be excluded from Soviet or indeed any other human experience. The poet Yevtushenko tells a story of his childhood.[6] In Moscow in 1941 his mother took him to see some twenty thousand German prisoners of war paraded through the streets of Moscow. He describes the crowd:

> The crowd were mostly women—Russian women with hands roughened by hard work, lips untouched by lipstick and thin hunched shoulders which had borne half the burden of the war. Every one of them must have had a father or a husband, a brother or a son killed by the Germans. They gazed with hatred in the direction from which the column was to appear.
>
> All at once something happened to them.
>
> They saw German soldiers, thin, unshaven, wearing dirty blood-stained bandages, hobbling on crutches or leaning on the shoulders of their comrades; the soldiers walked with their heads down.
>
> The street became dead silent—the only sound was the shuffling of boots and the thumping of crutches.
>
> Then I saw an elderly woman in broken-down boots push herself forward and touch a policeman's shoulder, saying: 'Let me through.' There must have been something about her that made him step aside.
>
> She went up to the column, took from inside her coat something wrapped in a coloured handkerchief and unfolded it. It was a crust of black bread. She pushed it awkwardly into the pocket of a soldier, so exhausted that he was tottering on his feet. And now suddenly from every side women were running towards the soldiers, pushing into their hands bread, cigarettes, whatever they had.
>
> The soldiers were no longer enemies. They were people.

Fourthly, we should try to make our prayers up-to-date and well-informed. Sometimes this criterion can be fulfilled from the person's own experience, as when Mother Teresa visited Taizé and co-operated with Brother Roger, the Prior, in composing this prayer:

> O God, the Father of everybody: you ask all of us to bring love where the poor are humiliated, joy where the Church is downcast and reconciliation where people are divided—the

father with his son, the mother with her daughter, the husband with his wife, the believer with whoever cannot believe, the Christian with his unwanted fellow Christian. You open this way for us, so that the wounded body of Jesus Christ, your Church, be leaven of communion for the poor of the earth, and in the whole human family. Amen.

But we do not require the personal qualities of such heroes of the faith to enable our own prayers to be well-informed. Christian Aid's published 'Prayers for the People'[7] for example may help us, even though at a more prosaic level. Here is the first of the series:

Christian Aid has allocated £2,000 towards temporary care and maintenance of refugees from mainland China, and old Russian refugees too, as they travel through Hong Kong in transit to a third country.

Pray for these people and for all who experience the sense of rootlessness, feeling that no-one cares or wants to know. And for the work of the Hong Kong Christian Service through whom this grant is channelled.

'In the name of Jesus Christ.' 'Lord, hear our prayer.'

The search for water in India goes on. Christian Aid approved a further grant of £25,000 to AFPRO (Action for Food Production) in Delhi, to provide for teams to investigate likely water sources.

Pray for those who work with AFPRO and in particular for the people involved with Groundwater Investigations Ltd in the vital work they are doing. And remember those for whom the discovery of water means new life and hope.

'In the name of Jesus Christ.' 'Lord, hear our prayer.'

In the islands of the South Pacific, a project involving furniture making, woodwork and boat-building has been supported by a grant of £7,600 from Christian Aid. Those employed are ex-lepers. Such a project may provide new purpose and dignity for people who, cured of leprosy itself, need direction and opportunity for taking up a full life once more.

Pray for the work of the Foundation for the Peoples of the South Pacific who administer the grant, and for those directly involved in the project itself, in Western Samoa. And that men and women everywhere may have opportunities of healing and purpose and worth in making their contribution to the common life.

'In the name of Jesus Christ.' 'Lord, hear our prayer.'

One of the simplest (and most effective) forms of meditation on the scriptures (and in particular on the Gospels) first involves the imagination. You are invited to imagine that you are there in person and that Jesus, if it is a Gospel passage, addresses Himself directly to you. Then you ask yourself, what is He saying about God, about yourself and about the society in which you live. Then finally you resolve on some action or some spiritual advance and pray to God for strength to fulfil it.

Similarly, such prayers as Christian Aid's 'Prayers for the People' require of us periods of silence in which our imaginations get to work. Imagine those tired old Russian refugees in Hong Kong, victims of great winds of change over which they had no control. What tales they must have to tell. How wonderful if a mere £2,000 can give them a chance of a new life.

Then there is that search for water in India. The distribution of water, in particular clean water, is the key to victory over famine and malnutrition. I have some photographs of members of the St John's College, Palayamkottai, Social Service Team, led by the College Bursar, Mr Bedford Solomon, helping a team of villagers to enlarge and deepen the village well. How hard they are working, stripped to the waist. Such visual aids help us in our prayers to imagine the skilled and eager search for water, 'remembering those for whom the discovery of water means new life and hope'.

How about those ex-lepers in Western Samoa? A friend of mine, visiting India for the first time, stayed at a village near Madras, given over to the rehabilitation of cured lepers. One man said to him: 'I love the Lord Jesus. He is the only God who has ever touched a leper.' What healing lies in that opportunity for those Pacific islanders to make furniture and build boats. And all again for a mere £7,000, to supplement no doubt the efforts of local Christians and others. Less than that mink coat I mentioned in the West End store catalogue!

Let Christian Aid also provide my final illustration for this section:

Lord Jesus, if I love and serve my neighbour
Out of my knowledge, leisure, power or wealth,

Open my eyes to understand his anger
If from his helplessness he hates my help.

When I have met my brother's need with kindness
And prayed that he could waken from despair,
Open my ears if, crying now for justice,
He struggles for the changes that I fear.

Lord, though I cling to safety or possessions,
Yet from the Cross Love's poverty prevails:
Open my heart to life and liberation,
Open my hands to bear the mark of nails.[8]

This hymn is strong meat, worthy of a second reading. I think
that I can pray it, but I am not sure that I would dare to sing it.

Prophecy. The Second Response

Prayer, then, comes first. But prayer by itself is not enough. For
most of us it has to issue in words (Prophecy), deeds (Political
Action) and a way of life (Personal Moderation). As an
anonymous writer has put it: 'Man can glorify his gods in two
ways: by building great houses of worship; and by accepting
responsibility for the care of all Creation. Prayer alone cannot
safeguard our common heritage. Man's gratitude and praise are
best shown by his good husbandry of Nature.'

These words seem to me however to set up in opposition to
each other what should be complementary. Such a 'great house
of worship' as Chartres Cathedral for example, sets out incom-
parably for those who can 'read' the windows and the sculptures
a grand design of creation and redemption in which Man has a
distinctive and essential part. In Chapter Three of *Enough is
Enough*[9] Dr John V. Taylor firmly anchors the call to live more
simply to its Biblical roots. 'The dream of shalom' to which he
refers establishes and expresses the harmony between the People
and the Land which is the gift of God. This harmony has to be
realized both in legislation and in proclamation, the Law and the
Prophets. Law and prophecy are distinct but not divergent. To
the people of Israel, Moses the Lawgiver remains not only the
first but the greatest of all the prophets.

Once when Moses was overburdened with administration he
cried out: 'I wish that all the Lord's people were prophets and
that the Lord would confer his spirit on them all!'[10] And so say
all of us. You do not have to speak from a pulpit or public
platform, radio or television studio, nor write a book, to be an

effective prophet in the cause of living more simply that all of us may simply live. Grandparents can and do teach their children and their grandchildren both by precept and by example, for many of the older generation cannot but live simply. They learned to do so in any case in the hard times of the thirties and during the Second World War. Similarly, parents can teach their young children. One of the best gifts you can give a child today is the ability to live cheerfully and contentedly without the psychological necessity of amassing consumer goods.

Children can teach their parents too. Many of the younger generation put their elders to shame by their joyous detachment from the rat race of the acquisition of money and the things that money can buy. Their life style can be a shining light. Teachers can and should take their opportunities of sharing the values we have in mind or at least of presenting them as a valid and attractive option. In a Report to the Planning and Environment Group of the National Council of Social Service we read:

> We think that it is desirable that the next generation should be aware of the implications of the Blueprint for Survival. The problem is how on earth this is to be done, since all the other social and political pressures are pushing in a diametrically opposite direction.
>
> The implications of the Blueprint are revolutionary in every sense, political, social, economic and philosophical; and it is not by spelling out the policies that this will be understood (although that will have to do in the meantime), but by helping the new generation to exercise the imagination needed to think up far more radical proposals than any of us have the nerve (or the imagination) to do at present!
>
> It is, after all, the teacher who is conscious of the importance of these issues who will, because of his own priorities and his own sense of responsibility, introduce these themes into his teaching.

Those whose daily work appears to give them no specialist opportunities for such Prophecy can often put in a word of truth in the club or in the pub, at the meal table or round the fire or in the momentary intervals between television programmes. 'I wish that all the Lord's people were prophets and that the Lord would confer his spirit on them all.' And that goes, in the present context, also for all those who doubt or deny the Lord's very existence but who share these values which we believers think that we derive from Him! This is the point, too, at which to recall that, as in Prayer so also in Prophecy, the Buddhist, the Hindu, the Jew, the Muslim, the Sikh and every other man and woman of faith, all have their part to play, their contribution to make and their insights to share. Here, for example, is the parable of a Sanskrit sage:

> Three children of the Lord of Creatures—gods, men and demons—lived with their father as students of sacred knowledge. After some time as students the gods said to him: 'Speak to us, sir.' He uttered one syllable: '*Da*,' and asked if they understood.
>
> They replied: 'We did understand. You said: Restrain your-selves (*Damyata*).'
>
> Then the men said to him: 'Speak to us, sir.' He uttered one syllable: '*Da*,' and asked if they understood.
>
> They replied: 'We did understand. You said: Give (*Datta*).'
>
> Then the demons said to him: 'Speak to us, sir.' He uttered one syllable: '*Da*,' and asked if they understood.
>
> They replied: 'We did understand. You said: Be compas-sionate (*Dayadhvam*).'
>
> This is how the divine voice rolls in the thunder: *Da, Da, Da*. Restrain yourselves, give, be compassionate. One should practise this threefold command: Self-restraint, giving, com-passion.[12]

Self-restraint, giving, compassion; these are precisely the building blocks required for the Life Style we seek; these are the precise fruits of the prophecy we must utter.

Political Action. The Third Response
As deeds are to words, so is Political Action to Prophecy. More and more of us are coming to realize that,

> in the words of Julius Nyerere, 'Poverty is not the real problem of the modern world. We have the knowledge and resources which could enable us to overcome poverty. The real problem . . . is the division of mankind into rich and poor.' The significance of this division lies not just in the uneven distribution of resources or of wealth. It is that 'the reality of the problem arises because the man that is rich has power over the lives of those who are poor and the rich nation has power over the policies of those which are not rich. And

even more important is the fact that our social and economic system, nationally and internationally, supports these divisions and constantly increases them so that the rich get even more rich and more powerful, while the poor get relatively poorer and less able to control their own future.'

It is therefore quite clear that the power to eliminate poverty lies with those who are rich, and not with the poor. We can give the poor as much technology and education as we want, but unless there is a transfer of wealth and resources to them as well the plight of the poor will remain unchanged. So we come to the point where we have to make a decision, whether to side with the poor and try to bring about this redistribution of wealth and power, or to leave the power where it is in the hands of those who profit from poverty and just relieve some of the symptoms.[13]

My experience is that at student meetings our personal duty to take political action is at once appreciated, even to the point in some cases of dismissing as irrelevant any complementary attempt to 'live more simply that all of us may simply live'. 'That's all very nice,' they used to say at question time, 'but what we need is the revolution.' Less has been heard of this revolution in recent years than previously. Many members of church groups on the other hand are scared of any form of political involvement. Even today there can be found those who say: 'But religion and politics don't mix.' I suppose that this is largely because political action in favour of the conservation of resources and their more equitable distribution appears, in the short term at least, to be contrary to the material interests of most of us in the Western World; particularly of those of us in positions of some power, whether in Government, in the ownership or in the management of the means of production or in the more powerful Trades Unions.

These material interests are pinpointed by Bishop Hugh Montefiore when he formulates 'some current dogmas of our technological culture':

1. Everyone has a right to a rising standard of material living.
2. There is no upper limit to the standard of living that we can achieve.
3. Man has the wit and the power to control his environment. There may be crises, but science and technology can get us through in the end, as they have done in the past.

4. A rising standard of living means greater happiness.
5. The chief aim of government should be material prosperity.[14]

Consumers of the World Unite!

These current dogmas are already obsolete as we move from the exploitative era of human history into the conservationist era; that is, from the period when it was broadly our human destiny to exploit the resources of our planet into the period when it is broadly our human destiny to continue to develop them, yes, but only within the context of conserving them and distributing them more fairly. Since the Reformation period we Europeans have moved from a Feudal society, in which a small landowning minority held sway by force, by custom and no doubt to a real extent by consent, into a Capitalist society in which the owners and managers of the means of the production of goods and services held and still hold massive power and influence.

For more than a hundred years this Capitalist society has been giving way in many parts of the world to a more Socialist style of society in which the Trades Unions represent the growing power of the organized workers who actually produce the goods and services. The strife which this shift of power engenders is real enough. From the sidelines, however, much of it looks today like shadow boxing. After a show of resistance to wage and other demands, the owners and managers generally give in, safeguarding their own position by passing on any consequent price increases to the hapless consumer. Inflation follows thick and fast all over the world.

Speaking as a professional economist, Dr E. F. Schumacher[15] commented on this situation:

> People ask what causes inflation. A very easy question to answer. There is only one cause of inflation: prices are put up. Unfortunately the language of most people who talk economics is so sloppy that they prefer to say, prices rise. It is an incorrect way of speaking—as if prices were balloons. No. Prices are *put* up, and when you put it that way, you can ask who puts them up. Those who have the power to do so and can get away with it. The powerless cannot get away with it.

How then are the powerless, the hapless consumers, to obtain and exercise political and economic power? Since we are all consumers and since the majority in any known society are the less conspicuous consumers, it follows that both in any effectively democratic nation and in the end within the Human Family as a whole it ought to be possible for the consumers of the world to unite to eliminate inflation on the one hand and the production of socially useless goods and services on the other. We have nothing to lose but the chains of our own greed.

By and large, the Capitalists won power by withholding capital from kings, princes and barons who resisted their demands. As the history of the English Civil War reveals, the cost of this transfer of power in terms of suffering was very high. As usual the poor and the powerless paid the highest price, staining the shires with their blood in defence of or in opposition to the Divine Right of Kings. Similarly, and again at consider-able cost, for example, to the coalminers and others who pioneered this movement, the workers continue to win power by withholding or threatening to withhold their labour. And now, as the exploitative era gives way all over the world to the conservationist era, we consumers must learn how to withhold our only power, our purchasing power. As the workers learned to unite in the nineteenth and early twentieth centuries, so we richer consumers must take the initiative in uniting with the poorer majority in order to concentrate our joint purchasing power on socially useful goods and services for all; food, clothing, housing, yes, and health and education services too. The list of socially useful products will be a long one today. We should not, for example, neglect music and the arts for all. We have not yet learned how to achieve an informed consensus on how to distinguish degrees of social utility. We shall need as powerful a solidarity with our 'mates' in the developing countries as Trades Unionists have achieved among themselves in our own land, if the consumers of the world are to unite to defeat inflation, to free trade from discriminatory restraints and to compel the producers to concentrate on what the whole Human Family so urgently needs and wants.

When those student questioners used to say, 'That's all very nice, but what we need is the revolution', they probably had in mind some form of alliance between students and workers such as so signally failed to materialize in the late sixties. The revolution that I propose is far more radical and has the great advantage of being wholly non-violent. All we have to do is to refuse in disciplined solidarity with each other and with the poor to consume what we neither need nor want. There would inevitably be a wide range of degrees of commitment to the Movement but some generally agreed guidelines would be essential.

Is this a practical possibility or merely an Utopian dream? Well, most if not all revolutions start with the bourgeoisie. Moreover I suspect that what is loosely called 'The Women's Movement' has a crucial part to play. But let us not pretend that no conflict of interests is involved.

Meanwhile it is again Bishop Montefiore[16] who reminds us that:

> All this demands unprecedented legislative action, introduced so as not to destroy our delicate economies; laws about paying for the social costs of pollution, laws that discourage large families, laws governing the use of materials, laws about conserving precious soil and air and water. It is no good one country going it alone, or it will simply price itself out of the international market. (The redesigning of motor engines for leadless petrol is an important example.) Just because the West has a vast preponderance of capital resources, the West must initiate action, or its intentions will rightly be suspect in the developing countries. We desperately need international agreement, co-operation and enforcement.

> A vast popular movement is urgently needed to achieve this. It must be international. It must sweep the world like a forest fire, for time is short. Fortunately many young people seem ready to fan the flames. Their world is at stake. No new law is of use unless it rests on consent. No organization has much force unless constituent members believe in it and can make it work. It is therefore necessary that there should be a colossal reorientation of social attitudes—a new way of living —if we are to change course.

> Despite our inbuilt delight in fertility, we must have a new attitude to procreation. And we must look for happiness not from things but from people. The only possibility of these huge changes taking place is under the compulsion of strong religious conviction (using religion in its proper sense of sacredly binding). More than education is needed; something akin to religious conversion alone can alter these deeply entrenched attitudes.

Your Political Action and Mine

Such general considerations, vital as they are, must not distract us from the main question before us in this section, our own personal political action. Each individual must answer for himself or herself. But it is possible to distinguish three main areas of opportunity: local, national and international.

In each sphere you and I become more effective when we combine with others. Locally, for example, the Bristol Cathedral Life Style Cell (of which more later) was able to give some corporate support to the local branch of the Conservation Society in its campaign to persuade the City Council to collect waste paper separately for recycling in areas where it was economic to do so. More recently we appointed a representative to liaise with the local branch of Friends of the Earth, and have supported their pilot project for the collection and recycling of bottles.

The daily work of some people gives them a particular opportunity to influence local affairs and raise the level of civic consciousness. Others may have the energy and ability to serve as local Councillors. Others again are better suited to act as Socratic gadflies, both as individuals and also as members of local Civic Societies or the local branches of national development agencies or conservationist societies whose activities have political implications. More often than is usually realized a local church or, better still, a local Council of Churches, can take effective political action.

This reference to national development agencies and conservationist societies leads us on naturally to the national scene. Such an agency as the World Development Movement whose aims are overtly political demands our particular attention. We can also, as individuals or on behalf of groups, write letters to a Minister or a Member of Parliament. The Bristol Cathedral Life Style Cell, for instance, once wrote to the then Secretary for Energy, Mr Anthony Wedgwood Benn, who also represents a Bristol constituency. We wished to draw his attention to the 1975 Report of the Dag Hammerskjold Foundation, entitled *What Now?* One of the Papers in that Report, entitled 'How much is enough?', contained a Five Point Plan for affluent and industrially advanced Sweden, as follows:

1. A ceiling on meat consumption.
2. A ceiling on oil consumption.

3. More economical use of buildings.
4. Greater durability of consumer goods.
5. No privately owned automobiles.

In his thoughtful reply, the Minister brought together the issues of 'extravagant consumption' and 'unequal distribution' in a wholly acceptable way.

The General Election 1978

In a leading article at the time *The Guardian* defined at least part of our political task in these words: 'If we can't get a bigger cake and the old one is going to be cut differently, then someone's slice is going to be smaller. The problem is how to make that simple message acceptable to the electorate of the countries which have never had it bad.'[17]

As already indicated in Britain's General Election in 1978 neither of the two larger political parties tried. Both pretended that the 'cake' would be larger and fuller of goodies for most of us than ever. So it was open to some of us at least to try to bring the real issues to the fore. Such political action need not be confined to the run up to a General Election. The pressure needs to be continuous, not least as the public becomes more and more disillusioned at the inevitable failure to enlarge and distribute this hypothetical cake.

One form such pressure can take is the organization of political meetings at which the local Member of Parliament and the other parliamentary candidates are invited to answer questions from a common platform on selected issues. Local Councils of Churches are particularly well placed to do this, but Head Teachers of secondary schools can do the same as can Students' Unions, voluntary societies or indeed any concerned groups.

Under the heading 'What Parliament for the Poor?', Oxfam produced an apparently undated Election Special edition of 'Oxfam News' in which the answers given by spokesmen for seven political parties to seven 'development' questions were placed in parallel columns, with Oxfam's own answers in an eighth column completing the picture. The questions were:

1. How can the UK help ensure that everyone in the world has enough to eat?
2. How would you propose to increase the effectiveness of the Government's aid programme?

3. Would you plan to increase the size of the Government's aid programme?
4. How would you propose to safeguard UK jobs while at the same time encouraging manufacturing industries in the poor countries?
5. How would you propose to ensure that the poorest in the Third World are not harmed by UK trade and investment?
6. Are there any ways in which Britain can help to reduce the amount that poor countries spend on arms?
7. Would you plan to increase public awareness of the inequalities in the world—and of ways that the UK can help to remedy them?

On a more domestic note, Harford Thomas and James Robertson wrote a full-page newspaper article on 'An Alternative Agenda for Party Politics'.[18] They proposed the following 'selection of key questions for the politicians:

What about:
Sharing out existing jobs?
Shorter hours, a shorter working week, more time at home?
Help for labour-intensive industries to create more jobs?
Encouraging unpaid voluntary work—'useful employment'?
A social wage for all?
Help for small firms, small farms, worker co-ops?
Reviving rural life, resettling the country?
Villagizing the inner cities, with urban farms, part-time farming?
Local participation in housing, schools, hospitals, leisure services?

In another article, 'Top Marks for Fringe Group Manifestos',[19] Harford Thomas emphasized the failure of the two major parties to take alternative futures into account and it was he again who pointed out how the 'first past the post' system of election effectively disfranchises a great many of us who are dissatisfied with the old prescriptions:

The disfranchised are emphatically asking for reform. Majority opinion is now three to two in favour of proportional representation in some form, and only one in six are against it. But a majority of MP's remain against it—for reasons of self-interest in manipulating the present system to their personal or party advantage.

Parliament was shown by the opinion poll published by the *Economist* last year to be totally out of line with public opinion on this. On the question of a referendum on voting reform, four out of five said the people should decide. This view was spread evenly across the parties, 81 per cent Conservatives, 81 per cent Labour, 86 per cent Liberals, and 82 per cent other parties favouring a referendum.[20]

The British Council of Churches also published a list of questions, but rather late in the day and, some would say, giving Conservative opinion a legitimate cause for complaint of tendentiousness. My own 'examination paper' for those who were seeking to represent me in Parliament was as follows:[21]

A. *International questions*
1. How does Britain compare with other developed countries in aid (expressed in percentage of GNP) for developing countries? How in practice can our record be improved? Which are the best forms of aid? Generous reciprocal trade agreements? Low-interest loans? Private and public investment? Nation-to-nation or through multi-national channels?
2. How best can the people of Britain help the various peoples of Southern Africa to decide their own destinies? Please make specific reference both to the transfer of power in Rhodesia and to British investment in South Africa.
3. What do you think are the particular political, economic and cultural contributions which Britain should be making towards the development of the European Economic Community? And what should we be receiving from the Community in these fields?

B. *Domestic political and cultural questions*
4. How best can we safeguard our nation from the possibility of a totalitarian takeover, whether of the extreme right or of the extreme left? What bearing have such issues as devolution, proportional representation and others on the maintenance and development of our tradition of parliamentary democracy?
5. How best can we ensure and increase the welfare of those citizens who belong to ethnic minorities (i.e. Asians, West Indians)?

6. What exceptions, if any, should be allowed to the principle of comprehensive education in the maintained sector? What is the role of independent schools and in particular should they retain their charitable status? What do you think to be the aims of religious education in a secular society and how are they to be pursued?

7. How best can we reconcile for our citizens the claims of equality of opportunity and of excellence in performance? And how best can we protect the interests of consumers in a producer-oriented society?

C. *Economic questions*

8. In making use of the wealth that is expected to accrue from North Sea Oil, what balance would you wish to strike between the claims of:
   (a) repayment of our international debts?
   (b) investment in productive industry?
   (c) investment in such services as education, health, pensions, police forces and other contributions to the maintenance of justice, law and order, public transport and so on?

9. What approximately are the resources in men and money devoted to research and production of:
   (a) nuclear energy?
   (b) coal?
   (c) oil and natural gas?
   (d) wind, wave and solar energy?
   In what ways, if any, should this balance be altered in the next few years?

10. How can we reduce unemployment? Consider the various implications of a shorter working week, a partial ban on overtime, investment in technological improvements, overmanning, diversion of production to socially useful products, early retirement, etc.

International Action
Internationally most of us feel, and indeed in practice probably are, more or less powerless. But we need to remember the rapidly growing interdependence of the members of the Human Family with the result that the attitudes and actions of individuals do contribute to the wellbeing or otherwise of the whole family.

After careful thought, for example, and some discussion,

some members of our Bristol Cathedral Life Style Cell signed an
Open Letter to former U.S. President Carter in support of his
'effort to eliminate nuclear weapons . . . his new energy policy
which will steer the United States towards conservation of
energy and, hopefully, along a soft energy path, towards the
efficient use of a wide range of abundant, safe and renewable
energy sources; of solar energy, wind power, water power and
the energy from bioconversion . . .'[22]

This signature had an unexpected sequel: an invitation to be
shown over the Berkeley Nuclear Research Station; a
fascinating opportunity to become somewhat better informed
on a difficult and complex issue. We certainly became aware of a
highly commendable though not altogether reassuring
concentration of research on the safety aspect of the production
of nuclear power.

It would seem that in the international even more than in the
national and local fields, corporate action becomes essential. A
good example was provided by a motion before the Methodist
Conference in the year of the Queen's Silver Jubilee:

> The rules in Scripture for a jubilee include the remission of
> debts, the resting of the land, the liberation of slaves and the
> return of every family to its own land . . . So (the proposal
> was) 'that the Church should respectfully petition the Queen
> to celebrate the jubilee of her reign by encouraging her
> Government 'to remit those debts presently owed to this
> realm by governments of the developing world.'
>
> 'The Bible tells us that all debts are to be released in Jubilee
> year,' argues the Rev. David J. Moore, superintendent
> minister of the Bow Mission, East London . . . 'The debts of
> the developing world, which are not huge in our terms but
> crippling to the Third World, could be remitted as a
> gesture.'[23]

The cynic, who, I must reluctantly admit, would have a
point, might comment that such a proposal was a typically
unrealistic piece of ecclesiastical romanticism. Certainly there
are circumstances in which a march or other form of demonstration constitutes a more effective political action than mere
words. David Moore and his colleagues at the Bow Mission
have themselves given courageous evidence of this in their
opposition to racism in East and South-East London. I have only
ever taken part in three such events, one in Cambridge in favour

of an end to the Vietnam war, one in Bristol in favour of racial equality and one in London in favour of the whale. This latter march, featured in *The Guardian* under the headline 'Whale protest seeks big catch'[24] may deserve a brief mention.

Friends of the Earth invited me, as an unofficial representative of the Churches, to join Spike Milligan, the entertainer, Brigid Brophy, the author, Frank Windsor, the actor, Country Joe Macdonald, the singer and Neville Sandelson MP in delivering a letter of protest at the Japanese Embassy against the continuing slaughter of whales. Then some five hundred of us marched past Marble Arch and along Hyde Park to the neighbourhood of the Soviet Embassy, to whose gate three of us were accompanied by a senior police officer to deliver our letter. Mr Milligan insisted that on this occasion 'the Church' should be the spokesman. Our letter was accepted after a brief discussion by the Second Secretary who came to the gate to meet us. Our police escort told us that it was the first such petition to have been accepted there in two years. We finished up with a chilly but jolly picnic in Kensington Gardens where we learned that similar demonstrations had been planned for Washington, Vancouver, Paris, Honolulu and other cities.

Was it merely a coincidence that within a week 'The International Whaling Commission (meeting in Canberra) announced a 36 per cent reduction in whaling quotas for the next year . . . reducing the quota for all whales species by more than ten thousand'[25]? Since then, the campaign to 'Save the Whale' has gone from strength to strength.

There is, however, no cause for complacency. Mention of Canberra reminds me that even the question of the preservation of these magnificent, gentle and intelligent creatures, to which I remain wholly committed, is not without its problems. Under the heading 'Counting the Human Cost of Saving Whales', whaling men told reporter Geraldine Doogue what the decision to close down the Western Australian whaling industry meant to over a hundred men whose livelihood had gone. 'Down here it's only the people that matter. And look at their faces when I try to explain that some people believe the whale . . . shouldn't be used. They just don't understand. We all know our jobs are finished . . . We'll just have to change our lives completely.'[26]

Up To Us
There is a danger in this or any other attempt to relate the great,

complex theme of Political Action to what ordinary people like you and me can do, of trivializing it beyond recall. Nobody, of course, is precisely like you or like me, nor is anybody just ordinary. Even former U.S. President Nixon once observed:

In the final analysis, the foundation on which environmental progress rests in our society is a responsible and informed citizenry. My confidence that our nation will meet its environmental problems in the years ahead is based in large measure on my faith in the continued vigilance of American public opinion and in the continued vitality of citizen efforts to protect and improve the environment.[27]

To thes words W. D. Ruckelshaus, administrator of the U.S. Environmental Protection Agency, adds the comment: 'Unquestionably the public must not only be allowed to participate in environmental decision-making, it should be encouraged to do so. Often the sheer weight of public opinion is sufficient to force corrections without any need for legal action.'[28]

The Contents Headings of the booklet from which these quotations are taken give a clue to the means of appropriate Political Action: The new revolution—Get informed—Know the law—Pick your targets carefully—Yes, lobbying—Fight for funds—Telling your story—Know your rights—Some final words.

The hypothetical student, with whom I was in dialogue at the beginning of this section, may remain unimpressed by this practical check-list of how to get things done. He or she knows that political action involves party politics. He or she will want to know where I stand. My answer is unexciting and may please neither my friends on the Right nor those on the Left. But then, as a Coventry Cathedral colleague once said to me, 'If you attempt reconciliation, you are liable to be bashed by both sides.' I would put my faith in some form of parliamentary social democratic party as best equipped to represent the universal consumer, hold the middle ground, protect the powerless against the concentration of power in the hands of the violent and achieve that for which the Australian Prayer Book so convincingly prays: 'Give wisdom to those in authority in every land, and guide all peoples in the way of righteousness and peace, so that they may share with justice the resources of the earth, work together in trust, and seek the common good.'[29]

To put the point in another way, despite my belief that large-scale radical action is required if the resources of our planet are to be distributed more equitably, I would still far rather live in Western than in Eastern Europe, in the United States than in the Soviet Union, in India rather than in China. I like to think that my preference for non-violent change and peaceful persuasion derives from Christian principles. I know that it also derives from a personal, though wholly undistinguished participation in the mass violence of the Second World War. Two young German friends once asked me politely: 'Are you old enough to have fought in the Second World War?' 'Yes,' I answered diffidently. 'Did you fight in any famous battles?' 'Yes,'—even more diffidently—'I began at El Alamein and ended up just outside Monte Cassino.' 'Oh, yes,' the girl replied, 'We've read about those in our history books!' Under the heading 'Even the Goriest of Carnage Has To Be Shown', Nick Downie, a journalist who has filmed four guerilla wars and twice won the Royal Television Society's news feature award, has put the point well:

> More than fifty millions died in the Second World War, and there are grounds for believing that the reason Europe is still at peace is that the men in charge remember what it was really like. Unfortunately the years are starting to take their toll.
>
> A new generation is growing up in Europe—a generation that will soon be twitching the reins of power—that knows nothing of saturation bombing, artillery barrages or hand-to-hand fighting. Furthermore it is a highly politicized generation that has been fed a diet of such slogans as 'Political power comes out of the barrel of a gun', and 'You cannot make an omelette without breaking eggs.'[30]

My final words for this section are taken from the Foodshare Manifesto,[31] signed by a number of representative Christian leaders. The signatories urged Her Majesty's Government to:

1. Press the EEC to double its food aid commitment from 1.3 million tons to 2.6 million tons of grain.

2. Help with the necessary finance to purchase this grain.

3. Double Britain's existing commitment of 25,000 tons of fertilizer to the FAO's Fertilizer Supply Scheme and pay the cost of this additional fertilizer.

4. Initiate a high-level study to report within three months, to see what economies could be made in our food patterns to release grain to the hungry.

I have to say that each of the first three recommendations is open to question at least as aspects of long-term policy. Is it better to send free grain or by finance and technology to encourage and enable the beneficiaries to grow their own? 'If I give a man a fish,' says a Chinese proverb, 'I feed him for a day. But if I teach him to fish, I feed him for a lifetime.'

Is it better to encourage a temporary increase in the use of imported fertilizer by those farmers who can afford to buy and use it or rather to promote the methods of organic farming which use to the full the resources naturally and locally available? But about the fourth point there is surely no question. Under this last heading the signatories went on to call upon those they represented and 'all men of goodwill' to:

Lower their patterns of consumption (by family fasts, one meal less a week, a meatless day, etc.).

Channel the money saved to aid agencies for their food and agricultural development programmes.

This would be a symbol of our commitment for an immediate and effective Governmental response.

In other words, let us 'Live more simply that all of us may simply live'; a corporate political initiative that leads naturally into a personal response; from Political Action to Personal Moderation.

Personal Moderation. The Fourth Response

At St John's College, Palayamkottai, we used occasionally to receive official visits from 'big men', as they are colloquially called, politicians, philanthropists and the like. Some were 'big men' indeed, mentally and spiritually. But I remember at least one who addressed the students on India's need for heroic self-sacrifice, invoking such names as Vinobha Bhave or Gandhiji himself. With powerful rhetoric he summoned the prospective graduates to give the best years of their lives to the village poor. The lecture ended, and the lecturer duly thanked and garlanded, he set off by taxi to catch the next train back to the state capital.

The students were no more impressed than we would be by the Socialist Member of Parliament who sends his sons to Eton.

Even such a visitor of undoubted integrity as Dr Billy Graham received the same cold scrutiny. 'How can he possibly be a holy man,' a Hindu student asked me ingenuously, 'when he is obviously so very rich?' We ourselves and our four children lived on a stipend that approximated to that of an Assistant Curate in Britain—not a great amount twenty-four years ago. But we occupied an old colonial bungalow that a few years later was to be turned into a hostel for thirty students.

The point is that we dare not prophesy about the grossly inequitable distribution of the Earth's resources and their conservation, nor take public political action on these issues; above all we dare not pray to the all-seeing Heavenly Father about them, unless in our own life style we are committed to some measure of Personal Moderation. I use this phrase, 'some measure of Personal Moderation' advisedly. We are not talking about fanatical austerity. At Palayamkottai I once expressed to a wise and trusted colleague my own anxieties about the fact that we had a battered old refrigerator: a luxury possessed by no other member of staff. 'Please don't give it up,' he begged. 'If you do, we won't be able to have ice cream any more.'

As Gandhiji exemplified to the full and as some Christian and other leaders in Africa and elsewhere have also shown, these considerations apply equally to political leaders.

> If you are one day called upon to diagnose the degree of development of a non-industrialized country, make it your business to find out about the diet of the Prime Minister or the Head of State.
>
> If the menus are drawn up in the style of Malossol caviar on toast Melba or filet de boeuf Wellington, and if the national dishes are only served as an amusement, a weekend fantasy, then you can tremble for your mission. You will, in fact, have reason to fear that the country is launched on a road to development which is not designed to favour either its local resources or the basic needs of its people. For, from the President's table down to that of his servants, and from them down to their families and friends, the tendency will be to prefer an 'aristocratic' diet . . .
>
> On the other hand if preference is given to yams rather than to potatoes at the President's table, even when he entertains distinguished foreigners, if proper consideration is given to maize, millet, cassava and cowpeas, then you can be sure that

full use is being made of local resources, and that the peasant has some chance of participating in a development plan which really involves him.[32]

These reported words of Josue de Castro may overstate the case. But they are parabolic of the attitudes and life-styles required of Western expatriates in developing countries as well. In the Yemen Arab Republic (North Yemen) my wife and I saw a good deal of the British Volunteer Programme (mainly Community Medicine, Adult Literacy and Agricultural Development). We were impressed by the simple life style of the volunteers, living as they did in small houses in the former Jewish quarter of the capital, Sanaa, or else in remote country places, and sharing to some extent the standards of living of many of their neighbours. They employed no servants, for example, and enjoyed the delicious local food. But this is by no means always the case.

The most immediate challenge to the World Bank, indeed, comes not from the left but from the right. Within the United States a common charge has been that the salaries and expenses of World Bank staff are too high, and only last week a US news agency published a study of the bank's travel costs, leading to criticism of the amount of use bank staff made of Concorde. This might seem rather petty when viewed against the broad problems of world economic development. But it is just the sort of issue being used by some US Congressmen as an excuse to try to deny the bank further injections of US funds, or to tie up the funds being granted in such a way that the bank would be unable to accept them.[33]

A twelve-verse poem in the *Washington Post*,[34] from which this selection follows, makes the point with venomous accuracy:

Excuse me, friends, I must catch my jet—
I'm off to join the Development Set;
My bags are packed, and I've had all my shots,
I have travellers' cheques and pills for the trots . . .

In Sheraton Hotels in scattered nations
We damn multinational corporations;
Injustice seems easy to protest
In such seething hotbeds of social rest.

We discuss malnutrition over steaks
And plan hunger talks during coffee breaks.
Whether Asian floods or African drought,
We face each issue with an open mouth . . .

After a tilt at 'Consultants who . . . borrow your watch to tell
you the time', and at the esoteric language of this Development
Set, the poem concludes:

Development Set homes are extremely chic,
Full of carvings, curios, and draped with batik.
Eye-level photographs subtly assure
That your host is at home with the great and the poor.

Enough of these verses—on with the mission!
Our task is as broad as the human condition!
Just pray God the biblical promise is true:
The poor ye shall always have with you.[34]

To which some readers might reasonably react with a quotation
from Hamlet: 'We that have free souls, it touches us not: let the
galled jade wince, our withers are unwrung.'[35]

It may be, therefore, that the first step on the road to Personal
Moderation for any who have not yet taken it, is to realize just
how rich most of us are.

How Rich Are We?

Attempting to answer the question, 'Where are the rich?',
William Davis proposed some years ago that 'No-one is rich
unless he has considerable assets, as well as a good income. Here
again one must adjust one's ideas to allow for inflation: given
today's house prices (for example) total assets of £100,000 do not
make a man rich or even wealthy.'[36]

Fantastic as it may seem, there are many people who would
agree with this estimate. To me, however, Victor Keegan's more
recent analysis of 'Riches Beyond Dreams' is more realistic:

You almost certainly haven't counted it. And you may not
believe it, anyway, but you and your family (if you are
average) have a personal wealth of around £27,000.

This startling information can be gleaned from an esoteric
Whitehall article published this morning by the Central
Statistical Office, called Personal Sector Balance Sheets.

On December 31st, 1976, the wealth of the personal sector

(all 55.9 million of us plus non-profit making bodies) was estimated at £339.4 billion, which works out at about £27,000 for an average family with 2.4 children. We had £231.4 billion in 'physical assets' like land, houses and consumer durables, and a further £151.9 billion in 'financial assets' like bank accounts, building society savings, ordinary shares, pension funds and the notes in our pockets. Our liabilities came to £43.9 billion, mainly mortgages and bank loans.[37]

Keegan rightly goes on to point out that 'wealth is so unevenly distributed in this country (the top 10 per cent own 60 per cent of all wealth) that a simple division of total wealth by total inhabitants creates an illusion of prosperity in the middle.' But he is also right to conclude that 'statistics may lie, but not as much as we ourselves would if asked how much we were worth.'

This general conclusion is supported by Philip Jordan in an article entitled 'How Living Can Be All Cakes and Ale'.

All in all it seems a pretty cosy life being British. Over the past ten years we have worked less, earned more, spent more, holidayed more, drunk more, borrowed more . . . Couples are marrying younger and owning their own homes earlier (50 per cent of the population), owning cars (56 per cent) and television sets (10 million colour licences and 8 million black and white), and deep-freezes (20 per cent) . . .

Between 1965 and 1975 beer consumption went up by 32 per cent, spirits by 81 per cent, and wine by 113 per cent . . . About 38 million people took a holiday last year compared with 31 millions in 1966 . . . When we are not away our favourite leisure occupations are television, drinking, gardening, eating out and going out for the day . . .

We spend a good deal of time talking on the phone. With 16,000 million calls helping the Post Office towards a £264-million profit we are third in the world telephone league, behind America and Japan.[38]

To the objection that the call 'to live more simply that all of us may simply live' is relevant only to the bourgeois or middle classes and does not apply to the 'working class', we can oppose the fact that this overall prosperity is not at all confined to any particular social 'class'. Under the heading 'A New Class of Buying Power', Dennis Barker reminds us that the 'Middle Class Proletariat' has gone many miles further forward on its march into the blessed land of washing machines, transistors and Scotch on the rocks . . . The household income of manual workers was underpinned by the wife's earnings in ways not always so widely available to middle class wives . . . It was established, for example, that of those who spent £5 or more a week on beer, 86 per cent read the papers of the Daily Mirror Group . . . The Mirror group readers smoke more heavily too—they account for three-quarters of all expenditure on tobacco.[39]

The view that the so-called 'working class' ('All labels are libels', as Dean Inge used to say) were 'catching up with' the 'middle class' some years ago was also confirmed by John Davis. After looking into the situation of professional engineers, he continued:

Other professions have also fallen behind but none so much as the clergy, whose stipend is now less than 75 per cent of the average earnings statistic. But even the clergy have no reason to feel sorry for themselves by comparison with large numbers (five million) of their fellow men and women living in households in which income is only 25 per cent of the statistical average—that is £20 per week or less compared with more than £80 per week.[40]

So we are comparatively rich, and so, perhaps, are you who are reading these words. For all of us, therefore, except the genuinely poor, this realization that we are already at least moderately wealthy should free us from any of that stress and anxiety that so often attend the notion that we have to get richer than we are—and quickly too. To be freed from that anxiety is to be psychologically more prepared for a life style of moderation.

John Madeley[41] has related this personal moderation to the needs of the world's poor in an article which is too closely reasoned easily to summarize. He points out that 'one of the most practical ways that we in Britain could help is by cutting down on our use of energy. If we used less oil there would be less pressure for the world price of oil to rise and poor countries could afford more.'

Of the many ways of reducing our consumption of energy he selects three: home insulation; reduction of temperatures in our homes; and doing without the family motor car. The genuinely poor of course don't have a family motor car, live in houses that are already too cold for comfort and, in the absence of any Government subsidy, cannot afford proper home insulation.

Turning to food cash crops grown in the Third World for our benefit such as coffee, tea, sugar and bananas, Madeley argues that if we consumed less, the price might indeed drop, but in all probability the workers who actually pick the crops would not thereby be paid less than the subsistence wages they already receive: 'If we consumed less of these crops, it might encourage poor countries to use more of their land for growing food for their own domestic consumption.' He quotes James Bellini as saying that for labourers on banana plantations 'The collapse of the banana market could only hasten the beginning of a more equitable local economic structure.'

Madeley also points out that in the West we each consume on average the equivalent of a ton of grain a year. In fact our direct intake of grain-based goods is less than a quarter of a ton. But since it takes about eight pounds of grain to produce one pound of grain-fed beef, the meat most of us eat sharply escalates the total. A great deal of grain is also used in the production of poultry, eggs and milk as well as in that of bread and meat, to say nothing of beer and whisky.

In a short article Madeley only touches on the problem of unemployment that might be caused by Personal Moderation, a topic to which I shall return later. But he does point out that 'if we save money on energy or food, we can simply give the money we save to a voluntary agency such as "Christian Aid" and so directly benefit the poor.' He is right also to add that 'All large-scale reforms have started from tiny beginnings. If we feel that we can do justice to the Third World by consuming less, then we do it without knowing the shape of the final outcome. "If you pursue justice", says the writer of Ecclesiasticus, "you will attain it."'[42]

Ten Reasons for Choosing a Simpler Life Style
In all this, there is in a sense nothing new, unless it be a new realization of the interdependence of the whole Human Family. In 1699 William Sachaverell, formerly Governor of the Isle of Man, visited Iona and the Western Highlands and exclaimed with admiration:[43] 'I thought myself entering a new scene of nature . . . There appeared in all the actions [of the inhabitants] a

certain generous air of freedom and contempt for those trifles, luxury and ambition, which we so servilely creep after. They bound their appetites by their necessities and their happiness consists not in having much but in coveting little.'

The worthy ex-Governor may have been influenced by romantic notions of 'the noble savage', yet the same austere yet happy tradition which he records persists in an undated paper entitled 'What can you do?', published by the Scotland West Branch of the Conservation Society. Its paragraphs speak crisply of the definition of our needs; the interaction of our style of life with those of others; the avoidance of waste; the responsible use of energy, food, water and air. Other paragraphs are headed Garden, Noise and Sharing. The paper looks as if it is the product of group study and action; one of the best methods of effective learning.

The Sussex group of the Soil Association took their cue from the Environmental Handbook in composing their (also undated) sheet on 'Me Save the Environment? What Can I Do?'. Their headings are all the better for faithfully reflecting their largely rural environment: Consumers; Transport; Water; Noise; Trees; Wildlife; Gardeners; Country code. Yet for my money the Movement to 'live more simply that all of us may simply live' must remain firmly rooted in the primary and global need for a more equitable sharing of our Earth's resources among the whole Human Family if it is to retain its authority.

Another recent paper exhorts us to 'use only what we need; conserve heat and light; use public transport; make less waste; limit family size; grow more food; share possessions; give hospitality.' We are also urged to give priority where appropriate to well designed products which 'come from renewable resources in balanced supply; use recycled material; use little energy in construction; are long lasting; come from areas where there is high unemployment; don't cause pollution.' The whole brief paper is in the same sensible style. But the most cogently argued summary of the need for personal moderation that I have so far come across comes from the pen of Dr Jorgen Lissner, a Danish expert who works for the World Lutheran Federation. I do not have to accept in toto his phraseology or emphases to acknowledge thankfully his ten reasons for choosing a simpler life style:

1. As an *act of faith* performed for the sake of personal

integrity and as an expression of a personal commitment
to a more equitable distribution of the world's wealth;

2. As an *act of self-defence* against the mind-polluting
effects of over-consumption;

3. As an *act of withdrawal* from the achievement-neurosis
of our high-pressure materialistic societies;

4. As an *act of solidarity* with the majority of humankind,
which has no choice about life style;

5. As an *act of sharing* with others what has been given to
us, or of returning what was usurped by us through
unjust social and economic structures;

6. As an *act of celebration* of the riches found in creativity,
spirituality and community with others rather than in
mindless materialism;

7. As an *act of provocation*—ostentatious underconsump-
tion to arouse curiosity leading to dialogue with others
about affluence, alienation, poverty and social injustice;

8. As an *act of anticipation* of the era when the self-
confidence and assertiveness of the underprivileged
forces new power relationships and new patterns of
resource allocation upon us;

9. As an *act of advocacy* of legislated changes in present
patterns of production and consumption in the direction
of a new international economic order;

10. As an *exercise of purchasing power* to redirect production away from the satisfaction of artificially created
wants towards the supply of goods and services that meet
genuine social needs.

Dr Lissner appends a necessary explanation of the link between
the simpler style of life he proposes and the needs of the poor and
underprivileged:

The adoption of a simpler life style is meaningful and
justifiable for any or all of the above reasons *alone*,
irrespective of whether it benefits the underprivileged.
Demands for 'proof of effectiveness' in helping the poor only
bear witness to the myth that 'they the poor' are the problem,
and that 'we the rich' have the solution. Yet—if adopted on a
large scale—a simpler life style will have significant socio-

political side-effects both in the rich and in the poor part of the world. The most important side-effects are likely to be economic and structural adjustments and release of new resources and energies for social change.

So we urgently need a concerted movement among the richer members of the Human Family, including me and probably you, to promote the practice of Personal Moderation. The relationship between this fourth response and the other three, Prayer, Prophecy and Political Action, is analogous to the age-old relationship between Faith and Works. If, on the one hand, 'faith without works is dead',[44] on the other hand 'the just shall live by faith'.[45] If Prayer, Prophecy and Political Action are necessary works, so we also need Personal Moderation as the inspiration, the psychological and the moral basis of the other three. And time is short.

CHAPTER FOUR

WHAT MAY I HOPE?

Alongside the four P's, Prayer (I suggest Personal Alignment for those who do not believe in Prayer); Prophecy (i.e. Propagation of the facts and their consequences); Political Action and Personal Moderation, I now place three S's: Self-affirmative Hope; Secular Hope; and Spiritual Hope. If it is necessary in such a book as this from time to time to beat the drum of doom, it is at least equally necessary also to blow the trumpet of hope; not only lest the magnitude and complexity of our problem paralyse our minds and hearts, but even more importantly in the interests of truth. For there are in truth strong grounds of hope that we shall overcome.

Self-affirmative Hope
Not long ago I was introduced at a party to a charming lady whom my host reasonably enough designated as the wife of Dr X, a man of some local distinction. 'I'm me,' she said as she held out her hand. In the Bible even God Himself is represented as establishing and asserting His own identity. 'I am that I am'[1] or, as I believe, more accurately, 'I will be what I will be.' Jesus of Nazareth also, despite or rather within the context of a certain reticence, does not hesitate to affirm his own significance—a point which, once grasped, helps us to appreciate and understand such apparently abrasive self-affirmations as are recorded in the Fourth Gospel.[2]

If we are to love our neighbour as ourselves, an aim which unites many believers and unbelievers alike, it follows that we have to love ourselves, even as God loves us. As the poet and prophet known as 'the Second Isaiah' put it: 'Your name is engraved on the palms of his hands.'[3] I like to imagine that in his Babylonian exile the poet may have been inspired to this unusual and beautiful metaphor by the sight of the statue of some strange god, stretching out his hands in welcome to his worshippers.

We shall never know. But what I do know, as a believer, is that my name is engraved on the palms of his hands. So are yours and everybody's. For me those hands, stretched out towards me, are marked with the imprint of nails. For the Christian, the inexhaustible worth and significance of every individual who has ever lived is, as it were, signed and sealed by the belief that God chose to 'become flesh' in a particular individual member of the Human Family.

I am me. I think, therefore I am. Anyone who is in the Humanist tradition, whether atheist, agnostic or believer, will assign decisive significance to the individual, not only in theory but effectively in the world. Speaking to an audience of ten thousand students at the University of South Africa in Durban, the late Robert Kennedy encouraged them with these words:

> Some believe there is nothing one man or woman can do against the enormous array of the world's ills. Yet many of the world's greatest movements of thought and action have flowed from the work of a single man. A young monk began the Protestant Reformation, a young general extended an empire from Macedonia to the borders of the earth, and a young woman reclaimed the territory of France. It was a young Italian explorer who discovered the New World, and the thirty-two-year-old Thomas Jefferson who proclaimed that all men are created equal.[4]

Nor does this significance of the individual apply only to the great and famous.

> In 1935 Paul Valéry gave away the prizes at Sête College. His speech was on the following theme. He explained that to mould the future is the simplest, the most profound and the most universal function of our existence. He showed how at the heart of the best equipped civilization, that which is richest in energy and most competent in terms of organization, personal life tends to become somewhat restless, worried and more anxious than was the life of our far-off ancestors. Correcting himself, he immediately added: 'I do want you, my young friends, to realize your strength.[5]

> Pierre Gaxotte comments: 'Valéry was right. We keep telling young people that they are confronted with evil days. We do not

tell them enough that they have within themselves whatever is necessary to make them better.'[6]

Robert Pirsig gives this argument an intriguing twist:

I think that if we are going to reform the world, and make it a better place to live in, the way to do it is not with talk about relationships of a political nature, which are inevitably dualistic, full of subjects and objects and their relationship to one another, or with programmes full of things for other people to do. I think that kind of approach starts it at the end and presumes the end is the beginning.

Programmes of a political nature are important end products of social quality that can be effective only if the underlying structure of social values is right. The social values are right only if the individual values are right. The place to improve the world is first in one's own heart and hands, and then work outward from there. Other people can talk about how to expand the destiny of mankind. I just want to talk about how to fix a motorcycle. I think that what I have to say has more lasting value.[7]

Whereas I have tried to make clear my belief that Personal Moderation and Political Action are complementary (like faith and works), Pirsig appears to set 'programmes of a political nature' over against 'talk about how to fix a motorcycle'. But his appeal to start with 'one's own heart and hands' should evoke a universal response. The prime significance of the individual applies not only to the educated young of the Western world who have inherited a tradition of individualism. That tradition indeed has been from time to time misleading and excessive. I have already written of the hope that keeps bubbling up, warm and fresh, in the highways and the byways of Calcutta. This hope is firmly rooted in the individual dignity and intrinsic worth of the city's swarming inhabitants. Listen to the late Canon Subir Biswas:

Ultimately Calcutta will not live by what is planned at a very high level in a detached way, or by those who wish to control the power, but Calcutta will live largely because the small people have never given up hope . . .

For the dignity of man can never be given to him—it can only be recognized. And if in the streets of the city, in its slums and its pavements, we cannot recognize the dignity, we cannot see the hope born anew, if we cannot see in the struggle of the unemployed and the struggle of the poor the aspiration and the passion of God, then where will we be?[8]

The pages of history are crowded with effective examples of such self-affirmative hope. Many more never reach those pages. Here is one which, since 'the forests come before civilizations, the deserts after them',[9] is highly relevant to our main theme.

Wendy went to Tiznit at the edge of the Sahara and rented a small castle (for £4 a month) and forty-five acres of desert, with her own money. She hired a tiny fraction of the town's permanently unemployed and set them breaking up the rock-bound land and digging holes for tree seedlings. They planted them all round the perimeter of the plot and a belt of them, a hundred metres, by the track. In four years, the seedlings grew from eight inches to twelve-foot trees.

With the protection of the tree belt she grew wheat and barley. It was the first time a tractor had been used in the Moroccan desert. In spite of the Agadir earthquake and of two plagues of locusts and the establishment of the dictatorship which finally drove her out, she planted two thousand trees here.

Algeria was newly independent, with a programme of reconstruction. She put her dogs and books in a car and went to Bou Saada, the oasis town which is called 'the gateway to the Sahara'. The Sous-Préfet and the Mayor welcomed her and the Government promised her a thousand seedlings and the help of the district forestry service to plant them, to see if her plan would really work. Eighty per cent of the trees survived.

Seven years later, two hundred and sixty acres of the barren plain have a hundred and thirty thousand forest trees on them, with citrus fruits, olives, tomatoes, potatoes, beans and grain growing in their protection. Because of the increased surface humidity from these, the ground is covered by grasses and shrubs which have sprung up by natural regeneration.

Her long-term dream is of a Green Front round the Sahara, a barrier of trees on the arid land between fertility and the desert, to hold back erosion and later to advance. 'It would have to be an international organization of course.' Wouldn't that mean that she herself would be squeezed out? 'Plenty of people have tried to squeeze me out already.' If they succeeded? 'I would go and find another place to grow trees. I doubt if I'll ever get stuck for deserts in my lifetime.'[10]

Wendy Campbell Purdie rented her castle at the age of thirty-three. The pen is rightly said to be mightier than the sword (how about the ploughshare?) and General Wolfe would rather have written Gray's *Elegy* than have taken Quebec. But at the time of writing I would rather have been able to organize the planting of all those trees than to be trying to bring some order into the unwieldy material of this book! But let us take heart. I read somewhere that only eight people attended the funeral of Karl Marx!

Secular Hope

There is no expert consensus as to whether in fact the Human Family, or rather the more powerful section of it, is more likely than not to learn in time to distribute our planet's resources more equitably and conserve those resources more sensibly. Even if there were such a consensus, it might well prove wrong in the event. Just at the very crisis point, however, at which we need them, we do find ourselves globally equipped with immensely developed resources of scientific knowledge and technological skill, of rapid and massive transport and communications, of managerial and organizational ability and of educational qual-ifications. It has often been observed that over 90 per cent of all the scientists who have ever lived are alive today.

Furthermore, there is an immense resource of increasingly well-informed goodwill towards our fellow members of the Human Family. There cannot be many people who have given the matter a moment's serious thought who are positively pleased that so many of their fellow humans are so desperately poor. Despite many senseless cruelties including deliberate torture, it can be maintained with some reason that in general people are kinder to each other and more sensitive to each other's needs than ever before.

'We are so much accustomed to the humanitarian outlook,' concluded Sir Kenneth Clark towards the end of his *Civil-ization*,[11]

that we forget how little it counted in earlier ages of civil-ization. Ask any decent person in England or America what he thinks matters most in human conduct: five to one his answer will be 'kindness'. It's not a word that would have crossed the lips of any of the earlier heroes of this series. If you had asked St Francis what mattered in life, he would, we know, have answered, 'chastity, obedience and poverty'; if you had asked Dante or Michelangelo they might have answered 'disdain of baseness and injustice'; if you had asked Goethe, he would have said 'to live in the whole and the beautiful'. But kindness, never. Our ancestors did not use the word, and they did not greatly value the quality—except perhaps insofar as they valued compassion. Nowadays, I think we underestimate the humanitarian achievement of the nineteenth century. We forget the horrors that were taken for granted in early Victorian England—the hundreds of lashes inflicted daily on perfectly harmless men in the army and navy—the women chained together in threes, rumbling through the streets in open carts on their way to transportation. These and other even more unspeakable cruelties were carried out by agents of the Establishment, usually in defence of property.

I am already straying from the area of secular into that of spiritual hope—an indication of the fact that there are no clear borders between them. That there are strong signs of Secular Hope even in the most uncompromising analyses of our predicament may be illustrated from the 'Blueprint for Survival', described by Sir Frank Fraser Darling as 'the sanest statement I have seen in the popular press and a good deal saner than many in the scientific press . . . not over-dramatic.' The authors express their hope in these words:

> We believe it possible to change from an expansionist society to a stable society without loss of jobs or an increase in real expenditure. There is every reason to believe that the stable society would provide us with satisfactions that would more than compensate for those which, with the passing of the industrial state, it will become increasingly necessary to forgo.[12]

In the field of development we can now read with satisfaction that

> in the thirty-six poorest countries the expectation of life has risen from thirty-nine years in 1960 to forty-six years in 1977; per capita calorie intake as percentage of daily requirement from 89 to 96; percentage enrolment of children in primary

schooling from 37 to 50; percentage literacy from 33 to 43.'[13]

Moreover as life expectancy increases, the global birth rate is actually declining 'for the first time in recorded history to 29 for each thousand people from 30 per thousand a year ago.'[14]

Of course, even if the birth rate does continue to decline or at least becomes stable, we are not out of the wood. According to the most recent information at the time of writing:

The world's population is expected to increase by about 50 per cent—from just over four thousand millions to more than six thousand millions—by the end of the century. Most growth will occur in the less developed parts of the world, where about two hundred million people are already under-nourished.

Yet the director of the United Nations Fund for Population Activities, Mr Rafael Salas, sees the major problems as those which arise from fertility decline, such as the increasing proportion of elderly and aged people in societies which cannot support them . . .

The trend towards smaller families is parallel with higher survival rates and a much increased life expectancy, now approaching that of the developed world . . .

What is taking place is not the elimination or even a substantial reduction of the 'population problem', but a transformation of its character and magnitude. Both the developing and the developed world need new perceptions of the problem and a new willingness to design policies and programmes to deal with the consequences of change![15]

So our Secular Hopes must be sober, qualified by vigilance. But they need not be quenched.

Small is Beautiful

Responding to an exposition of these 'Three S's' at a conference, a friend proposed instead three further P's. For 'Self-affirmative Hope' read 'Persons Count'. For 'Secular Hope' read 'Power is Available'. For 'Spiritual Hope' read 'Providence of God'. Certainly power, its use and abuse, is the key to the validity of our Secular Hope: 'Never before has man had such a capacity to control his own environment', proclaimed John F. Kennedy, 'to end thirst and hunger, to conquer poverty and disease, to banish illiteracy and massive human misery. We have the power to make this the best generation of mankind or to make it the last.'

Alongside this continuing advance of scientific and technological power, the late Dr E. F. Schumacher discerned a new mood of anxiety which paradoxically contains the seeds of hope. He wrote:

The late President Kennedy set a target; that by the end of the sixties man would visit the moon—and he did. The week of this fantastic feat was referred to by President Nixon as 'the greatest week since genesis'. It cannot be said that science and technology have suddenly lost their power. But somehow the glory is gone. At the height of success there is a smell of bankruptcy.[19]

Schumacher later continued:

The limits-to-growth debate is in full swing. The possibility of severe fuel shortages in many parts of the world, which only a few years ago was laughed out of court, is becoming a reality. Concern over environmental degradation and the dangers of ecological breakdown is no longer confined to a few minority groups. Most important of all, many people are beginning to take an overall view of the condition and prospects of life in an industrial society and to feel that we may be moving into a real crisis of survival.[20]

In this hopeful shift of opinion, whose ambiguity we have ruefully to recognize, Dr Schumacher himself played a distinguished part. His slogan that 'small is beautiful' found brilliant expression for example in this little parable:

Imagine a small island community of two thousand people. One day a boat arrives and unloads a man who has just been released from prison on the mainland. The discharged prisoner returns home. Will this community have any difficulty in looking after this one man, giving him a bit of human contact, finding him work and re-integrating him into society? Hardly.

And now imagine an island community 25 thousand times as big, of some fifty million people, and every year 25 thousand discharged prisoners return home. It is then the task of various ministries to get them back into normal life together with a number of harassed and over-worked probation officers. What a problem! In fact a problem that has never yet been satisfactorily dealt with.[1]

Dr Schumacher's basic method of reducing a problem's scale in order not only to study it but also effectively to deal with it appears to me to correspond with the general and spectacularly successful procedure of scientific experiment. By this procedure, data are extracted from the general environment for study under controlled conditions. Generalizations can then be made which are based on accurate observation of their behaviour.

Of this process the story of Isaac Newton's observation of the apple falling from the tree provides a classic myth. In using this word 'myth' I am not casting any doubt on the truth of the story; only pointing out its significance as an example of the principle that 'small is beautiful'. The falling apple becomes the key to the dance of the galaxies.

Spiritual Hope

I shall have cause to refer later to the proceedings of Commission Eight on 'Man's Stewardship of God's World' of the Church Leaders' Conference at Selly Oak in 1972. It was as a member of that Commission that Archbishop Donald Coggan made the point in discussion that, whatever the ambiguity of our Secular Hope, for the believer the Spiritual Hope is ultimate, universal and unassailable. I am not competent to judge how far such adjectives are applicable to the Marxist's millenium, nor to assess the assortment of spiritual hopes that are integral to faiths other than my own. But for the Christian, St Paul's words which form part of the main climax of his most formidably theological letter continue to ring true:

> With all this in mind, what are we to say? If God is on our side, who is against us? He did not spare his own Son, but gave him up for us all; and with this gift how can he fail to lavish upon us all he has to give? Who will be the accuser of God's chosen ones? It is God who pronounces acquittal—then who can condemn? It is Christ—Christ who died, and, more than that, was raised from the dead—who is at God's right hand, and indeed pleads our cause. Then what can separate us from the love of Christ? Can affliction or hardship? Can persecution, hunger, nakedness, peril, or the sword? . . .
>
> I am convinced that there is nothing in death or life, in the realm of spirits or superhuman powers, in the world as it is or the world as it shall be, in the forces of the universe, in heights

or depths—nothing in all creation that can separate us from
the love of God in Christ Jesus our Lord?[22]

As a trained Rabbi, Paul was a legal expert. As a Roman
citizen he was well acquainted with the rule of law. So the legal
metaphor which came naturally to him at the beginning of this
quotation need not obscure from us the ultimate and universal
dimension of his hope. He was writing to the members of the
puny, persecuted church of his day who lived in the Eternal
City, seat of the mighty Roman Empire. Yet his words apply to
the whole panorama of human life today. Even if we were
totally to destroy each other in our folly, that would not be the
end of everything for those who accept 'the love of God in Christ
Jesus our Lord'.

Distinct though it is from Secular Hope, this, our Spiritual
Hope, is not to be wholly separated from it. For the believer it
goes without saying that God wants the members of His Human
Family to use all the secular means available in order to live and
love and have our being, and not destroy each other in senseless
greed. Nor is this Spiritual Hope to be estranged from Self-
affirmatory or Personal Hope. The individual whose name is
engraved on the palms of His hands is of infinite worth, not just
as a theoretical doctrine but in the rough and tumble of the
secular world. In a rich cornucopia of inspired stories in the
Bible, God is revealed as personally meeting, challenging and
comforting a wide diversity of individuals—Abraham, Moses,
Elijah, Isaiah, Jeremiah and the rest; Peter, Andrew, James and
John; Mary, Martha and the Women at the Well—and Paul
himself. A sonorous roll-call of some of these is sounded in the
Letter to the Hebrews.[23] In this passage it is not easy to distinguish faith from hope. They are in fact inextricably
intertwined.

A Common Account of Hope

In the context of our contemporary global concerns, the
Commission on Faith and Order of the World Council of
Churches issued a 'Common Account of Hope'.[24] 'Called to
account for the hope that is in them,' the members begin
imaginatively, after an introductory paragraph of thanksgiving, with this Latin American song:

> Since He came into the world and into history;
> Broke down silence and suffering;

Filled the world with His glory;
Was the light in the coldness of our night;
Was born in a dark manger;
In His life sowed love and light;
Broke hardened hearts
But lifted up dejected souls;
So today we have hope;
Today we persevere in our struggle;
Today we face our future with confidence,
In this land which is ours.

They go on to 'distinguish between one level where specific things are hoped for—for example to have enough to eat—and another level where the question emerges, 'Why do you hope at all for what you cannot see?'[26] In a clear reference to the Letter to the Hebrews, they recognize that they

are not the first to express such faith and hope. Many have gone before us. A cloud of witnesses surrounds us who gave their testimony even at the cost of their lives. The faithful witness of the human hope in God is Jesus Christ. And every time we celebrate the remembrance of Him, we receive grace and power to give our testimony . . . The ultimate judgement of the world is His, our assurance that the murderer will never ultimately triumph over the victim. This ultimate hope in the lordship of Christ and the coming kingdom of God cannot be divorced from, or identified with, our historical hopes for freedom, justice, equality and peace. Our struggles for human well being are judged and transfigured in a life with God marked by the free gifts of forgiveness and (the knowledge that) their ultimate outcome is in God's hands.[27]

This section on 'Our Hope in God' is followed by one on 'The Church; a Communion of Hope', and that in turn by one on 'Shared Hopes in the face of the Common Future':

Our common hope is threatened by increasing and already excessive concentrations of power with their threats of exploitation and poverty. They are responsible for the ever widening gap between rich and poor, not only between nations but within individual nations. Political exploitation and dependency, hunger and malnutrition are the price paid by the poor for the superabundance of goods and power enjoyed by the rich. Concentration of power also leads to the preservation of the existing and the formation of new class distinctions. Nevertheless we share a common hope; for we believe that God has taken sides in this struggle.[28]

For this Commission also 'small is beautiful'.

The problems seem overwhelming. The cry for realism is deep in each one of us, and it expresses a kind of ultimate question about Christian hope. But we believe that each rightful action counts because God blesses it. With the five loaves and two fishes which the young man brought to him, Jesus fed the multitude. Hope lives with special power in small actions.[29]

Finally, this kind of Spiritual Hope, for this Commission, of course, specifically Christian Hope, is significantly described as 'the invitation to risk'. This kind of ultimate, universal and unassailable hope can afford to risk struggle, the use of power; affirming the new and re-affirming the old; self-criticism as the channel of renewal; dialogue; co-operation with those from whom we differ; scorn; and finally even 'death for the sake of that hope'.

As I read through these somewhat extended quotations I am bound to ask myself whether you, particularly if you are not yourself a believer, share my enthusiasm for this style of corporate writing. It is not without elegance. 'Hope lives with special power in small actions.' Nor is it without substance. The scope, to take but one example, of 'the invitation to risk' would afford any preacher material for more than one sermon. But what appeals to me is the conjunction in this writing of the Self-affirmative, the Secular and the Spiritual Hope.

This is good theology. And I suspect that it owes much to a particular theological book, Dr Jurgen Moltmann's *Theology of Hope*.[30] Having already quoted so much in this section, I must ration myself by taking from Dr Moltmann only three points.

Hope alone is to be called 'realistic', because it alone takes seriously the possibilities with which all reality is fraught. It does not take things as they happen to stand or to lie, but as progressing, moving things with the possibility of change . . . Hope will itself provide *inexhaustible resources* for the creative, inventive imagination of love. It constantly provokes and produces thinking of an anticipatory kind in love to man and the world, in order to give shape to the newly dawning possibilities in the light of the promised future, in order as far as possible to create here the best that is possible, because what is promised is within the bounds of possibility. Thus it will constantly arouse the 'passion for the possible', inventiveness and elasticity in self-transformation, in breaking with the old and coming to terms with the new. Always the Christian hope has had a revolutionary effect in this sense on the intellectual history of the society affected by it.

So it is 'realistic' after all 'to live more simply that all of us may simply live'! Secondly, however, Moltmann recognizes that such 'realism' involves 'every Christian and every Christian Minister' in conflict:

> If the God who called them to life should expect of them something other than what modern industrial society expects and requires of them, then Christians must venture an exodus and regard their social roles as a new Babylonian exile. Only when they appear in society as a group which is not wholly adaptable . . . do they enter into a conflict-laden but fruitful partnership with this society.[31]

Thirdly, in his discussion of Christ's Resurrection, Moltmann has this to say about Kant's famous three questions:

> The question, 'What can I know of the historical facts?' cannot here be separated from the ethical and existential question. 'What am I to do?' and from the eschatological question, 'What may I hope for?'—just as the other questions in turn cannot be isolated. Only when concerted attention is given to these three questions does the reality of the resurrection disclose itself.[32]

This means for us that what we can know is not mere knowledge but a springboard for action, what we ought to do. But we shall only do what we ought to do if we may hope, as surely we may, that what we do is full of meaning, both now and for ever.

> Leave this chanting and singing and telling of beads.
> Whom do you worship in this lonely dark corner of the temple with all the doors shut?
> Open your eyes and see that God is not in front of you.
> He is there where the farmer is tilling the hard ground and where the labourer is breaking stones.

He is with them in the sun and the rain and his garment is
    covered with dust.
Put off your holy cloak and like him come down onto the
    dusty soil.
Deliverance?
Where will you find deliverance?
Our master himself has joyfully taken on the bonds of
    creation—he is bound with us for ever.
Come out of your meditations and leave aside the flowers
    and the incense—
What harm is there if your clothes become tattered and
    stained?
Meet him and stand by him in toil and in the sweat of
    your brow.[33]

Tagore calls this poem *The Hidden God*. What is the name of
the Hindu poet's 'Hidden God' and what does He require of you
and of me? I believe that I know the answer to the first question.
'His Nature and His Name is Love.'[34] The second is more
difficult. But at the very least, 'as an act of solidarity with the
majority of mankind, which has no choice about life style',[35] He
surely requires us 'to live more simply that all of us may simply
live'.

CHAPTER FIVE

THE LIFE STYLE MOVEMENT

Six Points of Personal Development

As long ago as 25 November 1970 I wrote to *The Observer* in response to an interview with the American economist Professor J. K. Galbraith which had been published in the paper the previous Sunday. Professor Galbraith was quoted as saying:

> Expanding consumption isn't the guarantee of utter happiness that my friendly critics once held it to be. A new generation is becoming quite wise on that point. It realizes that a great many people consume what they are persuaded to consume . . . Why do we consume? To a point, because of physical need and satisfaction—no one doubts that. But beyond that, consumption is partly a matter of persuasion by the advertisers and partly a matter of competition—keeping up with one's neighbours. And partly, consumption is a measure of achievement. The more one consumes, the more one is, or seems to be. Now people are beginning to realize that a life style that depends on such consumption is contrived and rather silly.

In my letter I maintained that 'if a substantial minority of the richer half of the nation would agree voluntarily to limit their consumption, at least for a time, the psychological incentive which lies at the root of inflation would be decisively blunted.' I went on to acknowledge that we would find this much easier to do as 'members of a substantial company with a clear, uncomplicated commitment'. So I proposed 'the formation of an association for the limitation of personal consumption' which would consist of individuals who would 'undertake that during the year 1971 they and their dependents would not spend more than 90 per cent of their gross income.' Finally I asked: 'Which of your readers would be interested in the possibility of forming such an association?'

I was never to know the answer to this last question as the Editor did not choose to publish my letter—one of my many failures to communicate what I believe. In the opening paragraphs of this book I gave you due notice that this had to be a personal book, attempting to evoke a personal response. And this means in turn from time to time putting my personal cards on the table for you to see. I now therefore go on to discern six points of development which led me to write such a letter and so in due course to found the Life Style Movement.

In the course of more than a decade of attendance at two boarding schools, the one preparatory to the other, I heard many, many sermons, and now remember hardly a word of them. But I do remember perhaps a dozen of the preachers, men who attracted me by their holiness, their humour, their simplicity or their fervour. Outstanding among these was Brother Douglas, founder member of the Society of St Francis, the Franciscan Order within the Church of England. So impressed was I by this man that within a few days of going up to Cambridge I called at the Society's house in Lady Margaret Road and in due course become a Companion of the Order, a modest obligation which I have most inadequately maintained for nearly forty years. The charisma of St Francis and of so many of his followers down the centuries continues radically to challenge the profligacy of the natural man and offers to us all an alternative life style of discipline and joy.

Secondly, I became more fully committed to the Christian faith, a commitment which included becoming a candidate for training for ordination when serving in the Royal Artillery in the Western Desert. It is this commitment which above all provides for me the inescapable motivation for attempting to live a little more simply that all of us may simply live. But it is to the desert environment, in which I entered into that fuller commitment, that I now refer. Soldiers in battle have to learn to share anyway. In addition, however, the desert appears to exert a mysterious influence in favour of a kind of sacramental sharing that is essential to the survival of those who live there.

On our truck in the desert my driver, Gunner Edwards, was usually cook and 'disher out'. I noticed that he would reserve for himself the smallest rasher of bacon, soya link or whatever it was in the sizzling pan. The Bedouin who live in the desert all their lives do the same as a matter of course; not bacon, you understand! Since the time of Abraham and indeed before him their survival and their dignity have depended on their willingness to share their food unconditionally with hungry and exhausted travellers. I was vividly reminded of this some thirty-five years after my wartime sojourn in the Western Desert when waiting for the daily plane at the desert airstrip at Mahreb in the Yemen Arab Republic, ancient capital of the Queen of Sheba. A Bedouin family was also there. The patriarch approached me with a smile. From a leather bag at his waist he produced a hard, old, dusty chunk of bread, broke it in half and gave me a piece. As on the occasion at Corrymeela, recorded at the beginning of this book, it was like a celebration of the Holy Communion; but a celebration of a particularly significant kind, transcending religious as well as linguistic and cultural barriers, a celebration whose priest was a Muslim, a poor man who knew me for a stranger in his land.

My third focus of development spreads over a period of four years. I refer to the formal theological education I received at Cambridge, an education that was firmly rooted in Biblical studies. The point I wish to make may be established by a quotation:

At His transfiguration Jesus was attended by Moses and Elijah, formidable political figures indeed, courageous and effective fighters for freedom from oppression. According to their lights, not all equally acceptable today, Abraham and Joseph, David and even the pompous Solomon, Isaiah and Jeremiah, Daniel and Esther, Ezra and Nehemiah concerned themselves with political freedom, economic justice or bread for the people. At great cost they obeyed the call to 'seek first the kingdom of God and His righteousness'.

Jesus Himself transcends our categories. Of Him above all men it is true that 'all labels are libels' . . . We must be content with echoing the centurion's verdict that 'this was a just man' (Luke 23:47) and remind ourselves that Jesus appears to have been the most liberated and most liberating Man who ever lived. He was in favour of feeding the hungry, providing water for the thirsty, welcoming the stranger (the refugee?) and visiting the sick and the prisoners (Matthew 25:31f). Indeed He attached eternal significance to such activities as well as making them the theme of His first and representative sermon (Luke 4:16ff).

These words from an article I wrote under the title 'Christianity and the World—which God so loved. A Comment on the First Reith Lecture 1978'[1] illustrate my conviction that countless numbers of us, Christians and Jews and others for that matter, derive our commitment to sharing the Earth's resources more equitably not so much from any bourgeois political idealism as from the Bible. Not that I am wishing to depreciate bourgeois political idealism. For it too owes much to the Bible!

Fourthly, my wife and I spent four years as members of the Church of South India, the best part of one year in Bangalore and then in Palayamkottai in the famous Tirunelveli Diocese. Two of our four children were born in India. In four years a man can begin at least to appreciate his own ignorance of another culture, another religion and another race; and experience some sense of solidarity with its members!

Indeed in four days or even in four hours he can so begin. On our way to South India on the old P and O liner, *SS Canton*, we spent about four hours in Bombay. We visited the famous Dhobi Ghat, centre, as we would now say, of a thriving service industry where thousands of dhobies, washermen, pound the clothes of tens of thousands of customers to snowy whiteness. How efficiently and cheerfully they perform their valuable task. But as newcomers we were daunted by the sheer numbers.

Having disembarked and entrained at Colombo we passed over by ferry to India and changed trains again in the middle of the night at Madurai. As we picked our way among the hundreds of recumbent bodies asleep on the concrete platforms, we imagined them as homeless and desperate as many doubtless were. But many were of course just waiting for a train. We had already caught a glimpse of the massive poverty of the majority of our fellow human beings.

The point I am making is that as John speaks in his First Letter of his personal experience of 'the word of life',[2] so I dare to speak of my personal observation of the need to share our beloved Earth's resources among all the members of the Human Family: 'It was there from the beginning; we have heard it; we have seen it with our own eyes; we looked upon it, and felt it with our own hands; and it is of this we tell.'

Fifth comes what is in this context a negative point of development although at the time I found it memorable and exciting. As one of two delegates from the Diocese of Sheffield I was invited to attend the First British Conference on Faith and

Order in Nottingham in 1964. As a parish priest I had inherited a tradition of working very closely with the local Methodist Church. Already further advance was being held up by the failure of our two denominations to unite at the national level. I came to the Conference armed with the conviction that the time had come for those Churches who were sufficiently committed to each other to do so, to fix a sensible target date for their reunion and then solemnly promise to God and to each other to work and to pray for the fulfilment of the target. The appropriate biblical name for such a solemn promise appeared to be 'covenant'.

I was delighted by the gathering enthusiasm with which this not particularly original idea was received at the Conference. In due course it was formulated in a five-point resolution. Each point was accepted by an overwhelming majority, the first and vital one with five votes against and twelve abstentions out of a total eligible to vote of four hundred and seventy-four. It read: 'United in our urgent desire for One Church Renewed for Mission, this Conference invites the member churches of the British Council of Churches, in appropriate groupings such as nations, to covenant together to work and pray for the inauguration of union by a date agreed amongst them.'[3]

I returned home full of joy and confidence. I had no doubt at all that the member churches of the British Council of Churches would appoint a weighty Commission to draw up the terms of such a Covenant and recommend a target date in good time to fulfil our second resolution: 'We dare to hope that this date should not be later than Easter Day, 1980.' I foresaw that this Covenant would provide the necessary spiritual basis of love and trust for the successful outcome of the negotiations between my own Church of England and the Methodist Church. I also believed that four or five Churches in all would probably join in. In the event these hopes were not realized. But it never occurred to me at the time that I had to do anything about it. And indeed I don't suppose that, as a parish priest, there was all that much that I could have done. But in retrospect I can see the relevance of the prayer attributed to Sir Francis Drake: 'O Lord God, when thou givest to thy servants to endeavour any great matter, grant us also to know that it is not the beginning, but the continuing of the same unto the end, until it be thoroughly finished, which yieldeth the true glory . . .'[4]

For what it is worth, this negative experience of failure to pursue what I am still convinced was a good idea has had, as we shall see, a decisive influence on the foundation of the Life Style Movement.

The sixth and last experience or point of development which lies behind the formation of the Life Style Movement involved the establishment of what came to be called 'The Common Discipline' at Coventry Cathedral. Shortly after I joined the Cathedral staff in 1965 the Provost asked me to spend a week at the Benedictine Abbey of Ottobeuren in Bavaria. As a characteristically pragmatic Englishman I asked him what he wanted me to *do* while I was here. 'You don't have to do anything. Just go and live there and see whether you discover something there that I discovered—or perhaps something else.' 'But I can hardly put together a dozen words of German.' 'I would hardly be asking you to go to a monastery if the object was for you to learn German.'

So I spent a week at Ottobeuren in May 1966. I imbibed something of the spirit of a community in which prayer has been offered under a common discipline for over twelve hundred years. I tramped the rolling Bavarian countryside and I sat, often alone, in the huge baroque basilica, interpreting the grand design of the magnificent paintings and sculptures which throng the walls and ceilings. Often my eyes would return to the Coventry Cross of Nails in its place of honour on the central altar and sometimes an unseen organist would fill the church with glorious music, music usually of the high baroque. In the cell allotted to me I read for the first time in my life and pondered on the wise, humane and charitable Rule of St Benedict; also the lively, shrewd and equally charitable Rule of the Taizé Community, that fine band of brothers within the Reformed tradition who have made the unity of all Christian people the ferment of their devotion. And I became convinced that amid the pressures, opportunities and problems of our work at Coventry Cathedral we too urgently needed a Common Discipline. Of course it would be a very different affair from the 'religious life' of monks and nuns. Our work team consisted of a variety of people, about half of clergy and half lay, about half of us married and half of us unmarried, spanning a very wide range of age and of religious conviction. Moreover we were bound together not by a common home, that which provides the greatly treasured stabilitas, the stability and security of a Benedictine Community but by the less pervasive bonds of a common work. On the other hand I found that some of the provisions of the two rules exactly fitted our Coventry situation. I found this for example in the Prologue to the Rule of St Benedict:

> We have therefore to establish a school of the Lord's Service, in the setting forth of which we hope to order nothing that is harsh or rigorous. But if anything be somewhat strictly laid down, according to the dictates of sound reason, for the amendment of vices or the peservation of charity, do not therefore fly in dismay from the way of salvation whose beginning cannot but be strait and difficult.

These words from the Rule of Taizé seemed particularly relevant:

> With the growing number of visitors, we run into the danger of cutting ourselves off from them, by reclusion, in order to defend ourselves. On the contrary, while preserving our deeper life, keeping a certain discernment and avoiding feverish dissipation, let us remember on every occasion how to be open and hospitable . . . People who come to us expect bread, and if we present them with stones to look at, we shall have fallen short of our ecumenical vocation. They seek in us men who radiate God. This implies a life hidden in God, so that the presence of Christ which is borne by each brother may be renewed in us.

But as both St Benedict and the Prior of Taizé would certainly have wished, in preparing a Common Discipline for Coventry Cathedral I found an even greater inspiration in the scriptures and, in particular, in St Paul's letter to the Christians in Galatia. It is an amazing testimony to the power of the Spirit in the life of the apostle that a letter which is conceived in so passionate a controversy should conclude in so charitable and penetrating an analysis of the common life.

It took us about two years of consultation to fix the first form of the Common Discipline for the Staff of Coventry Cathedral. This is printed as the appendix to the Provost's book, *Basics and Variables* (Hodder and Stoughton, 1970). It contained two parts, 'The Spirit of the Discipline' and 'The Practice of the Discipline'. The former consisted of a fairly full introduction which related the discipline to the Benedictine tradition and differentiated it from that tradition, plus one section 'For

Corporate meditation'. The second part contained the practical details including provision for prayer and worship, work, study, recreation, holidays, sleep, food and drink, use of money, consultants, common meals, membership and revision and administration of the discipline.

Since then this Common Discipline has been revised several times and widely adopted within the Community of the Cross of Nails, an international network of over seventy Christian centres committed to a ministry of reconciliation and renewal. I ended a paper on the Common Discipline, which I read to a small international symposium in 1972, with these words:

> Not that I wish to leave you with a false impression of a success story such as my personal enthusiasm for this development may well have conveyed to you. Whereas on the one hand a younger colleague once told me that she did not know how she could have managed in a personal crisis without the help of her Consultant, on the other hand I have reason to believe that this Common Discipline hardly impinges at all on the lives of others of us, apart from attendance at the common meals. The Common Discipline, like the sabbath before it, is made for its members and not vice versa. Its effects are largely invisible and its principle is completely adaptable to the felt needs of a very wide range of communities.[5]

In fact, the words 'Voluntary Common Discipline' are a key to the understanding of the Life Style Movement. Although in this instance they derive historically from the Christian experience associated with Coventry Cathedral, their application extends far beyond the bounds of the Christian Church. To achieve anything worthwhile in this world self-discipline is essential, particularly in an age in which so many of the restraints of traditionally imposed disciplines have been withdrawn. Moreover voluntary discipline has to be common or shared, for we need each other's comfort and support if the world is to be saved and ourselves within it.

Selly Oak 1972

The Church Leaders' Conference held in Birmingham in September 1972 was quite unlike any other conference held this century. Five hundred leading members of the British and

Irish churches met together for ten days, not to legislate, pass resolutions and agree messages, but to join together in considering in depth, with a minimum of formality, the crises which Christianity faces today.[6]

My Bishop, the Bishop of Coventry, was to have attended this conference but, to the great delight of his many friends, decided to get married instead and therefore could not come. He asked me to go in his place. On my application form I chose Commission Six on 'The Real God and Real Prayer', convinced that it was about that that I needed to learn most. But by the time that my belated application came in there was room for me only on Commission Eight: 'Man's Stewardship of God's World'. This, however, promised to be of absorbing interest with Bishop Montefiore in the chair, Dr E. F. Schumacher among the Consultants and Lady Barbara Ward in attendance. And so it proved. Discussion was at a high and well-informed level and we began to produce an excellent statement on this vital theme. Half-way through, however, I felt bound to summon up my courage and protest that statements on such a theme by Church Leaders, however well-informed, would cut no ice in the world at large unless backed by an explicit commitment at least to try to practise what we preach in terms of personally consuming less of the Earth's limited resources and thus enabling a more effective sharing of them.

I was not demanding an absolute correspondence between precept and practice. But my plea for some correspondence between the two was difficult, if not impossible, to oppose! In due course, after careful drafting, it emerged as the following invitation (there were no resolutions) to the whole Conference:

Commission Eight, convinced that environmental responsibility and social justice on a global scale demand changes in personal as well as national ways of life, recommends to each of its own members and invites all members of this Conference to pledge themselves to a simplicity of life which is generous to others and content with enough rather than with excess; and that each should privately review his or her life before God so as to implement this pledge, as necessary, by altered patterns of consumption.

By accident or providential design the commendation of this invitation which I was asked to make to the whole conference

occured immediately before the final summing up and therefore
had a fair chance of remaining in the memory of the delegates. In
his report of the conference, David Edwards[7] singles out 'two
attempts at this Church Leaders' Conference to sum up its
thinking in words which might be simple and powerful enough
to reach far'. The first was our initiative and David Edwards
quotes from the document 'Towards Simplicity of Life', which
some of us produced at the conference itself. Despite the haste in
which it was put together it may merit being quoted in full as our
first 'Life Style' Manifesto:

1. See yourself as a citizen of the planet:
   Questions of poverty and environment are distorted if seen
   only in local or national terms.
2. Waste watching—where you have a choice:
   Resist obsolescence; choose the longer-lasting.
   Support public transport (with your feet and your vote!).
   Question advertisements.
   Resist wasteful packaging.
3. Question your own life style—not your neighbour's!
4. If possible, work out your way of life with the help of a
   group (family, friends, congregation . . .), asking such
   questions as:
   How can we measure our real needs (by the standards of
     our neighbours or by the needs of the poor)?
   How can we be joyful without being greedy or flamboyant
     (e.g. in hospitality)?
   How far does our personal way of life depend on society's
     wealth?
   Can our society's way of life be simpler?
   Is there any one such change we ourselves can work for?
   How can we be good stewards without being over-
     scrupulous?
   What decisions about personal life are the decisive ones
     to make (e.g. budgeting; family size, etc.)?
   How can others benefit from what we have (our home,
     our car and other possessions)?
5. Points to ponder:
   'Happiness is knowing what I can do without.'
   'My greed is another's need.'
   'Am I detached from worldly goods if I keep what I have
     and want to add to them?'

6. Essential reading:
   Only One Earth, Barbara Ward and Rene Dubos.

The second attempt at 'words which might be simple and powerful enough to reach far' to which David Edwards refers concerns 'the young radical commentary 'Upside' which was distributed to delegates throughout the conference by members of One for Christian Renewal'.[8] This organisation, of which I have been a member since its formation, co-operated with a small group of us in Commission Eight and it was out of this co-operation that emerged the original form of our Movement's slogan: 'Live more simply so that others may simply live.' David Edwards comments:

> This is the last motto or slogan, and it is the most challenging of all. It calls upon Christians to avoid all extravagance because so many millions of people in the world today do not have enough. We ought to support movements such as Christian Aid and Oxfam even when it means self-sacrifice. As a nation we must be clearly a champion, not an exploiter of the poor. And this generation has to discipline itself in its treatment of the resources of the earth, so that food and fuel and delight may be handed on to those yet unborn. As members of the Christian church and as members of the human family, we must so live now that there will be a future.[9]

In this admirable reportage we can already observe the natural affinity between such a movement towards simplicity of life style and the well-established Development Agencies such as Christian Aid and Oxfam. We may note also the political implications in the words 'as a nation' and the reference to 'the human family', a phrase which has become so characteristic of the Life Style Movement that it merits a brief section on its own.

The Human Family
We have rejected the terms 'mankind' and 'the family of man' as having a sexist connotation to some sensitive ears. The human race sounds too clinical whereas the Human Family brings out the warmth of interdependent relationships which should characterize the Life Style member. Of us it must never be said that although we claim all men as brothers we are very selective in our views of who might properly become our brother-in-law. 'Home is the world,' writes Christopher Hall,[10] an active

participant in our consultations at Selly Oak,

> This at least travel to the moon has made clear. Jack Schmitt said, 'As soon as you see earth from space, nationalistic boundaries disappear.' Charles Duke commented, 'I'm still a hundred per cent American, but now I see earth and mankind more as a whole than as individual races, religions and nations.' From such a viewpoint, how trivial are our tribal loyalties of colour, creed and party, for which some would claim (blasphemously) even divine support. The human race is one, not many. There is one God, not many, even if our understanding of divine truth may differ from place to place and develop from age to age.

Cesar Chavaz, the courageous and dedicated leader of migrant farm workers in California; wrote: 'If we hold life close for ourselves and our children then—even as we live—life will stagnate and lose its purpose: but if we give life freely and fully on behalf of our brothers and sisters, we will discover life as God intended it to be.'

Equally authoritative are these words of a young Indonesian:

> As an Asian I experience just how great is the myth of Western culture and technology in the eyes of so many of us. We can feel so small and have such a sense of cultural 'guilt' that we expect 'help' from people coming from a foreign culture. Many of the Westerners who come to help us come with the best motivations, but I cannot help wondering how much they are really helping when, in their great eagerness, we are still considered, consciously or unconsciously, as being the weak. Does this not in fact tend to make the myth of the West even greater, and those who already feel weak become more conscious of their inferiority and limitations?
>
> Surely we need one another—we need to support one another, to welcome and be welcomed, to listen to one another. Both the attitudes of feeling small and wanting to help are deeply rooted within us. Only a meeting within the context of the 'universal family' can help us discover one another.'[11]

You may have noticed that we have changed our slogan from 'Live more simply that others may simply live' to 'Live more simply that all of us may simply live'. This change was first proposed by Kenneth Turner, a delegate at the conference on 'Ecology and Christian responsibility' at Sewanee, Tenessee in

1975.[12] Ken pointed out that the word 'others' appeared to imply that they were the problem, that we were not necessarily all in the same boat together. I am sure that he was right. Rich or poor, none of us will survive unless we learn to share.

Four Principles

The prominence of conferences in this account of the origins of the Life Style Movement should not obscure the obvious truth that even an idea whose time has come, conceived in conference, may remain stillborn between the pages of the official record. For reasons already given I was determined that the insights so hardly won at Selly Oak should not vanish into thin air. We needed a continuing movement.

After a courteous correspondence had made clear that the British Council of Churches which had sponsored the Selly Oak conference (as it had also sponsored the Nottingham conference to which I have already alluded) had no present intention of devoting resources to any follow-up, I knew that I must take some action myself. From the start I envisaged four principles which, it will not surprise you, all conveniently begin with the same letter, the four O's. They are: One sheet of paper; Ordinary people; Open to all; Offered to existing organizations.

These four principles have been set down in 'Life Style: a note of explanation' as follows:

> We do not need another organization. Life Style has to spread through existing organizations.
>
> Life Style must be simple enough to be contained within one sheet of paper.
>
> Life Style must be designed for ordinary people, not for the heroic exceptions.
>
> Life Style is not for Christians only, but must be so worded as to be acceptable to men and women of goodwill of any ideology or none.

Now it has first to be admitted that more than five years later the only national or international organization that had taken Life Style into its system was the Pilgrims of St Francis, an imaginative group of people who organize national and international pilgrimages which are characterized by plain living, high thinking and a devotion to St Francis. It has been and remains my constant hope that Development Agencies such as Christian

Aid, Oxfam or War on Want might officially commend our Life Style Commitment as appropriate, but not of course mandatory for their supporters. I have had similar hopes for conservationist organizations such as the Conservation Society, Friends of the Earth or the Soil Association, or again for the already mentioned World Development Movement or One for Christian Renewal. Such a commendation could hardly harm such organizations and might indeed benefit them substantially, providing a focus of the kind of personal commitment by their supporters on which they ultimately depend. My hope that Life Style may prove complementary at the personal level to the public work of such agencies has however been greatly encouraged in recent years by a growing measure of co-operation with Christian Aid on the one hand and with 'One For Christian Renewal' on the other.

The containment of the Life Style Commitment within one sheet of paper has so far been maintained—just. This is to be desired not only to save postage on the one hand and the destruction of forests on the other, but also because in our hectic culture people are more likely to read and assimilate what is short and readily accessible.

In designing Life Style for ordinary people, we realize that fundamentally no one is ordinary; everyone is unique. We have not found it easy to steer a middle course between a Commitment that has no bite to it at all on the one hand, and so tough a Commitment on the other as to be rejected by many sympathizers as unattainable. We do well, I think, to err in favour of the needs of the unheroic. The heroic will tighten up the Commitment to their own aspirations in any case.

That the Life Style document is 'so worded as to be acceptable to men and to women of goodwill of any ideology or none' has proved to be the most controversial of the four principles. From time to time at church meetings Life Style has been roundly criticized for its lack of explicit reference to prayer, the Bible or the Holy Spirit. I remain unconvinced by these criticisms while recognizing that there might be a place for a parallel movement whose Christian reference is thus explicit. In fact over two years after the Selly Oak conference, 'That's the Style' was launched by *Crusade* magazine. Its founders consulted me before proceeding and I was in fact one of the first wave of those who signed its commitment in the following terms:

We acknowledge that:
1. One third of the world lives to excess at the expense of the remaining two-thirds who live in poverty; the earth's non-renewable resources are being ruthlessly and needlessly exhausted.
2. The Bible clearly teaches that we are stewards of God's world; good stewardship requires that we use no more of its resources than we need, sharing them generously with all men.
3. In the light of these facts we should adopt a simple, adequate, thrifty life style and encourage our families and fellow Christians to do the same.
4. We should try to influence public opinion within our churches and in the wider political field to press for changes to be made in both law and practice to improve man's stewardship and correct the present imbalance.'[13]

As we shall see, Life Style prefers to try to meet the specific needs and aims of its many Christian members and supporters by the addition to its Commitment of a 'Postscript for Christian Believers'.

Since it all began at Selly Oak, the Life Style Movement has advanced slowly and steadily, far too slowly for any complacency, yet steadily enough to encourage our belief that it does embody an idea whose time has come. Life Style received a great boost when the price of oil from the Middle East shot up dramatically, an event which inaugurated a new economic era and shook many thousands of people into a deeper understanding of the real world in which we all live. The Movement has benefited from a number of radio and television interviews not only in Britain but also in Australia, New Zealand and the United States. One tough reporter in Australia ended his interview with the comment: 'But that's just what Jesus taught isn't it?' There has also been a steady trickle of newspaper and magazine articles and the Movement has had encouraging commendations in several books, notably in John V. Taylor's *Enough is Enough*, Edward Patey's *Christian Life Style* and Patrick Rivers' *Living Better on Less!*[14]

But the main growth points are and have to be the nine hundred or so individual members who have signed postcards of acceptance of the Life Style Commitment and the fifty or so Life Style Cells of whose existence I have been informed. These individuals and groups are but the tip of a shining iceberg. The influence of such a Movement as this, whatever it may be, is bound to be largely hidden, by no means to be measured by the number of conscious adherents.

Nineteen Seventy-Five

February 1975, which saw the emergence of 'That's the Style', also saw the publication by Christian Aid of an simple but effective leaflet, 'Live more simply' . . .'. Without specific reference to our Movement, its authors 'offered advice to all who want to join the movement towards a more moderate life style'.[15] This leaflet, together with home collecting boxes which also carried our slogan, formed part of the 'Frugality Campaign' which Church leaders had begun to launch at the end of 1974: 'To give added point to eating a little less food or using a little less petrol and oil, they urged that the money thus saved should be given to food-production schemes in the world's hungriest areas.'[16]

1975 also saw the launching of 'Our Daily Bread. A Policy for the Diocese of Bristol'. On a visit to the United States early that year I had observed similar diocesan programmes at work in the Anglican Dioceses of Michigan and of Southern Ohio, the former known rather wordily as 'The Bishop's programme for concerned Episcopalians to help with hunger, energy, economy and church'. The latter was called 'Give us this day our daily bread. A response to the world hunger for the dioceses of Southern Ohio'. Our Bristol Diocesan Synod responded promptly and warmly to a proposal that we should officially adopt our own policy document for development education and support, a document which included a commendation of 'Life Style, Bristol Cathedral's own movement to bring hope and a sense of purpose to ordinary people who may feel helpless before the complex forces which threaten even the survival of the human family.'[17]

In due course the implementation of this policy in the Chippenham area produced a useful result: an unanimous vote in our Church's General Synod in favour of a motion sent up by our Diocesan Synod. Meanwhile in Newcastle, New South Wales, Bishop Ian Shevill addressed his Diocesan Synod on 30 May 1975 on 'A Christian Life Style for the 1970's'. The Bishop's methods and principles were similar to those of our Life Style Movement; but his headings were far more closely related to the specific requirements of church membership. His initiative facilitated a powerful 'pastoral care movement' which gives scope in a number of churches in Australia and New Zealand to a sustained programme of mature lay responsibility for the mission of the church.

Within the Life Style Movement itself 1975 was marked among other developments by the distribution of a question-naire to eighty-five Life Style members. We were greatly indebted for this to Oxfam and particularly to Philip Jackson, at that time their Communications Director on whose report I now largely rely: [19]

Most of those questioned had come to hear of the Life Style Movement through newspapers or radio . . . They liked the idea because it was simple and positive . . . It was encouraging for them to know that others shared their concern. In answer to the question 'What do you think is wrong with our present style of life?' the stupid emphases on competition, materialism, selfishness and waste of resources were all cited, plus the insidious attitude that luxuries become necessities within a decade. Several mentioned the almost total indiffer-ence of political parties to such matters as world population, resources and pollution. Consequently 'widespread famines' and 'the breakdown of orderly society' were to be expected, and everyone felt there was a strong connection between our life style and the problems faced by poorer countries . . . There was a marked, but understandable lack of mention of Latin American countries.

In answer to the question, 'What do you consider the most important causes of poverty in the poorer countries?' thirty-three out of seventy-six repondents placed 'Exploitation by the developed countries' in their first two choices. Next, but a long way behind, came 'Excessive population growth' (20) and 'lack of government planning and foresight' (10).

To help the people of poorer countries the changes in life style which people said they would be most prepared to make were: 'Eating less and more simple food . . . especially eating less meat', 'wasting less (of everything)', and 'refraining from luxury goods'. However, a large number said they were unsure whether such actions would in fact benefit the poor, and many expressed the need for practical and detailed guidance.

Policies which respondents said they would be prepared to support included, predominantly, an increase in Government aid to the Third World and a reduction in our own living standards . . .

A number of 'attitude statements' were listed in the questionnaire and each respondent indicated the degree of his/her agreement or disagreement. The statement given the strongest endorsement was, 'We in Britain consume more than our fair share of the world's resources so in future we may have to be content with less,' followed by 'There is only so much to go round in this world, so we must share what there is more equally.'

The two attitudes most strongly *dis*claimed were, 'What have the poor countries ever done for us?' and 'If people are poor or hungry they usually have only themselves to blame.' The statement upon which respondents were most divided— although a majority disagreed with it—was, 'The poorer countries would have few problems if only they would stop having so many children.'

Of the seventy-two who returned the questionnaire forty-one were women and thirty-one men. Only two were under twenty-five years old. Fifty-four said that they had gone on to college or university education after school. And many have obviously stayed in the academic life, for teaching or lecturing was the occupation (of self or husband) most frequently given. Housewives, those involved in medicine or in the Church were next best represented. Variety was provided by a crofter, a bowling green keeper, a cellist and a cane seat repairer. Fifty-four said that religion played an important part in their lives.

The questionnaires were all completed anonymously as had been requested.

Of the many interesting inferences that might be drawn from that report, I shall select just one: the urgent need for the Life Style Movement to get out into the world of the Trades Unions and of industrial management. Although the Movement may appear hostile to the short-term interests of the producers, particularly of luxury or otherwise socially useless goods and services, in the long term the only hope for our industry and commerce lies in the effective provision for the needs of the at present indigent majority of the Human Family.

A Workshop at Glay

In choosing the year 1975 to illustrate by means of examples how Life Style works, I have deliberately refrained from attempting a systematic history of this and the intervening years. So modest a Movement does not yet merit such a systematic treatment, though who knows whether it may come to do so? In the same spirit I have selected 1977 for illustration by means of three events.

The workshop which took place in February 1977 at Glay in France (but near Basel, Switzerland), was the second on 'The search for new life styles' arranged by the Commission on the Churches' Participation in Development, a constituent body of the World Council of Churches. One point that was immediately and properly raised was the propriety of applying the word 'new' to the issues under review. The Core Group appointed to follow up our discussion felt uneasy about the term 'New Life Style' and called for a name which would reflect the linkage between the personal way of life on the one hand and the need for systemic change on the other.'[20] This linkage rightly became a key concept of our discussions:

> A positive aspect of this search for new life styles is that it links the personal with the political, the superstructures with the transformation of the relationships of production. Oftentimes in the struggle to transform society, the patterns of individual behaviour and daily life are left untouched, leaving room for deeply-rooted and subtle forms of oppression (like that of women by men, or that of the traditional family pattern). Concrete experiences of alternative life styles, if seen in the global context of the struggle for systematic changes, help bridge the gap between these two levels.[21]

At Glay I learned both about my own life style and that of my church, and about the life styles of others. It was a pastor from West Germany (FDR) who asked me: 'Do you mean to tell me that you actually pay men and boys to sing in your Cathedral? When are you going to start paying the congregation to attend?' And it was two members of the Gossner Mission in East Berlin (DDR) who shared with us the positive aspects of the style of life which their Mission is promoting in their country. Central to this life style is the principle and practice of a solidarity which amounts to a political alliance with the revolutionary working class. This involves a massive change of consciousness if the revolution is to be completed and developed. It also involves a careful and continuing definition and redefinition of the relationship between the churches and various political agencies. Christians are encouraged to regard themselves not as the oppressed but as showing solidarity with the oppressed, not so much the Church for others as the Church with others. This involves repentance and humility, a sharing of the life of the poor, as followers of the poor and struggling Jesus. The Gossner Mission provides a service of solidarity (Programme of Church and Society in the DDR) which includes help to Vietnam and other developing countries. The centrally planned economy controls all purchases for the Third World. The Church may collect money but not itself send it abroad.

The speaker claimed that a socialist society with some prospect of moving towards communism was closer to the kingdom of God than other current forms of society. Solidarity with the international proletariat was strongly commended. The Programme to Combat Racism, organized by the World Council of Churches, is highly praised in East Germany where the need for a parallel programme to combat all forms of political and economic imperialism is widely discussed. There is little or no discussion of ecological questions, however, although a certain reaction against consumerism is to be observed. The speaker himself, formerly a full-time pastor, is now a factory worker, the leader of the Danilo Dolci brigade in his place of work, an active Trades Unionist.

You can imagine that all this did not go unquestioned. The questions were honestly answered and a considerable impact was made. Less controversial were accounts given or information supplied about Life Style Movements in France, Germany (FDR), the Netherlands, Norway, Sweden, Switzerland, the United States and our own 'Life Style'.

Life Style in the Netherlands

It appears that one of the most effective movements is the New Life Style Movement in the Dutch Churches. Unlike us in Britain, the enthusiasts were able to secure the official backing of the Churches, following a national conference in November 1974. The relevant resolution included the following statements and proposals:

The Council of Churches encourages all attempts to frame

new life styles in which a responsibility is expressed for present and future generations . . . In view of the very critical food situation in numerous parts of the world a revision of the composition of our food consumption as well as a sparing use of minerals and energy are necessary.

The Council of Churches addresses its member churches by asking them to appeal to their memberships to observe a weekly day of fasting. This day serves as a symbolic, but also a practical exercise in a more embracing new life style, focussed at a society in which the rights of the poor will be put first and foremost, both in personal and in societal life.

The energy and money saved ought to be destined to clear and transparent programmes for the renewal of society, both international and in the immediate neighbourhood.

The Council of Churches asks for a critical testing of the Bible on fundamental issues with regard to the social system as well as personal behaviour.[22]

A 'Working Group New Life Styles' (WNL) was formed to work under the authority of the Section for Social Problems of the Dutch Council of Churches. But this was never an exclusively Christian movement, even though both the Roman Catholic and a number of Protestant Churches were involved from the start. In January 1975 the Working Group began to initiate and stimulate church and other groups to search for appropriate life styles. The Working Group has also explicitly aimed at contributing to the development of a political climate in which structural changes may take place. Some fifteen members have met monthly, Hans Opschoor, who was present at Glay, being the first full-time secretary. The Group has published a number of brochures and (at the time of the Glay Conference) regarded itself as expendable with a limited life span. By May 1976 the Group already possessed the addresses of some three hundred and fifty New Life Style groups scattered among the one thousand or so distinct communities, municipalities and so on which constitute the Netherlands. There were probably, however, about double that number of groups, averaging eleven members each, more than half of them ecumenical. Nearly half the members were aged between thirty-five and fifty-five years of age, most of the others being younger. Membership of these groups has led in many cases to personal changes of attitude as a result of informed discussions on such subjects as developments in South Africa, recycling of materials, employment problems, food consumption and production. There have also been personal changes in behaviour in such areas as the use of a car, nutrition patterns, buying patterns and openness to the influence of others on the members' patterns of expenditure.

These NL Groups, the equivalent of our Life Style Cells, also share their ideas with others by means of publications in church and local news media, debates, panels, special church services and communication with like-minded groups. And they take action by financially adopting Third World projects, locally supporting nationwide initiatives, helping refugees who live in Holland, ministering to old people and organizing Third World shops.

No wonder, then, that the Netherlands in 1976 was equal top with Sweden of the league of developed countries in terms of the percentage of Gross National Product given to developing countries as Official Development Assistance (0.82% as compared with the United Kingdom 0.38%, West Germany 0.31%, the United States 0.25% and Japan 0.20%).[23]

Life Style Movements Elsewhere in Northern and Western Europe

As Hans Opschoor represented the Dutch New Life Styles Movement at Glay, so Margaretha Ringstroem represented the 'Life is More Than Affluence' movement in Sweden. The Swedish word for affluence, *overflod*, has an appropriately extravagant ring about it. This movement in its turn has the official backing of the Swedish Ecumenical Council. It concentrates its collective mind and action on an annual Development Week. Church leaders sign the documents prepared for the Week. But radical thinkers are said to write them. As in Britain it all seems to have started at a national conference in 1972, the Christian National Assembly at Gothenburg. The theme, 'Live responsibly in the world' gave an opportunity for self-criticism and reflection out of which a number of key concepts and slogans have arisen. 'Justice cannot wait', for example, was the theme of one Development Week, sponsored jointly by the Swedish Ecumenical Council and the Swedish Mission Council.

The Swedish movement calls for changes in the patterns both

of consumption and of production under the heading of 'A New Style of Living'. Some two hundred local ecumenical groups (1977 figures) took up the theme of development in terms of liberation, 'Freedom for the Oppressed'. As a result of this local activity, Church leaders presented a manifesto to the Government and to Parliament, signed by 75,000 members. This advocated for example international action to stop using for animal fodder any fish caught off the shores of developing countries. 'Life is more than Affluence'.

There are also in Sweden at the time of writing more than 20,000 members of the Norwegian movement, 'The Future in our Hands'.[4] In its first year under the enthusiastic leadership of Erik Damman, this movement is reported to have recruited 6,000 active members in Norway alone. This compares most favourable with our Life Style Movement's five hundred or so in the first six years drawn from a much larger population, many of whom in any case may not be all that active in the cause. An early undated document prepared by 'The Future in our Hands' poses the following 'Problems which have previously been unknown to human beings':

We shall soon not have any clean water, and seldom breathe the clean air.

We store up poisons in our organisms from the food we eat.

We are steadily destroying more natural areas, fishing waters and agricultural areas, ending that usage from which the country should live and increasing the pressure on the towns.

We long for peace, but the noise and tumult increase.

We have obtained more leisure time—but just the same we have less time for living. We feel the burden of growing demands and inhumanity where we work and in schools.

We have made a basis for social security, but developments frighten us, and we are worn out with increasing nervous problems.

We know that technology has gone awry and is creating enormous difficulties—but just the same we hope anxiously that *more* uncontrolled technology will remove them.

We live in a land of abundance, but just the same we have money problems—and do not give our handicapped, our old people and our problem families the living conditions they need.

We are on the way to losing control over our lives, our environment and our development.

These are *our* problems . . .

Personally, I always prefer to start in terms of opportunities rather than problems. But it has to be said that, as its name implies, 'The Future in our Hands' tackles these problems in a positive and practical way. The paragraph headings which follow the analysis in this document give the flavour of the approach:

Have we enough to perform the tasks before us? What can a little country do? What is wrong in Norway? How can a change be made? Must we develop a sense for other values? Who will begin? Consumer reduction is the key phrase. But what shall we cut down? We must support each other in a new view of consumption and ownership. We need a centre for meeting and support.

In another publication, 'The Future in our Hands' criticizes the vicious circle of the consumer society:

First we pay for a car or a motor boat to avoid walking or rowing and to save time. Then we have to pay for apparatus for exercising and to use up the time we saved.

First we pay for more food than is good for us, then we pay for slimming aids or medicines to repair the damage.

First we buy Cola and expensive lollies for our children, then we pay to repair their teeth and digestion. We pay to give them entertainment and everything they ask for, and then we have to pay for the damage because they feel a lack of challenge in life.

First we pay more than we need to follow the fashion, and then we pay for advertisements and marketing to alter fashion.

We pay for factories to make disposable products, and pay again for cleansing departments to remove the pollution they create.

We pay to keep up in the consumer race, and pay again for medical treatment because we are hurt by the pressures it creates.

We see that these circumstances damage us all. What is it that stops us from breaking our of this stupid spiral?'[25]

My impression, based on no detailed study, is that 'The Future in our Hands' is even more influential in Norway that 'Life is More Than Affluence' in Sweden or the New Life Styles Movement in the Netherlands. From Switzerland Hans Ruh informs us that,

> the very number of groups practising an alternative life style in one field or another is astonishing. A list of the ways in which these groups are active includes the following: house design, communities, communication, transport, recycling, technology, culture, agriculture, food production, animal husbandry and hunting, food and medicine, children, the complex housing-clothing-hygiene, kitchen, bathroom, crafts, energy, use and re-use of material resources, development aid . . . Central to the public debate are questions of energy, especially in connection with the planning of atomic energy plants.[26]

In Switzerland as elsewhere 'raising the level of awareness' of these matters has high priority.

Among the participants at Glay was Dr Manfred Linz from Hannover, the founder with others of 'One World', my final example of a Life Style movement in Western Europe. Adherents of 'One World' make a threefold pledge: to give away 3 per cent of income; to take part in political action; and to re-orientate their consumption patterns. A central secretariat of eight people meets weekly to produce information sheets on such positive aspects of a new Life Style as patterns of resource consumption and development education. Their concern is both ecological and ecumenical. Their intention to change society is clearcut. Members do not at all think of themselves as a moral élite. Their aim is to start a process of learning by beginning with themselves. Their starting point is founded in that kind of en-lightened self-interest which recognizes that if the members of the Human Family do not learn to live together they will certainly have to die together. 'One World' members reject the notion that the middle class label is a sign of reproach. Revolutions, they rightly claim, usually start from within the bourgeoisie.

Writing of his own Life Style, Dr Linz reports:[27]

At any rate, we have made a beginning. We have checked the

consumption of power in our house and discovered that we can easily save 10 per cent without great inconvenience. We have reduced our consumption of luxuries (mainly alcohol). Once or twice a week I travel to my office by bus, although it takes an hour and a half longer. We examine our purchases to decide what we really need. So far, it has all been less difficult than we expected. In fact we find it fun, because we see that we are still flexible. Time will show whether we can keep it up.

As a mature student of group dynamics and personal motivation, Manfred Linz realizes also that,

of course the new way of life does not mean only the reduction of personal consumption. Thanks to my thrifty up-bringing I have always largely escaped the compulsions of the consumer society. It is something else which has left its mark on me: the pressure to produce results, the very strong sense of self-fulfilment to be got from showing what I can do in my work and by reaping the laurels of professional recognition. And I have to be on my guard lest the work for a new way of life should subtly turn into its opposite, fortifying this ambition and desire for recognition—of course all in a good cause! One can only be saved from that danger by the group, working and thinking and rejoicing together and keeping one another on the right path.[28]

How apropos I find that confession as I sit here at my type-writer recording the quiet progress of a Movement of which, after all, I am myself the founder! I wonder how far I too have been motivated by 'the very strong sense of self-fulfilment to be got from showing what I can do in my work and by reaping the laurels of professional recognition'. Not that in the end it matters too much as long as the work itself is on the right lines and the amusing confusion of our motives is cheerfully acknowledged. Our desire for recognition does not necessarily diminish, I find, as we move on from that stage in life in which we may suppose ourselves to be promising to the succeeding stage in which we know ourselves to be disappointing! In any case there is no harm in candidly acknowledging that we all need to be loved, encouraged and recognized!

I shall end what I judge to be an encouraging look at the Northern and Western European scene by quoting the con-clusion of Hans Opschoor's *Case Study*: [29]

Finally, many people express a feeling of being powerless in view of the changes needed. Even a well co-ordinated network of NL groups might be incapable of building up enough pressure to change national policies. Even if that would be possible, what can one single small country accomplish on the world scene?

It is unlikely that a rational answer to such feelings is feasible. The beginning of an answer must rather contain elements of the faith and hope that may still be active . . . An immediate and practical consequence for groups like the WNL might be to join forces in an international network of movements searching for alternatives to prevailing life styles of individuals and societies of today, willing to change the structures behind them and to demonstrate their feasibility.

I like those words, 'immediate and practical'. The sooner such an international network is formed the better. In my own preliminary submission for the Glay workshop I proposed that,

the next stage of the process should be a study of Alternative Life Style Movements already in being with the clear aim of adopting or adapting or conflating material from such movements for active commendation by the Commission on the Churches' Participation in Development to its constituency. The matter is of such urgency that it would be far better so to commend a Movement which still needs a good deal of refinement in the light of further experience than to do nothing at all.

To the best of my knowledge my proposal has not been taken seriously or at least has not been taken up. But I remain convinced that what all these Movements need is a brief but comprehensive common statement of guidelines for the personal life style of all those who for whatever primary reason wish to commit themselves to living more simply that all of us may simply live; a Commitment that will be as acceptable to the Dutch as to the Germans, the Norwegians as to the Swedes. It should not be too difficult to draw up such a Common Commitment. It is even possible that we in the Life Style Movement have done it already!

The North Americans
In the preparation of any such statement, manifesto or

commitment it would be necessary to involve the North Americans from the beginning and representatives of the Third World too for that matter. Writing about the work of Hazel Henderson, 'the American counter-economist', as he calls her, James Robertson observes that the alternative movement in the United States is far larger than in Britain and has a far greater influence on politics and on public opinion:

> People coming out of the peace and counter-culture move-
> ments of the sixties have joined with environmentalists,
> women's rights activists, futurists, alternative technologists,
> consumerists (Nader's raiders) and—most remarkable to a
> British observer—some of the labour unions, to create
> throughout the seventies a continually evolving web of
> temporary coalitions, campaigning on one issue after
> another.[30]

Opinion polls show that this broad base facilitates a rapid increase in the numbers committed to 'voluntary simplicity'.[31] By 79 per cent to 16, Americans were (1978) reported to,

> think 'teaching people how to live more with basic essentials'
> is more important than 'reaching higher standards of living'.
> A clear majority of 59 to 33 per cent favour 'putting real effort
> into avoiding doing those things that cause pollution' over
> 'finding ways to clean up the environment as the economy
> expands'.
>   Research Institute analysts Duane Elgin and Arnold
> Mitchell found that some five million adults in the United
> States were full-time adherents of 'voluntary simplicity',
> defined as a way of life embracing 'frugal consumption, a
> strong sense of ecological urgency, and a dominant concern
> with personal growth'—what Ralph Waldo Emerson called
> 'plain living and high thinking' . . .
>   Messrs Elgin and Mitchell also found that another eight to
> ten million Americans were partial adherents of the 'vol-
> untary simplicity'. Study results show also that the number
> could rise to over twenty million by 1980, thirty-six million by
> 1985 and ninety-two million in the year 2000.

With these figures we may compare the statement in the *Los Angeles Times* (1978) that 'today, an estimated forty-five million Americans are living lives fully committed to the concept of voluntary simplicity, while perhaps twice that many more are partial adherents.'[32]

More facts about this considerable movement towards 'voluntary simplicity' is contained in *Futurist* magazine, 'a journal of forecasts, trends and ideas about the future'.[33] From the mass of contemporary information and advice contained in a single number of this magazine I select one basic quotation from Arnold Toynbee:

> These religious founders (Jesus, Buddha, Lao Tse, St Francis of Assisi) disagreed with each other in their pictures of what is the nature of the universe, the nature of spiritual life, the nature of ultimate spiritual reality. But they all agreed in their ethical precepts. They all agreed that the pursuit of material wealth is a wrong aim. We should aim only at the minimum wealth needed to maintain life; and our main aim should be spiritual. They all said with one voice that if we made material wealth our paramount aim, this would lead to disaster. They all spoke in favour of unselfishness and of love for other people as the key to happiness and to success in human affairs.

Voluntary simplicity is not a new life style. What is new is the urgency, or perhaps we should say our understanding of the urgency of the global need for its adoption on a truly massive scale. We may compare the figures already quoted with another estimate in *The Futurist* that the number of Americans fully committed to voluntary simplicity could advance from five millions in 1977 to twenty-five millions in 1987 and sixty millions in 2000. For partial adherents the corresponding figures might be ten, thirty-five and sixty millions, for sympathizers, say, sixty, fifty and twenty-five millions and for the indifferent or opposed seventy-five, sixty and fifty-five millions. So massive a shift might just suffice to enable the necessary political and economic changes to take place in time to avert global disaster. On the other hand I at least know of no parallel movement of voluntary simplicity in the socialist nations of Eastern Europe or in Asia. Perhaps no such movement has yet become necessary. In this, therefore, as in so many other matters, the main burden of global leadership rests with the United States.

Our own little Life Style Movement has a footing there, following a tour which included visits to nine states which I made in 1975. The Life Style Cell at Christchurch Cathedral, Louisville, Kentucky has published a broadsheet entitled 'Towards a

Simpler Christmas'. Full of sensible suggestions, this broadsheet ends with the following 'questions for family discussion':

How would you celebrate Christmas if you had no money to spend on gifts?

What could you do for your parents, relatives and friends that would be a gift of yourself?

What gifts can you make using natural and recyclable materials?

How can we help some people whom we may not even know be glad to be alive at Christmas?

How would Jesus want his birthday celebrated?

Is there something we can make together as a family that would have real meaning for us? Or something special a parent could make for a child as a surprise?

Have you ever thought about sharing a talent of yours (music, speech, a skit) as a gift?

What in the past has meant the most to you at Christmas?

How can our celebration focus more on people than things?

Do children really expect as much at Christmas as we think we should give them?

Life Style and the Church of South India

The notion of voluntary simplicity of life is no stranger to India in general nor to the Church of South India in particular. Many of Mother Teresa's Sisters of Charity are South Indian girls and it was a South Indian woman who made what I think is the best contemporary statement relating a Christian's life style to his or her propagation of the gospel that I have come across:

People are no longer converted to a doctrine, they can only be attracted to a way of life which they can see as a practical alternative to the values and assumptions of our competitive, alienated, materialistic society. We have been presenting Christianity (the system) and not Christ the person . . . We have to present to the world a living Christ, fresh, always life-giving and nourishing . . . Christianity is life in the Spirit and it can only be experienced in the loving, forgiving, sharing and liberating Fellowship.[34]

In adapting this statement, as we shall see later, for inclusion in the Life Style Commitment I am not in any way wishing to imply a depreciation of systematic doctrine. It is to the Church Missionary Society again that I now turn for further evidence of involvement by the Church of South India in Life Style concerns.[35] Mrs Daisy Gopal Ratnam, Honorary Secretary of the General Synod of the Church of South India, is being interviewed:

> How are you working out the question of life style, Mrs Ratnam? What are the practical implications for the Church of South India?

> We unanimously decided at our last Synod meeting that we should all voluntarily reduce our standard of living so that we would be nearer to the poorer sections of the population. We said we would forgo one meal a week and contribute to a social welfare project. Those who are earning will voluntarily give one day's salary, or half a day's salary if they have too large a family. We will invite a poor family in the neighbourhood to a meal, treating them the same as we would others that come to our homes.

Under the heading 'the British Life Style Group that received Aid from India', John Madeley began his article about our Life Style Movement with these words:[36] 'In the autumn of 1976, the Church of South India voted to give £1,000 to an organisation in Britain which "promoted the solidarity of the human family, rich and poor alike". The choice fell on the Bristol-based Life Style Movement.'

I myself commented on this beautiful yet humbling gift in my annual Life Style Newsletter for 1978 as follows:

> It is a very practical sign of support from the so-called 'Third World' for a movement which has been dismissed by some of its critics as irrelevant to that world. I am hoping that for the time being the interest that accrues from the investment of this gift will pay the travel and other expenses of Regional Correspondents, one each for Ireland, Scotland and Wales and for each of the economic regions in England.

At the time of writing these honorary Regional Correspondents have been appointed. On receiving the gift which enabled these appointments to work effectively, we wished to honour it in some way. In India tree planting is an acceptable, significant and appropriate sign of celebration. So in honour of the gift from

South India we planted an oak tree on College Green outside our Cathedral.

The Life Style Movement and Christian Aid

The third significant development in 1977 may be said to have started with a letter I had received three years previously from a member of Christian Aid Headquarters Staff expressing interest in Life Style 'because it is basic to our own motivations and aims'. This basic affinity had also been exposed in a Christian Aid leaflet entitled 'Action for Justice'. After describing the root cause of world poverty as 'an unjust social and economic order of which each of us is part', the leaflet concludes with 'the vision of a new style and quality of international living, a new pattern of relationships in which we recognize our mutual inter-dependence, a new understanding of the words "injustice", "responsibility" and "community". There is no moving from old world to new without radical changes in our attitudes and priorities. What the vision calls for is repentance.'

Such a total response by the individual is what Life Style is all about. So it is encouraging to record that the Christian Aid Board has generously authorized their Area Secretaries in the South West Region to give what aid and comfort they can to our Movement. At the time of writing no decision has been made to extend this co-operation to the whole country.

Life Style is doing what it can in return. Even in terms of hard cash I was much encouraged to receive a letter from a correspondent in Lincoln enclosing a gift of £50 for Christian Aid as a sign of approval of its association with Life Style. By the beginning of 1980 our own Bristol Cathedral Life Style Cell had collected over £500 for Christian Aid at its meetings, including generous contributions from those who are not committed to the Christian faith. An encouraging letter from the Portsmouth co-ordinator for Christian Aid and another (from which I now quote) from the Chairman of the Truro and District Council of Churches Christian Aid Committee confirm me in my conviction of the value of this alliance: 'Life Style in the manner which you describe has, for several years, been the policy to which this Committee fully subscribes. Our belief in a simple lifestyle was particularly brought home to us after we spent some considerable time studying the publication "Food for Thought Pack". Please be assured that this Committee supports your project.'

Of course we have to recognize that, as things are, a number of Christian Aid supporters will not be interested in Life Style. Similarly a number of Life Style members will prefer to support other Development Agencies.

What of the Future?
That the Life Style Movement embodies an idea whose time has come is axiomatic for the writer, as I hope by now for many readers of this book. This axiom receives support from a number of unexpected quarters. Paul Shay, for example, Director of Business Research Intelligence at the Stanford Research Institute International, painted a startling if ironic picture of future trends of consumption at the 1978 Advertising Association Conference at Brighton:

> Mr and Mrs Average 1987 are going to be the most boring, socially responsible, aggressive individualistic freaks ever known.
>
> Speeding to work in their millions on their custom-built, fuel-saving motorcycles, clad in their hand-woven denims, the new, well-educated masses will be the biggest threat yet to the multi-million consumer market in Britain, America, Germany and Japan.
>
> Eating home-made bread and into macrobiotics, drinking home-made beer and wine, and renovating semi-derelict Victorian and Georgian houses, the only boom they promise is even bigger sales for *Zen and the Art of Motorcycle Maintenance*, or Schumacher's *Small is Beautiful*.
>
> Weekending on pollution-free camp sites, or hang-gliding over the countryside, this new generation—dubbed 'the inwardly-directed consumer'—is going to be in the majority in the mid-1980's.'[37]

The hang-gliding and the motor cycling apart, I think I recognize myself and my fellow Life Stylers in this ironic picture. Mr Shay probably knows what he is talking about. Industrial companies, it appears, are willing to pay six thousand dollars a year for access to the research his company undertakes. Whether our Life Style Movement plays a significant part in any such transformation of values and of patterns of consumption need not be important. It is the idea of living more simply that all of us may simply live and its practice that are important, not the success of any particular organization.

Wanted—A Charismatic Leader?

Meanwhile the comment of an old friend at a meeting in Sheffield some years ago presents a challenge. 'Your movement will make no impact until it has obtained its first hundred thousand members.' He did not join.

A comparison at this point may throw light on the question he raised. The growth of membership of the National Trust has been as follows:

Year	Members	Year	Members	Year	Members
1895	100	1930	2,000	1960	97,109
1900	250	1940	6,800	1970	226,200
1920	700	1950	23,403	1975	539,285
				1980	778,070

So far we have done a good deal better than the National Trust; from one member at the end of 1972 to nearly nine hundred at the end of 1980! It took the National Trust twenty-five years to reach its first seven hundred members, nearly seventy years to arrive at its first hundred thousand.

I am convinced, however, that we have not got all that time to play with. The four horsemen of the contemporary apocalypse, Poverty, Population, Pollution and Profligacy, are on the march. At the end of the chapter on 'What can I know?' I made a virtue out of the necessity of my own lack of knowledge concerning the politics or the economics of development. A parallel disclaimer is appropriate at this point. I do not find in myself anything approaching the qualities of dynamic leadership that are needed to transform our Life Style Movement into the international secular reformation that is urgently required. I see myself only as a rather unsuccessful forerunner to such a charismatic enabler if he or she is to be found. Pierre Trudeau, former Prime Minister of Canada, once speculated on the crucial problem of inflation: 'Inflation has not found its Keynes. I personally think the Keynes of inflation will not be an economist [but a] political, philosophical or moral leader inspiring people to do without the excess consumption so prominent in the developed countries.'[38]

It may well be that this person is reading these lines at this moment, unaware of the opportunity until circumstances call him or her to the unremitting task. An alternative, but not at all mutually exclusive, way forward would be by means of some already well-established agency, Christian or otherwise, national or international, governmental or non-governmental, adopting the Life Style Movement, or something like it, as integral to its own life and being. Our present rather tentative association with Christian Aid may well be leading us in this direction. Time will tell.

In either case, the terms of the crucial document, the Life Style Commitment, will probably have to be revised; and that along lines which might well not secure my own complete approval. That could well be the decisive and creative 'letting go' which will soon be required of me. After all the Commitment is already in its eighth revision since that first 'Towards Simplicity of Life' was drafted at Selly Oak only six years ago. But before yet another revision is sanctioned we must understand in some detail what the present document intends. To that therefore we now turn.

CHAPTER SIX

THE LIFE STYLE COMMITMENT

Life Style
I have already quoted the Life Style Commitment in full at the beginning of this book. It is set down on one folded sheet of paper. Many of its points have already been made. Others have not; others again may need the further emphasis of repetition and illustration. On the front of the folded paper, under the heading 'Life Style', is the following statement:

> The Life Style Movement offers a Voluntary Common Discipline to those who are committed to a more equitable distribution of the Earth's resources among the members of the Human Family and to the conservation and development of those resources for our own and future generations.
>
> Life Style offers guidelines rather than rules. Those who accept in principle the Commitment inside this leaflet are invited to join the Community of the Life Style Commitment by sending the return card to the Movement's Central Correspondent, the Dean of Bristol, Bristol Cathedral, Bristol BS1 5TJ.

The story of Marcus Porcius Cato, the antique Roman Censor, is notorious enough. Jealous no doubt of the agricultural, economic and military potential of a revived Carthage, a potential which he rightly perceived as threatening his own ideal of an agriculturally strong and self-sufficient Italy, Cato is said to have interspersed all his speeches in the Senate with the words, *Carthago delenda est*: 'Carthage must be destroyed'. In our constructive as opposed to his destructive cause every opportunity has to be taken to emphasize the urgent necessity of personal commitment 'to a more equitable distribution of the Earth's resources among the members of the Human Family'. As we have seen in the chapter entitled 'What Can I Know?', to neglect that commitment is to connive at, if not actively participate in, mass murder of an appalling kind. What may not have emerged, however, is the point that, in rightly stressing the needs of the whole Human Family, we should not neglect the oppressed in our own country. David Sheppard no doubt has the cities of Britain primarily in mind when he writes:

> There are certain scarce resources in a big city. The scarcest of these are: land, good jobs, and good teachers . . . In all three cases the share which different groups in the country receive decides where advantages and disadvantages lie. In a just society it should be the aim that, if one group receives less than its share in one set of good things, it should receive more than its fair share in another. The unjust society is one in which one group always wins in the share-out of the land, the good jobs and the good teachers while another group always loses in these areas. Christian comment should recall that a distinctive mark of the mission of the Christ was that good news was announced to the poor. Jesus seems to have given priority to the poor and calls us to do so.[1]

The same writer is also aware of the linkage between 'a more equitable distribution of the Earth's resources . . . and the conservation and development of those resources for our own and future generations'. He sees the need (and also the limitations) of 'voluntary austerity now'.

> The social audit demanded by the developing countries and by new knowledge about the urgency of world conservation, questions whether we can any longer have (unlimited economic) growth. A call for 'de-growth' in standards of living—'consume less, enjoy it more'—must begin with those with more than average income. This may be voluntary austerity now; but there will need to be Government action to achieve any effective transfer of scarce resources from those who have more than their share. There can be no policy which begins by demanding that those further down the ladder start the process of asking for less.[2]

The addition in our text of the word 'development' to the word 'conservation' is important. To be committed to Life Style is not thereby and necessarily to be committed to 'No Growth'. Whether 'No Growth' is essential to the survival of the Human

Family is a highly complex and technical question. If they had the opportunity to vote on the matter, most of the world's poor would surely vote against it. On the other hand, they might well be mistaken in doing so. The key point is the need to develop the Earth's resources, at whatever rate of development is appropriate, with the needs of the whole Human Family, 'our own and future generations', as the controlling factor.

As was indicated at the beginning of the last chapter, the concept of the 'Human Family' is decisive for the Life Style Movement.

> One of the first people to think of the peoples of the world as a single community was H. G. Wells. His *Outline of World History* brilliantly attempted to trace mankind's story from pre-history to the present in all its global inter-relatedness . . . H. G. Wells, looking at the world as a single, global community, called for a World Thinking Centre, a World Brain, a World Ministry of Foresight, so that such cataclysms as World War I could be avoided, and nations could steer their courses intelligently and harmonize their policies for agreed purposes.[3]

Sadly, Wells died without faith and without hope. But his vision lives on.

Within the framework of a 'Voluntary Common Discipline', a principle and practice explored at some length in the last chapter, 'Life Style offers guidelines rather than rules'. Like the Sabbath before it, Life Style exists for the benefit of those who accept it (and through them for the world at large) rather than the other way round. To become a member of 'the Community of the Life Style Commitment', you do not have to accept every syllable of the seven points of the Commitment. It is the spirit of the Commitment that you accept when you sign the Life Style card.

This obvious point would hardly be worth the making, were it not for the fact that a person's unwillingness to accept every syllable can only too easily become an excuse for evading the challenge of any commitment at all. If you like (though not everybody does), Life Style is a modest way of joyful asceticism. As Charles Elliott writes:

> The search surely has to begin, for a new asceticism that puts as much emphasis on social inter-responsibility as an earlier

age put on spiritual purification. We have lost the joy of simplicity in an abandoned search for satisfaction. Always failing in that search, we reach out yet further for the latest gadget, the most recent model, the ultimate in luxury or technical sophistication or novelty. The ease of yesterday is today's deprivation: today's luxury is tomorrow's necessity. Robbed of spontaneity and gaiety by the pressure to consume not less than our neighbour, we the rich have lost our humanity.[4]

That is well said. To recapture our lost humanity we have to recall our sense of solidarity with the whole Human Family. Of Western man, Alexis de Tocqueville observes:

The first thing that strikes the observation is an innumerable multitude of men, all equal and alike, incessantly endeavouring to procure the petty and paltry pleasures with which they glut their lives. Each of them, living apart, is a stranger to the fate of all the rest; his children and his private friends constitute to him the whole of mankind. As for the rest of his fellow citizens, he is close to them, but he does not see them; he touches them but he does not feel them; he exists only in himself and for himself alone.[5]

My last comment on this introductory section concerns the invitation to 'join the Community of the Life Style Commitment by sending the return card to the Movement's Central Correspondent'. The word 'Community' is used in the broad sense of those who undertake a common commitment. The designation 'Central Correspondent' is preferred to more authoritarian or hierarchical names such as director or founder or even general secretary. So why fill in a form? Why not just get on with the job of 'living more simply that all of us may simply live'?

Not everyone wishes to join a movement, but there are at least two strong reasons for doing so. If we try to 'live more simply that all of us may simply live', we are swimming against a powerful tide of consumerism. There are immense and subtle pressures to which we feel we must conform, so we need all the encouragement we can get from like-minded friends. Secondly, they also need our encouragement and support, and this we give them by joining the Movement, particularly if we help to form a new Life Style Cell or take part in an existing one. In the article on 'The British Life Style Group that Received Aid from India', already quoted, John Madeley makes the point:

> As the movement's co-ordinator is well aware, the growth-orientated British society will not easily accept the idea of living more simply and consuming less. 'Opposition, both implicit and explicit to such ideas remains immensely powerful . . . This really does mean that those who are committed to live more simply so that others may simply live, have to be active in sharing that commitment with others and if possible forming a cell to promote their convictions.'[6]

The back of our leaflet contains 'A postscript for Christian Believers', to which we shall return. Inside are set out the seven sections of the Commitment.

Commitment One

> I recognize that the peaceful development and perhaps the survival of the Human Family are threatened by:
> The injustice of extremes of poverty and wealth.
> The excessive growth of population.
> The widespread pollution of natural resources.
> The profligate consumption of these resources by a substantial minority.

This first section states a conviction rather than a commitment. Nearly all of what I would wish to say about it has been said in previous chapters. But is the 'survival of the Human Family' really threatened? Is not that pitching it rather high? 'If the experts are right,' wrote Jackie Gillott, 'and we have only a generation in which to alter our view of what is desirable, maybe we should face up to the harsh priorities survival entails. They are unpleasant. They contradict a great many of those things civilization has taught us to value.'[7] Moreover, we have to recognize that even the most gloomy projections are unlikely to take all the adverse factors into account. For example, under the heading 'Will It Be an Ice Age?'[8] George Alexander investigated some recent research by Dr Leona Libby and Dr Louis Pandolfi in California. They believe that particular studies of the formation of tree rings over the last eighteen hundred years have enabled them to detect patterns of climatic conditions, which correspond with evidence from other sources and relate to comparatively small changes in the sun's output of heat. On the basis of this research they predict moderately cooler temperatures through the mid 1980's, followed by a warmer trend until about 2000 and then a significantly colder era, involving an average drop of up to three or four degrees Fahrenheit. As it only takes a drop of some ten degrees to bring on an ice age, this could have a disastrous effect on our use of energy to keep ourselves warm, our transport going and so on. Of course these predictions may be wrong. This is but one illustration of why we would be far better equipped for survival in the next century if we curb our profligacy in this.

Commitment Two

I therefore propose to:

Live more simply that all of us may simply live, understanding that my greed may already be denying another's need. Change my own life style as may be necessary, before demanding that others change theirs.

Give more freely that all of us may be free to give.

Accept that those who are poorer than I can teach me a style of life which offers a practical alternative to the values and assumptions of a competitive, alienated and narrowly materialistic society.

Enjoy to the full such material goods and available services as are compatible with this commitment. Enjoy also the consequent freedom from the tyranny of possessions.'

Ivan Illich begins his *Celebration of Awareness*[9] with a challenge:

I and many others, known and unknown to me, call upon you:

To celebrate our joint power to provide all human beings with the food, clothing and shelter they need to delight in living.

To discover, together with us, what we must do to use mankind's power to create the humanity, the dignity and the joyfulness of each one of us.

To be responsibly aware of your personal ability to express your true feelings and to gather us together in their expression.

We can only live these changes: we cannot think our way to humanity. Every one of us, and every group with which we live and work, must become the model of the era which we desire to create . . .

But we must also recognize that our thrust towards self-realization is profoundly hampered by outmoded, industrial age structures . . .'[9]

Illich has memorably expressed that to which our Commitment is both a response and an enabling. Simply to 'understand that my greed may already be denying another's need' is not enough: 'We cannot think our way to humanity'. But to 'live more simply that all of us may simply live' is precisely 'to become the model of the era which we desire to create'.

Illich's emphasis on celebration, delight and joyfulness is precisely relevant to our Commitment to 'enjoy to the full such material goods and available services as are compatible' with it. I shall refer later to this paragraph but wish now to make the point that such joyfulness is also a sovereign antidote to the temptation that our earnest resolve might make us over-critical of others. I became aware of this temptation in writing not without irony of Concorde aeroplanes and Jaguar cars. Each one of us, therefore, has to take care to 'change my own life style . . . before demanding that others change theirs'. This does not disqualify us from making such demands in due course. But these demands will carry no authenticity unless we are at least attempting to practise what we preach. It is a question of priorities: 'First take the plank out of your own eye, and then you will see clearly to take the speck out of your brother's.'[10]

I was once trying to make this point at a meeting of a Diocesan Synod, most of whose members would be found within the management or professional classes. I illustrated the point by reference to two groups who were currently demanding large wage and salary increases, consultant surgeons and physicians on the one hand and coalminers on the other. I said that, when confronted with the challenge of Life Style, we should not try to evade it by condemning the miners on the one hand or the consultants on the other. A lady doctor present completely missed the point and angrily and publicly rebuked me for having criticized the consultants. She did not mention the miners. So comprehensive a misunderstanding was impossible to remove in public. But we sorted it out afterwards over the obligatory cup of tea.

This need for sensitivity in our comments on the life styles of others may be further illustrated. In *The Ice Age*, Margaret Drabble gives us this picture of Len Wincobank, whose name she borrows from a Sheffield neighbourhood:

> A war baby, an adolescent of the years of austerity with an
> invalid father and a mother who worked in the municipal
> wash-house in one of the worst paid jobs known to women,
> he had certainly appreciated every blessing of the material
> life. The day they had electricity installed. He could actually
> remember it. The addition of bathroom and lav by the
> council. The day that his mum had bought a new table lamp,
> with a base like a dancing woman, and a plastic rippled shade:
> how he had loved that lamp, the elegant glow of it, the
> discreet pool of warm light, the intense homely charm, the
> safety, the beauty. The turkey at Christmas, the extravagant
> Sunday roasts and Yorkshire pudding, the odd bar of scented
> soap, the trip to Scunthorpe, the piece of stair carpet—second
> hand but good as new—the whipped Carnation milk, as a
> treat, on the tinned fruit, for Sunday tea. Every little luxury
> Len had enjoyed, admired, and as he and his brothers started
> to work, began to bring home pay packets, how miraculously
> easy and warm life had become, with a hired television set, a
> new radiogram, and even, finally, a telephone, which had
> frightened his mother at first so much that whenever it rang
> she would jump up in her seat, rigid with alarm, and say im-
> ploringly, 'You go, Len'—or you Kev, or you, Arthur. How
> Len had loved the slow easing of the fifties, the glories of the
> sixties.[11]

I lived in Sheffield long enough, though on the other side of
the city, to appreciate how accurately, indeed lovingly that is
recorded. Who dare cast the first stone at our Len? Certainly not
I. I need his help. He and his mates have to discover for themselves how the other two-thirds of the world lives in Burundi,
Brazil and Bangladesh. And they must share their knowledge
with others. By writing this book, and in other ways, I and
others like me can help a little. But the Life Style Movement will
really have come of age when a majority of its members are
weekly wage earners.

We turn again to that other two-thirds of the world to illustrate the next paragraph of Commitment Two: 'Give more
freely that all of us may be free to give'.

Listen for a moment to the voice of Mikhil Ram, one of the
many beggars in Calcutta: 'My whole life, even when I was a

baby, has been spent begging. My mother lived on the streets
and she broke my legs so people would take pity on me and
give me more money. When I grew older she died. Every day I
ask to be put in the shade but they do not listen. It is terrible to
be in the sun and not able to move.'[12]

When we visited Calcutta Cathedral in 1976 with a joint choir
made up of adult members of Bristol Cathedral and Clifton
(Roman Catholic) Cathedral Choirs, the members of our party
did what we could to take part in the programme of the
Cathedral Relief Service. One of us took part in 'Operation
Twilight'. Every night a jeep leaves the Cathedral with about
thirty food parcels aboard to be distributed to the hungry on the
streets. There are plenty of such people. But it is also true that
some of those who have to camp out on the pavements have jobs
and therefore just about enough to eat; but no home.

I asked the girl who took part in Operation Twilight to tell me
about it. Her eyes filled with tears as she replied: 'Our last parcel
was offered to a poor man, thin and ageing, with only a loin
cloth on him, lying on the pavement. "No," he said, "I have
eaten today. There is a man round the corner who has not. Give
it to him."'

That man was probably a Harijan, a 'child of God', as
Gandhiji so beautifully called those without caste. His practice
of his Hindu religion therefore may well have been of the
sketchiest. Quite probably he had never heard the name of
Jesus. Yet, as a Christian myself, I am entirely convinced that by
that action he became one of those who, in Jesus' own words,
come from the East or from the West and sit down in the
kingdom of God before us formally accredited believers.[13]
However that may be, by that touchingly generous action he
established his human dignity and became an example to us all.
The Cathedral Relief Service, supported by Christian Aid and
other development Agencies in the West, by the offer of a
simple, inexpensive gift enabled that poor and powerless man to
become free to give. 'Give more freely that all of us may be free
to give.'

How shaming, therefore, that according to the *Guardian*,[14] in
the five years 1961-1965, years which brought such welcome
prosperity to Len Wincobank and millions of others, national
incomes in the West rose by 35 per cent while our contributions
to international aid rose only by 1 per cent a year. Even now we

need a fresh theory and practice of such international aid, a distinction between three main types. First there is Charitable Aid, not to be despised by intellectuals and sophisticates, the simple and practical outpouring of compassion by the rich for the poor. Second comes Development Aid, currently promoted with much skill, and rightly so, by the development agencies. This aid is given by the rich to the poor, when possible in patient consultation with the recipients, with the express aim of enabling the poor to become more independent, more and more masters of their own destinies.

But thirdly, not yet I believe so fully understood, comes Mutual Aid. Now the rich continue to help the poor materially, preferably in terms of imaginatively planned Development Aid. In return the poor teach the rich how to live cheerfully and creatively in a world whose resources have to be conserved more carefully and distributed more fairly. This is a lesson which we, the rich, need urgently to learn. The poor know how to live joyfully on less, once the basic necessities are secured. Given a chance, they can teach us. We must learn to listen to their voices and heed their examples.

That is why I propose also 'to accept that those who are poorer than I can teach me a style of life which offers a practical alternative to the values and assumptions of a competitive, alienated and narrowly materialistic society'. As has already been mentioned,[15] this statement is based on words written by an Indian Christian lady. The word 'narrowly' has been added to 'materialistic' lest it be reasonably objected that there is a sense in which Christianity is the most materialistic of all the major faiths.

Now this acceptance 'that those who are poorer than I can teach me' has to be applied at the public as well as at the personal level. Dr Conrad Gorinski,[16] an ethnologist working at St Bartholomew's College of Medicine in London, has called for an international, ethno-botanical programme to make available all that is known about our planet's botanical resources. This means consulting the experts, primitive people whose 'authority should not be dismissed out of prejudice on the grounds that their sages and doctors happen to be wearing feathers rather than suits . . . We should involve the primitive in the vital task of securing our biological heritage . . . Only by acknowledging the authority of these people and being seen by them to be doing so will it be possible to escape the devastating trauma that they are encountering. Shame can be as great a killer as disease, and they may both be linked in the mind of the primitive . . . All that we know about plants has been handed to us by primitive peoples. We have produced nothing in spite of our ingenuity. Take the potato. It was being grown by Indians in a small place in the Andes. From this a bigger and better potato was bred. One could say that the Industrial Revolution was made possible by the potato's intensive foodbase. That pathetic group of Indians, now forgotten, in fact helped to launch the most impressive civilization the world has seen.

Medicines 'borrowed' from primitive peoples include cocaine used as a local anaesthetic for dentistry, curare essential for surgery, quinine, opiates including morphia and rauwolfia used for the reduction of blood pressure. All have been 'discovered' comparatively recently. Many more probably await discovery. 'The idea of consulting witch doctors,' concludes Dr Gorinsky, 'is completely offensive to many scientists. I do not find it so in my work.'

Let us therefore give thanks for and to the South American Indians and identify ourselves with their struggle against odds 'simply to live', next time we munch a packet of crisps or tuck into a bag of chips. Life Stylers shouldn't be eating crisps or chips in any case! Let us rather bake in their jackets these gifts from some of the poorest members of the Human Family and, if we are believers, praise the Lord!

Now you do not have to be sold on that dubious myth of the 'noble savage' to appreciate the urgency as well as the long-term significance of Dr Gorinsky's thesis. I end this brief salute to the voice of the voiceless with a thought-provoking word from the poet Louis MacNeice:

> I am against bigness and greatness in all their forms—against big successes and big results; and in favour of the invincible, molecular, moral forces that work from individual to individual, stealing in through the crannies of the world like so many soft rootlets or like the capillary oozing of water, and yet—if you give them time—rending the hardest monuments of man's pride.

Tolstoy would have agreed. I believe that the Russian peasant soldier, embodied in Platon Karatayev, is the true hero of *War and Peace*.

Enjoy to the full such material goods and available services as
are compatible with this commitment. Enjoy also the
consequent freedom from the tyranny of possessions.

It has already been pointed out, but it bears repetition, that
the Life Style Movement is no killjoy process. In the preface to
'Alternative Life Styles in Rich Countries' we read:

> The call for reduced living standards in industrialized
> countries as part of a better life style and as an act of political
> realism with beneficial consequences for the Third World still
> receives a mixed reception in rich countries. This may be
> because, so far and for the most part, only the negative case
> has been argued: that world resources are limited, that
> overeating is unhealthy, that inequality is invidious, that
> over-consumption here means under-consumption there, and
> so on. Johann Gaultung points out that there are also positive
> arguments, not the least interesting of which is that people
> already do seek alternative life styles when they are free to do
> so. When they go on holiday for example they frequently
> adopt a simpler, more natural approach, often with reduced
> consumption. The evident failure of material prosperity to
> satisfy more than material needs and to meet such non-
> material needs as sociability and self-fulfilment may prove to
> be the spur towards a simpler but better life.[17]

Commitment to the Life Style Movement in fact is as full of
joy as going on holiday, a release from the tyranny of possessions. In our home for example we usually only drink alcohol
when we have guests; a small sign of celebration which also
serves to make the entertainment of guests even more pleasant. I
brew my own beer. It isn't always very good, but our guests give
every appearance of enjoying it. From a practising psychologist,
John Lickorish, I quote further evidence of the satisfaction to be
derived from a more simple life style:

> Inflation is usually considered to be a purely economic issue.
> But as a psychologist I would regard it as indicative of a deep-
> rooted dissatisfaction with life. The current demand for more
> and more money is due not only to rising prices but also to the
> desire to acquire more possessions and more power in com-
> pensation for the non-fulfilment of the basic needs of life.
>   By learning to satisfy one's basic needs in a reasonable
> manner a feeling of inner security develops and the urge to

seek the pseudo-satisfactions of power and possessions decreases. Along with this goes the willingness to forgo a rise in the 'standard of living' and even to accept a negative economic growth rate under present conditions. This would lead to an improvement in the general quality of life with less pollution, less psychological stress and breakdown . . .[18]

Life Style then looks like being not a dull and wretched deprivation but a joyful prescription for personal and social maturity and happiness. So be it.

Commitment Three

I pledge my active support to such political and social action and to such economic policies as tend to conserve, develop and redistribute the Earth's resources for the benefit of the whole Human Family.

Under the heading of Political Action in the chapter on 'What Ought I to Do? I stated the urgent need for a massive transfer of political and economic power from the powerful producers of a whole range of goods and services which the Human Family does not really need or want to the powerless majority of consumers of essential goods and services. And I proposed that we, the consumers, should unite in solidarity within that powerless majority and use the only power we have, the power to refuse to buy what is socially and culturally useless or even harmful.

In the intellectual minefield of economic policy we must therefore call for new ideas and new realistic definitions. In the field, for example, of the application of theology to industrial and economic questions, Simon Phipps has usefully observed: 'Perhaps what the children of light need, if they are going to become wiser, is more thought about the meaning of the word "love". C. F. Andrews' definition could be their starting point: "Love is the accurate estimate and supply of somebody else's need."'[19]

As a *quid pro quo* for this kind of thinking we need fresh definitions of 'wealth' from our economists and politicians which go beyond George Adam Smith's *Wealth of Nations* on the one hand and Marxist jargon on the other. No doubt there are philosophers of economics (as there are philosophers of science) who have written effectively on this vital issue. At least I hope that there are. For their researches have hardly penetrated the popular mind. The Concise Oxford Dictionary for example defines 'wealth' as 'riches, large possessions, opulence; being rich; abundance . . .'[20] No doubt the lexicographers have accurately represented current usage. But what an elementary error such current usage reflects. Do people still imagine that well-being, 'in health and wealth long to live', consists in 'large possessions, opulence', and the rest? For whom is wealth created if you build a Concorde aeroplane or an expensive car? For those who make it no doubt; possibly too for the very rich who travel in it; but not for the hapless taxpayer, nor for those who might otherwise have enjoyed the many socially useful products which these vast investments of capital, labour and technological and managerial skill might otherwise have made available.

At a less spectacular level, and by way of example only, a Bristol company with a number of socially useful products to their credit, set out their 'Cash Flow and Profits in 1977' in an attractive brochure. Under the heading 'The cash we created in 1977—and who benefited' the recorded facts are as follows: 'In 1977 materials and services cost us £291,700,000. We turned these into products which we sold to our customers for £431,500,000 so creating an additional £139,800,000 . . .'.

Now I have an instinctive feeling, which I am sure any alert student of economics could express more clearly than I can, that that word 'creating' is unintentionally but dangerously misleading. Was it not a redistribution of wealth rather than a creation of it? Or, rather, should not this notion of 'the creation of wealth' be applied only to the production of socially useful products (of which as I have said this company does make a number) rather than in a blanket fashion to all so-called goods and services? My instinct is decisively confirmed (for me at any rate) by the document's answer to the question, 'And who benefited?' We read: 'So creating an additional £139,800,000 which went to Employees (£109,700,000); Government (£7,200,000—tax paid on profits); Shareholders (£6,400,000); and the Business (£16,500,000).'

Bernard Shaw once wittily observed that all professions appear to be run for the benefit of the professionals. I suppose that he had the teaching and legal professions, medicine and perhaps the Church in mind. But these figures suggest that his thesis applies equally to trade and industry. Employees claim the lion's share of the wealth that is 'created', with 'the Business' coming a poor second.

My own amateur, but nevertheless I believe valid thinking on these complex questions has been helped by a project in which the Life Style Movement has been involved from the start. 'A Slim Guide to Economic Life Style' is indeed slim enough, just six cyclostyled pages. Its name in fact stems from the South London Industrial Mission, from whom it may be obtained. The Guide begins with this statement of the issue:

> World resource depletion and inadequate distribution are major matters. Because of that, much has been said about personal life style. A new recognition of what is 'enough' is likely to bring about changed behaviour in personal consumption and living. However, it may also lead to confusion and frustration at the work end of one's life where others hire us and set our priorities.
>
> It seems important therefore to devise sets of criteria by which to measure our behaviour at work (i.e. within the complex economic system).[21]

The Guide proposes five sets of criteria by which to judge the validity of any productive enterprise as follows:

1. Concerning economic 'goods'.
2. Concerning the economic Enterprise (the Company as a 'corporate person' in law)
3. Concerning emotive social issues.
4. Concerning indices of human happiness.
5. Concerning all organizations in society.

As they stand these criteria need a good deal of expansion, but at least they place the productive enterprise firmly in its social setting. I have also found helpful an article by a first year economics student, Nicholas Pye Smith. Under the heading 'GDP Spells Disaster' he has this to say: 'A thing called Gross Domestic Product (GDP) has been one of the most constant preoccupations of governments in Western industrial countries during the last thirty years . . . Its rapid growth is believed to herald universal happiness, while a static GDP foreshadows civilization's imminent end.'[22]

Pye Smith goes on to expose 'two serious failings' in GDP. (The more familiar GNP or Gross National Product is similar but takes into account production in one country from resources owned by people in another.) First, GDP goes up when we are compelled to buy goods or services we would prefer to do without. If crime increases, for example, we must spend more on prevention and punishment and so have less to spend on other things. But GDP stays the same. Secondly, it does not take into account goods or services for which we do not pay money. Thus, if you buy a washing machine for, say, £150 which lasts twenty years, GDP is increased by £150. But if washing machines are built to last for only five years and cost £100, then at the end of twenty years GDP will have increased by £400 but your standard of living will be the same as in the previous instance. In 'The Gas Man Cometh' a song by Flanders and Swann, the gas fitter comes to repair a tap and damages the woodwork. The carpenter who is called in cuts an electric cable. The electrician breaks a window and so on until the painter jams the gas tap again. So Flanders is back to square one with five days of skilled work added to the GDP.

Pye Smith's account of GDP illustrates simply enough for me to understand the errors into which conventional economics can lead the unwary. He concludes with an extract from the alternative economist Oswald Barraclough:

> It is very difficult to regard GDP as even a rough and ready measure of living standards. The Japanese people, for instance, have a higher GDP than we have, but their environmental conditions are so bad—almost continuous smog over Tokyo, bad housing, gross over-crowding and fierce social competition—that it would be hard to say that their true standard of living was higher than ours.[23]

Of course such 'alternative' economic thinking is making headway among the comparatively powerful as well as among such relatively powerless people as industrial missioners and first year students. Dr Sicco Mansholt for example once observed of the European Economic Community of whose Commission he had been President that 'a Community concerned with nothing but cabbage, cauliflower and motor cars condemns itself.'[24] In an article entitled 'Pollution Politics'[25] he listed four conditions that were 'necessary to ensure the survival of humanity':

1. Priority to food production by investment in the so-called 'non-profitable' farm produce;
2. Considerable reduction in the consumption of material goods per inhabitant, to be compensated for by the

extension of less tangible goods (social forethought, intellectual expansion, organization of leisure and recreational activities, etc.);

3. Marked increase in the life-span of capital goods, thus preventing waste and avoiding the production of 'non-essential' goods;

4. Struggle against pollution and the exhaustion of raw materials by the reorientation of investments towards recycling and anti-pollution measures which will naturally lead to a displacement in demand and thus in production.

Dr Mansholt proposed these measures 'on the assumption of a stable world population'. Agreeing that such an assumption was 'excessively optimistic', he went on to propose more radical solutions 'entailing highly centralized planning and fully de-centralized production'. I have become convinced that such planning and such production may well be the political and economic price we will have to pay for 'a more equitable distribution of the Earth's resources among the members of the Human Family.'

If we may apply the modest phrase 'comparatively powerful' to the President of the EEC Commission, we may equally apply it to our own Minister of Overseas Development. For neither officer can do more than marginally influence the general direction of political and economic decisions in the European Economic Community and the United Kingdom respectively. When she was in this latter office, Judith Hart would often make the obvious but crucial point that 'if two-thirds of the world's population begin to develop and want to buy, there is going to be enough trade for everybody'. But Harford Thomas has to comment: 'However persuasive this case may be, it remains the fact that the instinctive political reaction at a time of high unemployment is to keep the so-and-so's out. It would be better to create jobs by selling more of our goods to the Third World, but first of all we have to see to it that the Third World can earn the money to pay for them.'[26]

At this point the over-simplified slogan 'trade not aid' comes into its own. That it over-simplifies the issue may be illustrated by these words of the late President Allende of Chile:

Over the past twenty years the flow of foreign capital into the Third World has meant a net loss for us of many hundreds of millions of dollars, besides leaving us in debt to the tune of nearly seventy thousand millions. If to this debt we add our real, although invisible losses resulting from the decline in the prices of our exports and the increase in the cost of everything we import, it can clearly be seen that since the war international economic relations have caused a damage to the peripheral countries of over one hundred thousand million dollars.

Direct investment of foreign capital, often presented as an instrument for progress, has almost always proved most harmful. For example, between 1950 and 1967 according to data furnished by the Organization of American States, Latin America received three thousand, nine hundred million dollars and disbursed twelve thousand eight hundred millions. In other words, our region paid out four dollars for every dollar it received.[27]

Reference to Allende is bound to raise a further political, economic and ideological question of prime importance. On 'The Christian and the Marxist' John Tinsley, Bishop of Bristol, had this to say:

Because Karl Marx made serious strictures on religion and its role in society many Christians have not waited to hear any more. Many Christians in fact have the lazy feeling that somehow the Marxist questions have all been answered and in the negative. It may well be that in the long run Europe certainly and perhaps the rest of the world will have to choose between some form of liberal (or socialist) democracy or some form of Marxism. I agree therefore with a contributor to the preparatory handbook for the Lambeth Conference when he says: 'The most vital issue is to get Christians to clarify their attitude to Marxism which while it makes its appeal to human freedom and creativity and expresses concern with the poor and the oppressed has not yet shown itself able to do these things in terms which are compatible with genuine democracy and freedom.[28]

In the section of this book on 'Political Action' I have already recorded my own conviction that the style of a moderate Social Democracy is best equipped to hold the middle ground in that type of parliamentary government to which I remain committed both in my own country and, though with less confidence, in the world at large. I remain convinced that such a liberal 'socialism with a human face' is more likely than its more doctrinaire rivals either to the right or to the left to secure more justice for the underprivileged and political and economic freedom for the powerless.

Commitment Four

I intend to:

Make my decisions on what to buy, how much to spend and what to do without as one who wants fair shares for all.

Resist the pressures of advertising to buy what in fact I do not need or want.

Where possible, challenge wasteful packaging, built-in obsolence and bad workmanship.

Encourage the repair, renovation, re-use or recycling of materials and products as may be appropriate.

'I intend to make my decisions on what to buy, how much to spend and what to do without.' Have I that freedom? What usually happens is this:

> The seller in a dominant position will pass on cost increases in price increases on the assumption that the buyer will be willing and able and obliged to pay. The price will be fixed at a level to provide a profit margin sufficient to finance the activities of the enterprise.
>
> The kind of management concerned primarily with production achievement may find it preferable to concede wage claims rather than pay the cost of strikes. So price fixing becomes a matter more of business management rather than a response to market competition. And the dominant seller sets the prices for others to follow—and also as a supplier of goods and services to other companies puts up the costs of other big enterprises which do likewise . . . Result, price increases become desirable or even inevitable from the company's point of view (never mind the market) both during a deflation when operating below capacity, and during a reflation if it stimulates output above a realistic level of capacity.[29]

It is this 'assumption that the buyer will be willing and able and obliged to pay' that the Life Style Movement is committed to challenge. Those of us 'who want fair shares for all' must identify ourselves with the millions who are by no means 'willing and able to pay'. We are determined to secure for ourselves and others the freedom not to be conned into buying 'what in fact we do not need or want'.

The inclusion of the word 'want' is deliberate. The Life Style Commitment does not confine us to strict necessities. If, for example, you are an enthusiastic lover of painting and can afford to buy an agreeable little original work for the cost to you of, say, three days' wages, then why not? In any case your purchase will be of a 'labour intensive' product in whose creation there has been no inordinate loss of the Earth's resources. On the other hand, you could hardly be true to any Life Style Commitment if you are one of those who, as reported on the radio by a multiple store manager, spent an average of just over a hundred pounds (in 1978) in his toy department at Christmas time. In the context of Life Style's commitment to 'resist the pressures of advertising', I appreciated the irony of receiving some years ago some unsolicited advertising material from André Bernard, 'the first name in beautiful hair'. Entitled 'Life Style', this glossy little leaflet let me know that 'for us hair fashion interpretation is meeting what you really want in your life style and hairstyle. We know that this can only come from having the right philosophy . . .'.

On the correct assumption that in the end the consumer pays, the 'right philosophy' to which Mr Bernard appealed can turn out outrageously expensive:

At any one time there are anything from a dozen to eighteen people round the set—and the set consists of a table top covered with shiny black plastic that curves up to form a background. At the front of the table, facing the camera, sit the stars of the production: three tall, glossy cans of hair-spray.

It will be a very simple commercial, one day's filming. A shot of the cans, a girl turning her head to make her splendid red-gold hair fly through the air, another shot of the cans, first in silhouette, then in growing light, and a delicate hand that reaches in, presses the button to release a fine mist of hair spray. On screen, the commercial will last fifteen seconds. Making it will cost the hairspray manufacturer £18,694. Moment for sparkling moment, the most expensive productions of television are the natural breaks.[30]

The money thus spent on this one fleeting advertisement, if

diverted to socially useful goods and services could, for example, buy about eighty well-built family houses for pavement dwellers in Calcutta. In our anger and disgust, however, we must not fall into the trap of a blanket condemnation of all advertising. Advertising can and does perform the socially useful, indeed necessary function of bringing goods and services that are for sale to the notice of prospective buyers. As in the case of profligacy generally it is the inordinate use and misuse of advertising that we need to oppose and expose for the social evil that it is. Such excesses rather than all that boring pornography are the proper obscenities of our age.

An Australian friend of mine is a freelance producer of television advertisements. Some time ago the Sales Manager of a cat food manufacturing company phoned him. He had had the brilliant idea of an advertisement depicting a large number of cats frantically trying to enter a supermarket just before opening time. As soon as the doors were opened the cats were to burst in and swarm up to the shelves where the company's products were prominently displayed and then try to get at the tins and their contents. Could this be done?

Murmuring something about the difficult being done immediately and the impossible taking a little longer, my friend promised to ring back. He telephoned the local animal protection society. 'No trouble at all. Thirty thousand stray cats pass through this place every year. How many do you want? Did you say, fifty? I'll set aside a hundred cats today, remove those who fight, leaving you with, say, eighty. We've got a secret chemical formula which cats find irresistible. Select your supermarket and we'll mix this formula in with some sardine oil and smear it on the inside of the doors. The cats will be desperate to get in. Then we'll paint a trail of the stuff round and about and lead it up to your client's product. No trouble at all. You'll need half a dozen strong men to catch the cats afterwards. We'll supply some special handlers' gloves but try not to have too many retakes. The cats won't be in the best of tempers when thwarted of their expectations. They'll need a meal afterwards. No doubt your client will provide the necessary. But his product had better be good!'

After naming a suitable sum as a donation to his charity he rang off. At the time I met my friend the job had not been done. I wonder how it went. What an absurd parable of contemporary values! Incidentally it raises the question of whether it can be right in today's world to acquire or replace a cat or a dog and then feed it on tinned meat or worse still butcher's meat. Possibly the tinned meat need not offend our Life Style commitment. In Britain at least it no longer entails the slaughter of whales though it may involve much cruelty to horses, including nowadays New Forest ponies and other such semi-wild creatures, all of which of course have their price.

A much more sinister example is to be found in the allegation that:

> Drug companies spend fourteen millions a year on advertising and promotion to doctors, which is 10 per cent of the value of their home sales. That amounts to about £400 spent on every doctor in the country . . . The *Health Rights Handbook* revealed that certain drug reps divided doctors into categories: 'Gullible', to whom anything could be sold; 'Pseudo-sophisticates' who could be conned; 'Motherly types', 'Opinion leaders', 'Snobs' and 'Ignorants'; which says something about their wolf-life approach to the medical profession.[31]

In doing her research for this article, its author, Polly Toynbee, approached a member of the staff of one of the advertising agencies. 'I just want you to know we earn five hundred million pounds a year in exports for this country,' was his only comment. Her article concludes:

> About seventy new drugs appear each year, with many different brand names offering almost the same thing at different prices. Only three or four genuinely new products come on to the market . . . Vallium, which gets eight-ninths of the tranquilizer market, sells ten pills for every adult each year in this country. Sales of aspirin indicate every man, woman and child in the country consuming one aspirin a day. The money spent on drug advertising in this country exceeds the entire amount spent on educating doctors.[32]

With the help of the British Code of Advertising Practice, however, monitored by the Advertising Standards Authority, we in Britain do have some hope of 'resisting the pressures of advertising to buy what in fact we do not need or want'. We are supported also by a steadily increasing body of legislation. I believe that teachers have a vital part to play in helping their pupils to learn to discriminate more successfully in their buying and spending. The subject could be made so interesting, amusing and practical, not least for the less academically inclined school leaver.

That arrogant reference to 'five hundred million pounds a year in exports' reminds us that many of our friends in the developing countries are less fortunate in this respect. An advertisement widely distributed in India featured an attractive young mother with her child and a tin of Bournvita. The caption reads:

> Our whole family drinks Bournvita. My husband insists on it because, besides having malt, milk, glucose and sugar, Bournvita is so rich in cocoa. He says cocoa is the most concentrated energy food available . . . My little girl just loves it —and I know it's giving her all the precious nourishment she needs for her growing muscles and bones and brain.

Dr David Morley of the London University Institute of Child Health commented as follows:

> This is a dishonest statement. It says it provides all the nourishment needed and this is quite wrong. I'm sure it's lacking essential nutrients like heavy metals. And anyway to 'nourish' means to feed satisfactorily and that means calories as well as nutrients. As for the statement that cocoa is the highest energy food available, this again is nonsense. Oils and fats have more energy.[33]

That is a great pity, because for its proper purpose as a bedtime drink this product compares favourably enough with its rivals.

The *New Internationalist* claims and deserves credit for its strong initiative in exposing what has come to be called 'the baby milk scandal'.[34] But the criminal cruelty of irresponsible advertising extends far beyond baby foods.

> Families who live in dirt-floor hovels buy floor wax; skin cream is sold to Africans as 'the magical white cream'; the cost of protein in essence of chicken . . . sold in Malaysia is about twenty times the cost of protein in eggs there . . .
>
> Cornflakes or Weetabix promoted in Kenya can cost a hundred times more than locally available staple foods . . . the misuse of Reckitt and Colman's Patent Barley Water in Bangladesh may have resulted in severe malnutrition and death.

Drugs containing Phenacitin were banned from over-the-counter sale in Britain five years ago and the British committee on safety of medicines is now considering a total ban on the drug because it can cause severe kidney damage. But in the Far East it is sold freely by Boots, though a warning about harmful side effects is now given on the pack.

There is intensive promotion of British food and drug products to consumers in the Third World who do not need them, can barely afford them, and who are in no position to benefit from them.

Beecham's Indian subsidiary promotes protein-enriched Brylcreem hairdressing in a country in which protein/calories malnutrition is rife . . . Infant formula milk powders are drastically overdiluted by mothers of poor families in order to make them last.[35]

It is only fair to add, as my source does, that 'there is no suggestion that the companies involved are acting illegally. Some, under pressure, are changing their practices. Reckitt and Colman has suggested that what is sold as 'Robinson's' barley water may not be the company's product at all.'[36]

In the midst of all this, the key phrase in Commitment Four, as in a sense throughout the Life Style Commitment, is 'make my decisions'. Since no man is an island, this immediately implies an active concern for all those whose ignorance or poverty (in many cases illiteracy) make such decision-making difficult indeed.

This particular Commitment ends with what are intended to be some practical guidelines:

Where possible, challenge wasteful packaging, built-in obsolescence and bad workmanship. Encourage the repair, renovation, re-use or recycling of materials and products as may be most appropriate.

The words 'where possible' recognize the practical difficulties. Too often we cannot see our way clear to implement these guidelines. It is at this point that discussion within a Life Style Cell can be so helpful. Then again, the cards are so often stacked against us. If, for example, you buy gas for heating and cooking you are forced to pay substantially more for the first batch of units used and less for subsequent units. This system could not have been more effectively designed to penalise the small consumer, the single pensioner, for instance, and reward the extravagant. At a time when there is an urgent need to conserve energy, the system encourages its maximum consumption. In a sane world of course, not dominated by the producers' overriding desire to sell their products, you would pay less for the first set of units consumed and more for the next with a very high rate for what within any particular sector of consumers might be reasonably considered excessive.

Is it not curious, too, that when there is a shortage of petrol (a situation that is likely to become more common) the consumer is often not allowed to buy more than, say, four gallons at a time? This encourages him to keep his tank as full as possible by frequent topping up. If instead he was not allowed to buy *less* than four gallons at a time (with some concessions for cars with small petrol tanks) he would only buy when in real need and many thousands of gallons swilling around at the bottom of many thousands of tanks would become available.

As Michael Young, chairman of the National Consumer Council, has argued, 'when there was economic growth, critics used to attack the consumer society, as though the consumer was not only the king (as Adam Smith said he should be) but a corrupt one. The truth was the other way round. We were, and still more are, living in an anti-consumer society, dominated by the producer interests of the three-cornered corporate state.'[37]

But let us not despair. There are producers (and retailers) who have the consumers' real interests very much at heart; and just a few who actually conduct their businesses on avowedly ecological principles. Thus Earthcare[38] proposes the following 'criteria for environmental acceptability' in the conduct of its retail business:

1. *Use of finite resources*: the supply of metal ores and oil will not last forever. Earthcare encourages the use of alternatives and wherever possible re-use or recycling.

2. *Use of products or by-products of endangered species*: many cosmetics use oil and ambergris from the sperm whale, a species threatened by extinction. Earthcare will be selling cosmetics free of animal products.

3. *Energy used and pollution caused by manufacture*: Aluminium requires a large amount of energy for its manufacture. Earthcare will be selling cast-iron ware as an alternative. The manufacture of certain plastics involves

the use of chlorine and mercury, two dangerous pol-
lutants. Earthcare promotes the use of alternatives.

4. *Pollution in use*: detergents, aerosols and cleaners contribute to environmental pollution. Earthcare sells alternatives, e.g. soap flakes.

5. *High or low energy consumption in use*: many consumer
goods require large amounts of energy when in use, e.g.
some electrical goods. Many of these are unnecessary.
Earthcare encourages the use of manually operated household articles, e.g. grain mills and coffee grinders.

6. *Durability and flexibility*: durability and flexibility imply
the maximum use of an article. Earthcare looks for these
features in the articles it sells.

7. *Packaging*: Most packaging wastes resources and is
difficult to dispose of. Earthcare will be trying to
encourage minimum pre-packaging and encourage
customers to recycle and re-use containers.

Earthcare's promotional literature is printed, of course, on
recycled paper. They represent a most welcome sign of the new
age which is upon us. Probably the next step is for one or more of
the 'household names' in retailing to experiment with Earthcare-
style counters or departments within their stores. My guess is
that such developments, apart from their promotional value,
would turn out in fact to be excellent investments.

Meanwhile, let us get on with our decisions 'what to buy, how
much to spend and what to do without as those who want fair
shares for all'. Dr John V. Taylor's suggestions which follow will
not command universal support. I would dispute one or two of
them myself. But they are certainly worth debating in a Life
Style Cell:

Let's limit our family to one child of our own and one adopted
brother or sister. Let's black-list any product we see
advertised and buy an unadvertised brand instead—if we
need any at all. No second helpings unless there are guests. No
second car. Perhaps not even one. And the next car we buy
will be bought to last for its natural life, not to be junked or
given in part exchange after two years. Let's go for quality in
other things as well, and make them last, even if we have few
of them. Let's go for new-style hospitality: simple fare and a
much wider circle of guests. And let's develop the hospitality
of our car also.[39]

My last word on Commitment Four is a word of thanks to the octogenarian lady who heard me speak in Chicago of the four P's, Poverty, Population, Pollution and Profligacy; and the other four P's, Prayer, Prophecy, Political Action and Personal Moderation: 'I have four R's for you which have served me well throughout a long life: Repair, Renovation, Re-use and Recycling.'

Commitment Five

I shall decide (or have decided) what percentage of my net disposable income to give away for the benefit of those in need, especially in the developing continents. I shall review this decision regularly and intend to make this amount a first charge on the way I spend the money at my disposal. As an effective sign of this intention I shall decide (or have decided) whether regularly to do without a meal and gladly to give to the hungry the money so saved.

When the late Monsignor Ronald Knox referred to 'the acid test of the collection plate' he drew attention to the fact that our use of our money provides a useful key to our integrity and our intentions. And that, no doubt, is why most of us most of the time prefer not to discuss the question with others. This fifth Commitment requires little explanation for those who are accustomed to the theory and practice of the Christian Stewardship of Money. I do not know what the equivalent might be for Marxists or Muslims or Hindus, although I do know that both the latter faiths require almsgiving of their adherents. One vital aspect of such Stewardship (which of course has to cover all aspects of our use of money, not just almsgiving) is a conscious decision on what proportion of our net disposable income we are to give away. Such decision making is integral to the Life Style Movement and in direct contrast to leaving the matter solely to spontaneous impulse. That word 'solely' needs emphasis. The spontaneous impulse to generosity is by no means to be excluded. But it must be in addition to the conscious decision.

'Net disposable income' is a phrase capable of a variety of interpretations. Personally, I mean by it that income which remains to us after the payment of rates, taxes, National Insurance contributions and any other statutory contributions there may be. We may also deduct such expenses of office as are allowed to be so by our tax laws, but not of course mortgage payments, life insurance premiums, school or any other fees or indeed any regular payments which we have voluntarily undertaken in order to benefit ourselves or our dependents. It can be only too easy to cheat our consciences in these matters. 'Those who want to be rich fall into temptations and snares and many foolish harmful desires which plunge men into ruin and perdition. The love of money is the root of all evil things . . .'[40]

A young friend of mine told me that she was prepared to accept the whole of the Life Style Commitment except for this one point of a decision about a percentage of net disposable income. Her own life style is in fact far more generous to others and personally frugal than mine has ever been. But she prefers to think of the rather small amounts of money that come her way as disposable for the immediate situation; to give away, to spend, to save as the situation demands. I told her, I hope rightly, that as Life Style is a matter of guidelines rather than rules she should ignore this particular guideline as being too calculating and bourgeois for her and continue to 'do her own thing' in this matter.

In fact, of course, she is much nearer to the Gospel precepts, though not in fact a believer, than those of us who conscient-iously work out our percentages. On the other hand, most of us will in practice be much more effectively generous if we continue to do so. I know. When I was a parish priest ours was the first parish in the Diocese of Sheffield to run a Christian Stewardship Campaign. We doubled our income and trebled our giving away to missions and charities; thanks not least to our appointing a retired Inspector of Taxes, a devout Christian man, as our Campaign secretary!

To sum up: this particular Commitment, like the Life Style Commitment in general, is a matter for personal decisions, a word which, with its associated verb, decide, occurs no less than five times in less than a hundred words. This is also of course the key word in the reference to 'deciding whether regularly to do without a meal and gladly to give to the hungry the money so saved'. The Commitment does not insist on the practice of what it does claim to be an 'effective sign'. What it does enjoin is the making of a personal decision about it. For myself, I have practised this little act of self-discipline from time to time (a hot drink instead of a meal) but have found it humiliatingly difficult to sustain over a period; or rather Freudianly easy to forget to try again!

Commitment Six

I intend:

To be generous without ostentation and hospitable without extravagance. Neither to eat nor to drink to excess, nor to consume what in my judgement depends for its production on the deprivation or the exploitation of the poor.

To make time in my life for reflection; for the deepening of my understanding of the world in which I live and of the people in it; for recreation and for the sharing of simple pleasures with others; and for sufficient sleep for good health and good temper.

In my proper concern for the whole Human Family, not to neglect those near and dear to me or any others towards whom I have particular obligations.

This is the most wide-ranging of the seven Commitments and was in fact expanded to meet a legitimate criticism of former drafts, which concentrated too exclusively on our use of material goods. 'To be generous without ostentation and hospitable without extravagance' needs no further explanation. Its rhythm, if not its precise sentiment, is vaguely plagiaristic of the claim on behalf of the fifth-century Athenians which Thucydides puts in the mouth of Pericles: 'We cultivate refinement without extravagance and knowledge without effeminacy', a sentence that is more lapidary in the original than in any possible translation.[1] What counts is the motive. Generosity and hospitality call for extra consumption, and rightly so. But if our generosity is motivated by any desire to parade our virtue, or our hospitality designed to outdo our social peers, then each is soured and spoilt. 'Neither to eat nor to drink to excess' is both prudent and kind, both safeguarding our own health and our purse and releasing resources for others to enjoy. But 'nor to consume what in my judgement depends for its production on the deprivation or the exploitation of the poor' raises more complex questions and demands further explanation.

The words 'in my judgement' are the key to this guideline. I doubt whether anyone can know the answers to the political and economic questions raised by any decision we might make to drink less coffee or less tea and so make our personal contribution to the release of resources of capital, land and labour in East Africa, Brazil or Sri Lanka for the growing of more food for the village poor. But this lack of certain knowledge must never reduce us to inaction. In a world which is far from Utopian and massively complex, we must do the best we may with such insights as we have. I shall try briefly to deal with one such issue, our consumption of grain-fed meat, in the next chapter.

'To make time in my life for reflection; for the deepening of my understanding . . . for recreation and the sharing of simple pleasures with others; and for sufficient sleep for good health and good temper.' A quarter of a century ago in Bangalore I was trying to learn Tamil, that ancient, beautiful and difficult tongue whose very name means sweetness. Tamil Christians say that it was the language of Adam and Eve. Their critics reply that it was the language of Balaam's ass! My teacher, a jolly clergyman, was patiently guiding me through a lesson on the practicalities of travel; how to buy a train ticket, how to ask the bus driver to stop at your destination and so on. At one point I asked: 'How do you say in Tamil "to miss a train"?' He grinned broadly. 'We have no word for that. We don't have that idea. We just go to the station and take the next train that comes.'

No doubt I do not have to take that little story too literally in my attempts, in the words of Commitment Two, to 'accept that those who are poorer than I can teach me a style of life which offers a practical alternative . . .'. But it may encourage me to 'make time in my life' for other things than my work—or even the hard, if satisfying, grind of trying to finish writing this book! The Life Style Movement is always in danger of becoming too earnest, even Puritan, in the pejorative misuse of that term. This danger is compounded by the fact that Life Style was started by a clergyman, a body of men who are beset by the temptation to occupy ourselves with a round of useless tasks in a vain attempt to be free of the slander that we only work one day a week!

Many of those who are attracted to Life Style are from the same stable; full of good works, assiduous attenders of meetings. There is nothing wrong in this. Activitists and militants are essential if changes are to take place. But we do need this section of Commitment Six as we also need the further warning 'not to neglect those near and dear to us or any others towards whom we have particular obligations'. Life Style could so easily turn sour if it ever became primarily a means of assuaging our personal feelings of guilt about our comparative affluence at the expense of our children or spouses, or became a licence for our meanness, or a psychological weapon to promote our desire to dominate or get our own way in our own homes. We may not succeed wholly in eliminating such motivations. But to be aware of them is more than half the battle. Provided that our membership of the whole Human Family becomes a kind of permanent background to our way of life, we who are parents, for example, do well persistently and consistently to work for what really is the best for our children. And that includes, of course, as has already been said, the nurturing in them a capacity for cheerful enjoyment of life without any need to amass a superfluity of material goods.

CHAPTER SEVEN

THE LIFE STYLE CELL AND
A CHRISTIAN POSTSCRIPT

Commitment Seven

As opportunity arises, I undertake to:

Commend this Commitment to others and invite them to
join the Community of the Life Style Commitment by sending
a card to the Central Correspondent.

Join a 'Life Style Cell' or with others form a new one, to
meet regularly for mutual support, study and action.

Alternatively, invite a friend to support and advise me
from time to time in the working out of this Commitment.

I have already made clear why I believe that it is important for
those who support the aims and ideas of the Life Style Movement to commit themselves openly to the cause, both for their
own sake and for the sake of others who may need their support.
By the same token Life Style has to be a missionary movement.
How else will it achieve its aims? So let us 'commend this
Commitment to others and invite them to join'. But the question
of 'joining a "Life Style Cell" or with others forming a new one' is
important enough to demand the opening of a new chapter.
What are these Cells and how do they work?

From the fact that, as far as is practicable, Life Style is a
Movement rather than an organization, it follows that normally
Cells develop from groups or organizations that are already
established. Of the thirty-two Cells listed in February 1976,
eleven were local church groups. Three were associated with
Cathedrals—Bristol, Chelmsford and Louisville, Kentucky.
One was an Iona Community Associates' Group, another a
World Development Movement Group, another a county
branch of the Conservation Society and another a Christian Aid
Study Group. Other Cells had been formed by the Ammerdown

Study Centre; the Eighty Acre Group; the Monastic Community of San Miniato al Monte in Florence; the New Villages Association; the People Group; the Pilgrims of St Francis; the Presbyterian Community Centre, Belfast; the United Church Group, Port Moresby, Papua, New Guinea; and the Vauxhall Motors Recreation and Christian Fellowship, Luton. Life Style Cells appear to come and go, often being dependent for their continuation on an individual's enthusiasm. They have been known to die off without letting the Central Correspondent know! On the other hand there may well be such Cells of which I have never heard. The number increased slowly in the three years from February 1976 to a list of fifty-one.

The Correspondent of the Cell associated with the Victoria Methodist Church in Bristol wrote to me some time ago as follows:

> We have been meeting now, roughly every month, for just over a year. At present we have twenty-two members; of these about fifteen are really committed. We have just come to the end of a series of meetings based on Edward Patey's book *Christian Life Style* and on the 17th of this month we shall begin the Christian Aid programme 'Food for Thought'. Speaking personally, the group is the most helpful one I have ever belonged to in terms of fellowship and commitment to a common aim.

In 'The Life Style Movement. Notes for Speakers', compiled in November 1978, I quoted this encouraging letter in full and commented as follows:

> The best way to join or start a Cell is by means of an already existing organization—a local church, a local branch of the World Development Movement, the Conservation Society or the Campaign against the Arms Trade or whatever it is you may support; a school staff room or a students' society; a men's or women's group; whatever you may belong to. To meet monthly seems about right for most groups. It is best to start with the members' own Life Styles. Study programmes as mentioned in the letter quoted above are good. Occasional visiting speakers are helpful. The Cell can also seek invitations to visit other groups and hold small group discussions after an introductory talk by one member.

The Bristol Cathedral Life Style Cell

This advice was distilled from the experience of our Bristol
Cathedral Life Style Cell. Our first evening meeting was held at
our home. A dozen of us sat around the room after a cup of
coffee. I asked them: 'How shall we begin?' A retired doctor
said: 'We must begin with ourselves.' It was agreed that we
should share information about our personal consumption of
resources, but without putting anyone too much on the spot,
without the necessity of too much self-exposure. This incipient
self-contradiction was resolved by the production from my file
of some slightly out-of-date figures for the National Average
Percentage of Expenditure[1] as follows:

	%
Food	28.6
Consumer goods	11.5
Clothes	9.6
Housing	8.7
Insurance	8.3
Alcohol	6.4
Tobacco	6.2
Fuel and light	4.9
Entertainment	3.5
Running cars	3.2
Travel	3.1

For several reasons these categories did not entirely suit our
purpose; but they sufficed to spark off a rather guarded
discussion of our personal use of the money at our disposal, the
first such group discussion in which I had ever taken part in over
a quarter of a century of Christian ministry. We finally agreed
that those of us who wished to do so should make a rough
estimate of our own personal percentages of expenditure on the
various categories, write it down and bring it to the next
meeting. It was emphasized that only those who wished to do so
should take part, that the estimates need be only approximate
and that all contributions should be anonymous. The reading
out of the contributions was to be the starting point of our next
discussion. We arranged to meet a month later at the home of a
member of the group.

There were a few newcomers at the next meeting. Most of
those who had attended the first meeting had remembered to
bring along their estimates. The various figures were read out

for each item and revealed surprisingly large divergences within the group. As soon as the discussion warmed up, anonymity was thrown to the winds. Individuals explained their own figures at some length, justifying some and expressing their anxieties about others. We discovered that not a single member of the group was a smoker (Average Percentage of Expenditure on Tobacco—Nil. National Average 6.2 per cent). Our average expenditure on alcohol was less than one half of 1 per cent. (National Average 6.4 per cent). On the other hand it soon emerged that the question of the under-use of housing was a real challenge for several of us.

A brief discussion centred around clothes. We had a good look round at each other as we agreed that clothes have a part to play both in expressing the personality of the wearer and in giving pleasure to those around her (or him). We also agreed that what is cheap, as in shoes for example, is by no means necessarily economical in the use of the Earth's resources. A good pair of shores, costing twice as much as a cheap pair, may well last five times as long. But we also agreed that there is such a variety of reasonably priced clothes available today that no-one has any need to fall a victim to the demands of expensive fashion. As a result of this conversation one lady eventually made a decision not to buy any major new item of clothing for the next few years and to give the money so saved to Christian Aid.

Such personal and practical consequences of our meetings have continued to be a feature of the life of our Cell; something which I fear is too often not true of church and other group meetings of this kind. Nor have such practical consequences always arisen from the formal business. In the conversation after one meeting a member was telling us about her visit to South Africa where she was deeply shocked at the conditions under which the African workers lived. Another member then and there decided to sell her South African shares. As a widow she lived on a fixed income and her Bank Manager strongly advised her not to sell, as her shares were doing well at the time. But she persisted.

Now whether this was or is the right thing to do remains a matter for debate. My own view is that it is so for most small shareholders with little or no influence on company policy. At our Bristol Cathedral Chapter I had already raised the question of selling our own rather profitable shares in a South African sugar corporation. My colleagues had agreed to my sending a questionnaire to the Company about conditions of employment. I based it on information supplied by Sir Robert Birley, an expert in these and indeed a number of other matters. But there was not much enthusiasm for selling until I told my colleagues what my friend and member of our Life Style Cell had done. As soon as the issue became thus personalized we immediately and unanimously agreed to sell.

I told this story in a sermon, not in order to recommend from the pulpit the selling of South African shares, a specific which I believe to be more appropriately recommended in a discussion group or public meeting; but rather as an illustration of how an individual, following the dictates of conscience, can influence a group or organization. Afterwards an investment expert in the congregation commented: 'I totally disagree with your motives in selling those shares; but from an investment point of view it was probably the wisest thing you could have done'!

One question of personal consumption which we have discussed in our Cell arises from the Life Style commitment not 'to consume what in my judgment depends for its production on the deprivation or the exploitation of the poor'. This question has been put well by the Rev. Leonard Golledge, writing in the Crewkerne Parish Magazine:

> Grain is the main source of protein, essential for body building. But the rich West aggravates the food shortage in one particular way. As societies become wealthier their consumption of animal products increases. This means that a greater proportion of such basic foodstuffs as grain and soya beans, that could feed humans directly, is instead converted into feed for poultry and large farm animals. Yet this conversion of feed into animal food for humans is far from efficient. Only 16 per cent of the calories fed to chickens are recovered by us when we eat chickens. In a poor country the average person feeds himself with some 430 lb of grain a year, of which about 312 lb are eaten directly as cereals, bread and other grain-based products. And the rest of the grain—more than 59 per cent of the total!—is used as animal feed. By eating less meat we are helping to make more grain available to the Third World, and so helping to reduce poverty. What

about a meatless day each week?

Mr Golledge makes out a good case. But it is at least possible that if collectively we ate significantly less grain-fed meat, the powerful agribusinesses which produce the grain in North America and elsewhere would simply produce less and still keep the price up beyond what the poor can afford?

We decided to study this matter at a meeting of our Life Style Cell with the help of a letter to Stephen Sykes, then Dean of St John's College, Cambridge, from Professor Sir Joseph Hutchinson, Professor Emeritus of Agriculture in that University, and a man of wide experience of Third World food production. Professor Hutchinson addressed himself to two preliminary questions. 'First, by what margin does the diet of affluence which we enjoy exceed the diet necessary to maintain us in good health and vigour? And, second, in what ways could we cut down that margin, and thereby benefit those who suffer a deficit?'

In answer to the first question he quoted (in February 1974) the national averages for India and for the United Kingdom in 1969: for the United Kingdom 3,180 calories and 88 grammes total protein; for India 1,940 calories and 48 grammes total protein. Estimates of calorie need are 2,520 for a temperate climate and 1,990 for a tropical one. Protein intake should be about 60 grammes.

In answering his second question Professor Hutchinson pointed out that 'First, we now know that we can devise adequate diets with much less animal protein than we now eat. Secondly, animal protein is, in terms of primary food sources, a very expensive human food.' He concluded that 'the cereals we use in modern, intensive, cereal-based meat production would go three times as far if we ate them direct, as they do when we eat the meat. This is the point at which we could revise our dietary habits and make a really significant contribution to feeding the world.' In support he gave a rough estimate that on average an American consumed sixteen hundred pounds of grain in a year, of which no less than fourteen hundred pounds had first been fed to livestock and converted into meat to eat. Parallel figures for Great Britain were eight hundred pounds and six hundred pounds; and for India three hundred and seventy-five pounds and seventy-five pounds. He continued: 'Evidently, the cereal supplies of the Western World are going disproportionately to

feed livestock. In a time of shortage this has very serious consequences. Less than a year ago, Canadian wheat for bread-
making flour cost us £35 per ton. It now costs us [1974] over
£100. We manage to pay it, but we are buying the food out of the
mouths of the world's poor who can't pay it.'

In the light of these facts, Professor Hutchinson recommended a reduction of our meat consumption. Poultry, he
further informed us, both eggs and meat, rely most on cereal
concentrates, followed by pigs. Beef and dairy products come
next but sheep of course are fed mainly on grass as are some
cattle. Our Life Style Cell spent a whole evening studying his
open letter. One member took a modest decision to continue to
eat and to enjoy whatever was set before him in his own home or
another's, but he would never in future make a choice of beef or
pork when such a choice was available. Another decided not to
spend more than fifty pence a week on meat. 'You can't get
much for that these days', a friend correctly commented. A third
decided there and then to become a vegetarian. It is such small
but successively more beautiful personal decisions that make the
world go round. In the nature of the case the examples I have
given are but the tip of a growing iceberg. Most of these
decisions rightly go unrecorded.

A bowl is provided at our meetings for gifts of money to feed
the hungry. At the time of writing, well over five hundred
pounds have been given to Christian Aid; some of it, I understand, the money saved by our members' voluntary abstention
from a meal on a regular or an occasional basis. Several
members have gone out to give talks about Life Style to various
groups, one of them once taking part with me in what turned out
to be a lively radio interview for BBC Radio's 'Woman's Hour'.

Like other Cells, we have engaged in study programmes such
as that contained in the 'Food for Thought' pack published by
the main Development Agencies. We have had talks from
various experts on such subjects as the possible economic effects
of any massive movement of voluntary simplicity; the
'computer chip revolution'; the Campaign against the Arms
Race; and so on. One evening we met a small group of industrial
managers and trades union leaders. We have enjoyed
wholefood meals, seen films and slide shows and set up our stall
in a large fair on College Green, the central open space alongside
the Cathedral and the Council House. Several members have
attended various regional and national conferences on Life Style

and other related themes. But we keep coming back to our original concern, that is our own personal Life Style, our own patterns of consumption. Despite the protests of at least one member that it was impracticable, we eventually formally addressed ourselves to the question: 'Can we define the forms of consumption which are not compatible with the Life Style Movement?' Provided that it is clear beyond misunderstanding that 'the list of suggestions made by individuals which follows does not necessarily represent any consensus of opinion', our collective answer which follows may be not only of interest but of practical usefulness to those who have persevered in reading so far.

Can we define forms of consumption which are not compatible with the Life Style Movement?
On 15 September 1977 the Bristol Cathedral Life Style Cell met to consider this question. We agreed that since 'Life Style' is about guidelines rather than rules, any suggestions should be considered as such and not as in any way judgmental.

As we 'went round the room' inviting such suggestions, some spoke of attitudes rather than forms of consumption, such as lacking awareness of others' needs or wasting tradespeoples' time. Others spoke of forms of consumption against which we ought to campaign; for example, the addition of lead to petrol.

The list of suggestions made by individuals which follows does not necessarily represent any consensus of opinion. It is based on the categories from a study paper issued by the Servants of Christ the King. The categories of Insurance and Travel are omitted as they attracted no suggestions.

1. *Food*
   (a) Excessive meat eating. Any consumption of veal.
   (b) Identifiable battery chicken meat or eggs.
   (c) Convenience foods, out of season foods or long distance foods (e.g. oranges in winter).
   (d) Adding sugar. (To use sugar in cooking is permissible.)
   (e) Excessive tea or coffee. (More than three cups in any one day?)
   (f) Excessive tinned goods, especially if alternatives are available.
   (g) Ice cream, cake or sweet biscuits (except for treats).

2. *Consumer goods*
   (a) Goods advertised on television.
   (b) Aerosols.
   (c) Heavily or expensively packaged goods.
   (d) Excessive and unnecessary toiletries and beauty aids.
   (e) Books, works of art etc. bought to enhance prestige or image.
   (f) Excessive expenditure on pets. (Tinned meat, toiletries, fancy goods.)
   (g) Sunday newspapers and unread or superfluous magazines.
   (h) Expensive cameras, hi-fi equipment or television sets.

3. *Clothing*
   (a) Fur coats or hats, crocodile or other skin products; whatever involves killing wildlife.
   (b) Expensive clothing generally, especially if expensive because fashionable (e.g. any item of clothing costing more than £50?, £75?).
   (c) Undue quantities of clothing. e.g. A man might limit his purchase of suits to not more than one every two years, with not more than six in stock at any time.
   (d) Man-made fibres if natural fibres are reasonably available.

4. *Housing*
   (a) Any under-use of housing (i.e. living alone in a large house or having more than one guest room largely unused).
   (b) Under-use of land (i.e. neglected gardens).
   (c) Excessive interior or exterior decorations (i.e. more than once in five years?).
   (d) Unnecessary replacement of furniture or furnishings.

5. *Alcohol*
   (a) Any excessive consumption.
   (b) Any alcoholic spirits.

6. *Tobacco products*
   (a) Any tobacco products (but particularly their use by those who have not yet formed the habit).

7. *Entertainment*
   (a) Gambling. (This was not defined in detail.)
   (b) Pornographic or otherwise trivial material.

8. *Fuel and light*
   (a) All excess and careless use (e.g. room temperatures above 65° except in illness).

9. *Running cars*
   (a) Large, fast cars (i.e. those with engine capacity of over, say, 1600cc).
   (b) Exclusive use of cars; unwillingness to share.

10. *Other categories*
    (a) 'Private' medicine, except in serious emergency.
    (b) Independent education, unless on grounds of some minority principle.

Of the thirty-three categories listed in our report, none would be considered in some quarters more controversial than this last. I found myself personally involved in this question shortly after the inauguration of the Life Style Movement. I was nearing the end of my first five-year stint as a governor of my own old school when it was decided to launch an appeal for a quarter of a million pounds or more for new and refurbished buildings; a School for Art, a Sports Hall and a renovated Study Centre. Members of the Governing Council would of course be expected to support the Appeal not only financially but by speaking on its behalf at public or private meetings. I was happy to make a modest financial contribution in gratitude for my own school-days. But I could not bring myself to promote an appeal for the benefit of boys who were already so privileged, knowing what I did about the educational needs of the underprivileged both in our own country and throughout the world. So I quietly asked that my name should not go forward for the formality of re-election for the next five years. Some of my fellow governors appeared to consider this a harmless eccentricity. Others were more understanding.

The Winterbourne Life Style Group
There are, at the time of writing, fifty other Life Style Cells. The Winterbourne Life Style Group, for example, exists

in order to foster awareness of where our civilization is heading and what we can do to change it. It is an informal group where individuals can co-operate with others who share the same concern for the world. We recognize that the situation calls for us to simplify our own individual and family life styles and to pursue a more creative purpose in life than just increasing our consumer consumption.

We act as a focal point for members of such organizations as Friends of the Earth, the Conservation Society and the United Nations Association, and it is through these organizations that we can best influence political and economic decisions. But as individuals seeking to increase public awareness and to carry out appropriate local projects we are encouraged and supported by others who also see that the time has come to do something about it. The group is closely linked with the Life Style Movement, Christian Aid and Oxfam, but the work we undertake is that chosen by our members as appropriate to our own local circumstances.

This quotation from the Group's information sheet reveals a proper independence of outlook and a healthy earthing in the local situation. Broadsheets published by the Group include 'Conserve It!'; 'People Matter'; 'The Theology of Enough'; 'One World'; and 'The Other Two Thirds'. The members obviously enjoy their meetings as, according to evidence received, do the Victoria Methodists and the Bristol Cathedral Cell. So why not 'join a "Life Style Cell" or with others form a new one, to meet regularly for mutual support, study and action'? Or, if that is not practicable (as for many it is not immediately so), then 'alternatively, invite a friend to support and advise you from time to time in the working out of this commitment'. These final words of the 'Life Style Commitment' are inspired by the provision of 'Consultants' in the Common Discipline of the Community of the Cross of Nails. I know that they are effective. I have tried them. And, by the way, I do realize that in briefly personalizing the question whether the enjoyment of independent education is compatible with the Life Style Movement, I have not answered it. The omission is deliberate. For the particular thrust of Life Style is to encourage each of us to answer such questions for ourselves.

A Postscript for Christian Believers

The Life Style Movement is for all members of the Human Family without any reservation whatever their creed or lack of it.

It so happens, however, that many of those who accept the Life Style Commitment are committed also to the Christian Faith.

The words 'without any reservation' are important and explicit. But it appears that, so far, Christian believers form a large majority of those who are committed to the Life Style Movement. For this, I believe, there are two main reasons, one positive and the other negative. The negative reason is that I personally and a number of the others who promote the Movement have so narrow a range of contacts and influence. Much as I would have liked to, I have never had an opportunity of sharing the aims of the Movement with Trades Unionists, although I did once give a talk to a meeting organized locally by the Co-operative Movement. The positive reason is that, as I am convinced, Life Style is in fact a direct consequence of Christian faith and practice. The man from the *Sydney Sun* was right when he concluded his interview with the words: 'But that's just what Jesus taught, isn't it?'

In briefly justifying the *Sydney Sun's* conclusion, I wish neither to go over again the ground so admirably covered by Dr Taylor in *Enough is Enough*,[3] Chapter Three, 'The Theology of Enough', in my opinion the best chapter in a fine book, nor to anticipate what I wish to say later about parables of sharing. To root the question firmly enough in the Bible it may suffice to quote from O. R. Jewiss, 'A Scriptural Background to the Thinking of Theme Four—a monthly group interested in Christian Lifestyle and World Development'.[4] Jewiss quotes a key text from St Paul: 'He was rich, yet for our sake he became poor, so that through his poverty you might become rich.'[5] Under the heading 'Towards a Simpler Lifestyle and the Perils of Riches', he continues:

How much then do we need for ourselves? Should we give away all we have? The words of the Proverbs say 'Let me be neither rich nor poor. So give me only as much food as I need. If I have more, I might say that I do not need you (God). But if I am poor, I might steal and bring disgrace on my God.' (Proverbs 30:8, 9, TEV.) Paul's letter to Timothy warns us of the perils of riches. It also reminds us that we brought nothing into the world and when we leave it we can take nothing with us, but if we have food and clothing we may rest content (I Timothy 6:7-10).

Jesus himself warned us to be on our guard against greed; when a man has more than enough his wealth does not give him life (Luke 12:15). He suggests that we sell our possessions and give to charity and build up for ourselves wealth in heaven (Luke 12:33). We can learn much from the intervening verses in Luke's Gospel, too—notably not to worry—Luke 12:15-33. Some of these thoughts are repeated in Matthew's Gospel, where the impermanence of earthly goods and the lasting value of treasures stored in heaven are emphasized.

Jewiss develops the theme with a number of biblical references. At least for members of my own Church of England, however, the most familiar reminder may well be found in the Magnificat,[6] Mary's revolutionary song which those of us who still attend Evensong in this age of television serials continue regularly to say or sing:

He hath put down the mighty from their seat: and hath exalted the humble and meek.

He hath filled the hungry with good things: and the rich he hath sent empty away.

But God does not act in a vacuum. He requires His servants to carry out His purposes. And this the tradition of the Church has never wholly neglected. I quote, for example, from St Basil (A.D. 330-379):

The rich take what belongs to everyone, and claim they have the right to own it, to monopolize it . . . What keeps you from giving now? Isn't the poor man there? Aren't your own warehouses full? Isn't the reward promised? The command is clear: The hungry man is dying now, the naked man is freezing now, the man in debt is beaten now—and you want to wait until tomorrow? 'I am not doing any harm,' you say! 'I just want to keep what I own, that is all' . . . You are like someone who sits down in a theatre and keeps everyone else away, saying that what is there for everyone's use is his own . . . If everyone took only what he needed and gave the rest to those in need, there would be no such thing as rich or poor. After all, didn't you come into life naked; and won't you return naked to the earth? . . . The bread in your cupboard belongs to the hungry man; the coat hanging unused in your closet belongs to the man who needs it; the shoes rotting in your closet belong to the man who has no shoes; the money which you put in the bank belongs to the poor. You do wrong to everyone you could help, but fail to help.[7]

St Basil is often saluted as the father of monasticism in its corporate as distinct from its individual expression. St Ignatius of Loyola, founder of the Jesuit Order, associates a similarly radical precept and practice of voluntary restraint in consumption to the Christian doctrine of Man:

> Man was created to praise, reverence and serve God our Lord, and by this means to save his soul: And the other things on the face of the earth were created for man's sake, and in order to aid him in the prosecution of the end for which he was created . . . (Whence it follows) that man ought to make use of them just so far as they help him to attain his end. And that he ought to withdraw himself from them just so far as they hinder him.[8]

In our own day Hans Kung tells us that:

> Jesus invites his disciples to practise inward freedom from possessions (consumption). If anyone wants his behaviour to be inspired in the last resort by Jesus Christ, he will not be forced to renounce in principle possessions and consumption. But in the wholly concrete case he will be offered the opportunity to make this renunciation for the sake of his own and others freedom.

Later he continues:

> The Christian message provides no technical solutions: not for environment protection, distribution of raw materials, town and country planning, noise abatement, elimination of waste; nor for any kind of structural improvements. Nor do we find in the New Testament any instructions about the possibility of bridging the gap between rich and poor, between the industrialized and the industrially under-developed nations. Least of all can the Christian message offer any decisive models or devices for solving the enormous problems which a change of policy would create: for instance the problem of freezing the national and international economy to zero growth, without causing a breakdown of the different branches of industry, loss of jobs, chaotic consequences for the social security of whole population groups and for the underdeveloped countries.
>
> But the Christian message can make something clear which is apparently not envisaged at all either in the economic

theory or in the practical scale of values of the modern consumer and efficiency-oriented society, but which perhaps could have a part to play; replacement of the compulsion to consume by freedom in regard to consumption . . . In the light of Jesus Christ . . . it makes sense not to be always striving, not always to be trying to have everything; not to be governed by the laws of prestige and competition; not to take part in the cult of abundance, but even with children to exercise the freedom to renounce consumption. This is 'poverty of spirit' as inward freedom from possessions; contented unpretentiousness and confident unconcernedness as a basic attitude.

If Kung is right, as I know he is, 'to live more simply that all of us may simply live' is crucial to the specifically Christian response to today's world. This view is confirmed by the report of a recent Consultation on the 'Orthodox Approach to Diaconia':[10]

Christian diaconia today requires a revival of the spirit of asceticism, i.e. of self-denial and of concern for our neighbour, leading to a more simple life style . . . For this reason diaconia includes the necessity to liberate man from whatever oppresses, enslaves and distorts the image of God, in order to open the way for redemption. In this sense diaconia (service) is a liberation for salvation.

This particular note of 'liberation for salvation' is also struck by the Presbyterian theologian Ian Fraser:[11]

According to the root meaning of the word 'Salvation' in the Old Testament, the deliverance of human beings has to do with 'having or getting space in which to move', breathing space, space which gives the possibility of choice, of growth and development . . .

'Oppression' is almost the exact opposite of 'Salvation' in the Bible. It gives the idea of being hemmed in, imprisoned, cornered, suffocated. Jesus set himself alongside the oppressed when he became a slave . . . Those who are unfree, cramped, without room to manoeuvre or liberty to shape their lives for themselves, cornered and helpless, are denied their basic human status and calling. Salvation is related to the provision of a door of escape and through it ground on which they can walk as a people free to participate in making their own future.

God calls us today to be His agents of deliverance from being 'hemmed in, imprisoned, cornered, suffocated'. Rich and poor alike, but in different ways, can become 'unfree, cramped . . . cornered, and helpless'. The young man of great wealth whom Jesus loved and so invited to sell up and follow Him. 'went away with a heavy heart'.[12] He was as certainly trapped by his great possessions as the poor man may be trapped by his lack of any possessions at all. Liberation comes to the variously oppressed, rich and poor alike, when the rich learn to share with the poor, 'understanding that our greed denies another's need; changing our own life styles as may be necessary before demanding that others change theirs'.

Such liberation requires an inner change in the hearts of the affluent and the would-be affluent both individually and collectively. As Carl Jung sadly commented:

> Christian civilization has proved hollow to a terrifying degree; it is all veneer but the inner man has remained untouched and therefore unchanged . . . Too few people have experienced the divine image as the innermost possession of their souls. Christ meets them only from without, never from within the soul: that is why dark paganism rules there.[13]

Those of us who feel chastened by Jung's strictures may find that 'the supplementary Commitment which follows for Christian Believers will help us to do better:

1. I intend to nourish God's gift of faith in me and the practice of the Life Style Commitment within it:
   By regular prayer, faithful witness, study of the Scriptures and participation in public worship. For most Christians this means regular and joyful sharing in the Eucharist.

The words 'for most Christians' are intended to remind us that, for example, the Salvation Army and the Society of Friends do not root their Christian commitment in the Eucharist and yet, in their distinctive ways, are rich and strong on 'Voluntary Common Discipline' and simplicity of life. The rest of this brief summary of essential Christian duties requires no further comment.

2. As a sign of this intention I propose regularly to pray 'Give us this day our daily bread' as an intercession for the whole

Human Family; and to do what I can towards the fulfilment of this prayer.

This provision takes up a point already made in the section on Prayer in the chapter of this book on 'What Ought I To Do?'. I have already discovered how bad I am at remembering this particular Commitment. But when the remembrance does come, more as a gift from God than anything else, then there comes with it a recollection of the countless poor for whom Christ also died; and a resolve to become less ineffective in advancing that for which all Christians regularly pray.

3. I commit myself also to work and pray for such changes within the Church as will promote an inner renewal of the Spirit; the mission of Christ in and for the world; the visible and effectual unity of God's People; and social justice, human dignity and freedom from oppression for all.

Here again there is nothing new. For the commitment to appropriate change is part of genuine Christian faith as Henri Nouwen has well said:

You are Christian only so long as you look forward to a new world, so long as you constantly pose critical questions to the society you live in, so long as you emphasize the need of conversion both for yourself and for the world, so long as you in no way let yourself become established in a situation of seeming calm, so long as you stay unsatisfied with the status quo and keep saying that a new world is yet to come. You are Christian only when you believe that you have a role to play in the realization of this new kingdom, and when you urge everyone you meet with a holy unrest to make haste so that the promise might soon be fulfilled. So long as you live as a Christian you keep looking for a new order, a new structure, a new life.[14]

Therefore, those who are committed to the Life Style Movement will often find themselves praying: 'God grant me the Serenity to accept the things I cannot change . . . Courage to change the things I can, and Wisdom to know the difference.[15]

To a considerable extent they will all be sharing in what Fr. Balasuriya characterizes as 'the dilemma of priests':

If the priest becomes involved in social issues he finds he has to take options on day-to-day problems. He sees that some of his parishioners exploit others. Some in fact take the food away from others who are hungry. Some have much land, others none. Some spend much on private transport, health and education, while others have broken-down, overcrowded, ill-staffed public buses, hospitals and schools. Some are black-marketeers. Some even torture others. As the priest perceives these incongruities his conscience becomes troubled. He asks himself if he is doing the right thing. Is he making the best use of his consecrated life? Can he afford to tell these things in his sermons? Will he be supported by his superiors if he does so? What will the 'faithful' say? Will he be 'reported' to the bishop as a troublemonger, an unbalanced person, one involved in politics, a 'Communist'? What will the bishop then think, say, and do? How will his friends, fellow priests, relatives, and parents react to such a social sensitivity? After all, many fellow priests who thought like him and tried to react conscientiously are now in exile, or have left the priesthood. Many are married. He may even begin to doubt his vocation . . .[16]

That was written in Sri Lanka by a Roman Catholic priest. But *mutatis mutandis*, it applies to some extent to all who challenge 'the values and assumptions of a competitive, alienated and narrowly materialistic society'. In so uncomfortable a situation Henri Nouwen does well to 'emphasize the need of conversion both for yourself and for the world'.

Such personal conversion finds a place in the Life Style Movement. After one of our Annual Conferences for the Movement at the Ammerdown Conference Centre a friend wrote to me: 'I think I can say without exaggeration that it was for me the nearest thing I have experienced to a 'religious experience'—joy, fellowship, feeling moved emotionally, fun and laughter. Not bad for a mixed-up pair of agnostic Christians!' As for the conversion of the world, Bishop Hugh Montefiore rightly prophesied, before the foundation of the Life Style Movement in fact, that 'if our species is to prosper, what is needed is not just an international popular movement with a definite and realistic political programme, but also a genuine religious re-awakening . . . To put it in Christian terms, if man is to pass from the world judgement of Advent, he must have the new start which Christmas brings to men.'[17]

A Christian, a Buddhist and a Hindu

In conclusion to this brief commentary on 'A Postscript for Christian Believers', I return to the key statement with which the Postscript begins, that 'the Life Style Movement is for all members of the Human Family without any reservation whatever their creed or lack of it'. Here, then, are three quotations from three deeply religious men which interpret their various faiths in a Life Style manner.

In a message to the Secretary General of the United Nations, Pope Paul VI declared: 'We appeal to the developed nations to make great efforts to forego their own immediate advantages, and to adopt a new life style that will exclude both excessive consumption and those superfluous needs that are often artificially engendered.'[18] In a message to the International Youth Festival of Hope for Mankind, sponsored by the Ockenden Venture in 1977, the Dalai Lama made this point:

> Most important of all, those of us . . . who share these thoughts and who are concerned about these human issues, must in our own way set an example to the others by practising what we preach. It is not sufficient to introduce a new method and a new path; we must ourselves use the method and follow the path and thus show the way to the others. By doing this we will be able to convince and persuade others more effectively in what we believe in.

Let Gandhiji have the last word (as he usually did):

> To the poor man God dare not appear except in the form of bread and the promise of work. Grinding pauperism cannot lead to anything else than moral degradation. Every human being has a right to live and therefore to find the wherewithal to feed himself.[19]

CHAPTER EIGHT

FOUR AWKWARD QUESTIONS

1. *If we do learn to consume less what about those who become unemployed as a result?*
Quietly, I enjoy the irony of the situation in which at almost every meeting about Life Style this question is triumphantly raised as if it were both unanswerable and new. Other hardy perennials are: 'Will what I do make any difference to anyone?' and 'What should I personally be giving up?'. But I find that the most difficult of all is: 'Are we not just playing games, avoiding the real tough economic and political issues?' I set up these questions, not as Aunt Sallies. You will see that I cannot claim to answer them with complete satisfaction.

Those of us who, like myself, are thought to be in 'safe jobs' have to handle this question of unemployment with great sensitivity. Indeed I find the question so sensitive that in the first instance I must take it right out of the context of current controversies (about the car industry or the steel industry in Britain for example). I have to try to examine in principle what happens and what ought to happen when patterns of consumption, and therefore of production, change as a result of technoloigcal advances or of cultural changes or of a combination of both these factors. Such changes have been taking place throughout human history. Some have been massive, abrupt and painful. Others have happened gradually enough to allow time for adjustment. On the face of it, it seems likely that any changes brought about by Life Style and other similar movements will be gradual, allowing plenty of time for adjustment. If, however, as has been stated, millions of people in the United States are already practising some form of voluntary simplicity, the impact on some patterns of production must already be considerable.

A convenient example of what happens when patterns of consumption change is found in the Acts of the Apostles. 'Now about that time, the Christian movement gave rise to a serious disturbance . . . A man named Demetrius, a silversmith who made silver shrines of Diana and provided a great deal of employment for the craftsmen . . . called a meeting of these men and the workers in allied trades.'[1] Demetrius made an impassioned speech in which he rightly predicted that 'this fellow Paul with his propaganda' would not only discredit 'our line of business' but before long bring down 'the great goddess Diana who is worshipped by all Asia and the civilized world'. This transparent association of personal interest with religion and civilization produced the effect of a violent demonstration, characterized by repetitive shouting of the slogan: 'Great is Diana of the Ephesians!' Eventually the Chief Executive in the city's local government persuaded them of their folly and advised them to have recourse to the courts.

Demetrius was correct in his analysis of the situation. If successful, the Christian movement would radically change the patterns of consumption, and therefore of production, not only in Ephesus but, in due course, 'throughout the civilized world'. So would the Life Style Movement! Now if we attempt to transpose the genuine predicament of the silversmiths to the latter part of the twentieth century, we may consider the following possible ways of dealing with it.

First, it is possible to try to root out the causes of changes in the pattern of consumption by threats and by violence. This is as immoral as it is ineffective. It didn't work then and it doesn't work now: 'There is one thing stronger than all the armies in the world; and that is an idea whose time has come.'[2]

Secondly, it is possible to try to restrain by means of moral and intellectual arguments those who are making changes. This is entirely legitimate. As Paul was always willing to debate the claims of the Christian Faith, so we in the Life Style Movement should always be willing to debate with those who disagree with us.

Thirdly, society in general and Government in particular can adopt an attitude of *laissez-faire*. The producers of socially useless or obsolete goods and services are then allowed to become unemployed in accordance with the laws of supply and demand. I suppose that this is what in fact happened to the Ephesian silversmiths, perhaps over a sufficiently long period of time to mitigate large-scale hardship. But today it is morally unacceptable as the primary solution of the problem. The English are notorious for giving a French name for what we find unacceptable as, vice versa, are the French.

Fourthly, it is possible to subsidize the production of silver statues of Diana at the expense of society as a whole, that is, the taxpayer. This solution is also of doubtful morality. Why should we all be forced by the Government of the day to help to pay for other people's luxuries, supersonic aeroplanes, expensive cars or, as some would add, independent schools or private medicine? Such subsidies are of course most helpful to the producers of unwanted or socially ambiguous goods and services in a transitional period. But as a long-term solution of the problem they are absurd.

The fifth option seems to me to be the only acceptable one, both morally and practically; and that is to retrain the un-employed silversmiths with the help, if need be, of public money to make socially useful goods, such as kettles, pots and pans; or even knives and forks. The increasing numbers of the followers of 'this fellow Paul with his propaganda' will provide a ready market. In broad terms, it would seem that the advance of the Christian faith over the face of the world has coincided with an improvement in the material standard of living of its adherents both in Europe and elsewhere. I am similarly convinced that a massive adoption of Life Style principles and practice in the Western world would be of great material benefit to the whole Human Family. In the present context of our discussion of unemployment, this conviction has to rest on a global view. Charles Elliott gives us the following insight:

I am sure all of you are aware of the unemployment on Merseyside . . . But unemployment in developing countries makes even Liverpool's problems seem small. During the summer I was in the Caribbean; there, even in Trinidad which, with oil, is the richest island, rates of unemployment among those under twenty-five rise to 50 per cent in the towns. In Sri Lanka, unemployment among university graduates under thirty is over 40 per cent and as you go down the schooling levels the rates increase. Now perhaps these are unusually high, even extreme examples, but they are nevertheless examples of a universal phenomenon which is that the younger, particularly the less educated people in the

Third World are finding it extremely hard to get, not a well paid job, but any kind of job at all. So they are obliged, especially in urban areas, to get their living in what we euphemistically call 'the informal sector'; that is, peddling, portering, begging, water-carrying, haircutting under a tree on the street, or as a pavement artist, whatever it may be. This is life on the edge of formal society, in extreme insecurity. A study of the informal sector in Kampala suggested that about 20 per cent of younger people looking for jobs had not had a meal for twenty-four hours and about one in six had nowhere to sleep at all—and that in what was a relatively prosperous country.[3]

Unemployment, therefore, is a global problem, affecting the whole Human Family. It can only be solved by a massive switch over to the production of goods and services which are socially useful to us all. I would hazard a guess that the basic needs of the whole Human Family in terms of food, clothing, shelter, transport, education, health and so on are so vast as to be sufficient to supply employment for all who need it, notwithstanding the progress of automation and the computer chip. In imagining the silversmiths of Ephesus turning their skills to the manufacture of pots and pans, knives and forks I was of course being deliberately anachronistic. But it cannot be too difficult today for the producers of large, fast cars to be making buses instead. Anyone who has tried to use the bus service in Calcutta (or in Bristol for that matter) will know that there is an enormous potential world market for buses; provided only that we make it possible for those who need the buses most to buy them with the wealth created from the use of their own land, labour and capital. As has already been said, we need a new definition of 'wealth', whereby it is no longer assumed that the production of everything and anything creates wealth, whether or not that production in fact contributes to the 'common wealth' or well-being of us all.

I must now place a contemporary illustration alongside the story from Ephesus. On 30 June 1977

President Carter cancelled production of the B1 bomber, at £100 millions each the most expensive combat plane ever planned . . . Senator John Culver said: 'It is the most constructive and courageous decision on military spending in our time . . .'.

On the other side the gloom was profound. Rockwell International, the main contractor for the bomber, said that about 10,000 employees in the Los Angeles area would be laid off . . . .[4]

Ten thousand employees and their families is a substantial number of members of the Human Family. And it is right for us to try to imagine the shock and the anxiety which the President's decision brought to them. We may presume however that he made that decision, which Senator Culver so warmly applauded, primarily as a contribution to international peace and détente; and, secondarily, in the hope that it would release very substantial resources of materials, technological skill, labour and capital for other, more constructive uses. If his decision was a good one on these grounds, then he was right too not to defer it because of the consequences of immediate and substantial unemployment.

In demanding that industrial production should be subordinated to the 'common wealth' of the Human Family, I am not of course subscribing to that depreciation of industry and commerce, not uncommon among intellectuals, to which Kenneth Adams, Comino Fellow of St George's House, Windsor, rightly draws our attention:

> There is a divergence between education and the means whereby we as a nation earn our living, and it increases as the education reaches its higher levels. Many educators dislike to the point of contempt the activities and the values of the industrial sector. They see it as having little respect for human values, little recognition of human attributes, committed only to the rising production heedless of value, unconcerned about the extent to which people are dehumanized or the earth's resources are ransacked in the process. They see it as dependent for its success upon pandering to the baser human emotions of greed and envy.[5]

While I hope that Mr Adams would agree that these criticisms of 'the industrial sector' are not altogether without substance, I agree in turn with his subsequent and positive conclusions:

> As co-heirs with Christ and fellow-workers with God, we are called and enabled to co-operate with Him through our human endeavours towards the relief of poverty everywhere and towards the coming of His Kingdom.

We Christians need to be able to affirm and celebrate the activity by which we principally earn our living. We need God's blessing on it, we need to be able to give thanks to God for it, we need to be able to confess our failures and short-comings in performing it and we need the sense of God's judgement on it.[6]

So let the Life Style Movement 'affirm and celebrate the activity by which we principally earn our living' wherever we find it to be genuinely working 'towards the relief of poverty everywhere'.

2. *If we do learn to consume less will what I do make any difference to anyone?*
I have to confess straight away that I do not think that it is possible to prove any direct link between your refusal or mine of a second helping today and any particular member of the Human Family receiving his or her daily bread tomorrow. At the end, however, of his 'Ten Reasons for Choosing a Simpler Life Style' which I have already quoted in full, Dr Lissner makes this important point:

> The adoption of a simpler life style is meaningful and justifiable for any or all of the above reasons *alone*, irrespective of whether it benefits the underprivileged. Demands for 'proof of effectiveness' in helping the poor only bear witness to the myth that 'they the poor' are the problem and that 'we the rich' have the solution. Yet—if adopted on a large scale—a simpler life style will have significant socio-political side-effects both in the rich and in the poor part of the world. The two most important side-effects are likely to be economic and structural adjustments and the release of new resources and energies for social change.[7]

The crucial words 'if adopted on a large scale' mean that the practical difference which your voluntary simplicity of life or mine may make to anyone else may depend on whether a sub-stantial number of others are following our lead. And this in turn depends on our own missionary enthusiasm and effective-ness in our cause.

I have already referred in Chapter Four, 'What May I Hope?', to the vital significance in the global scheme of things of each individual. The broad consequences of the adoption by an in-

creasing number of individuals of an idea whose time has come
are global, irreversible and incalculable.

Returning abruptly from such lofty considerations to that
'acid test of the collection plate', I have already reported that a
single Life Style Cell, the Bristol Cathedral Cell, raised well over
five hundred pounds for Christian Aid; a small sum but sufficient, I am informed, to build and furnish two brick-built
'pukka' family homes in Calcutta. On the other side of the
balance sheet the imaginative and generous gift of a thousand
pounds by the General Synod of the Church of South India to
our Movement is a most encouraging sign of confidence in what
we are trying to do. It has in fact been decisive in enabling us to
pay the expenses of a network of regional representatives.

While we are on this subject of money, can we be sure that any
money which we may save because of our commitment to Life
Style and give away to the poor will in fact reach them and so
make any difference to them? No, we cannot. It would be
incorrect, as well as unwise, for me in my capacity as a member
of the Life Style Movement to try to persuade otherwise those
who ask this particular question. For some at least of them are
consciously or unconsciously looking for reasons for not giving
money to the poor and for not committing themselves to Life
Style. To ensure a detailed and accurate reply, this question
should be referred to the Development Agencies, Christian Aid,
War on Want, Oxfam, Tear Fund and so on. By and large these
are efficient organizations and will be glad to supply facts and
figures to any serious enquirer. And they will be the first to
admit that there is many a slip between the cup, not always such
an overflowing cup by the way, of the more affluent giver and
the lips of the thirsty poor.

However that may be, one fact is certain. If we do not give the
money, it will not reach the poor. And if we do, it is more
probable than not that it will. I have personal knowledge of a
number of examples of excellent stewardship of resources that
have been made available, in part at least, by voluntary giving. I
have already drawn attention to the Calcutta Cathedral Relief
Service, substantially supported by a consortium of European
agencies, including Christian Aid. With initial resources far
more slender than those of any English Cathedral, and in
addition to an ambitious ongoing programme in Calcutta itself,
this Relief Service was able to complete the following projects in
war-devastated Bangladesh: 19,600 houses built; 9,860 acres

brought under cultivation; 836 tubewells dug; 25 new pump sets installed and 20 pump sets repaired; 13 new schools built; 12 hospitals and 6 dispensaries established; nearly 50,000 items of clothing and 32,000 blankets distributed; 11 tile factories and one orphanage built; 11 carpentry shops in existing orphanages equipped[8]. Even now I have only mentioned half the items.

3. *If we do learn to consume less, what should I personally be giving up?*

Recently I suggested to a friend, a former Professor of Theology, that Jesus seldom gave a direct answer to a direct question. 'Never, I would have thought,' was his immediate reply. Jesus certainly encouraged those who listened to Him to think and to decide for themselves. Far be it from me therefore to presume to tell anyone what he or she should personally give up. In any case the question is too negative. The question to be asked is more positive. 'What do I need or want for a full and happy life?' Life Style, like the Sermon on the Mount (if I may compare a small thing with a sublime one) is about being happy. The only viable answer which you or I can give to so personal a question is an equally personal testimony about the Life Style which we attempt or envisage (and fail to achieve) for ourselves.

On Ash Wednesday 1977 I typed out the following programme (subsequently amended) for myself:

1. Food. As a general rule, but with occasional exceptions, no breakfast cereals, sweet biscuits, cake or cakes, sweets (except boiled sweets on journeys), added sugar, snacks between meals. At breakfast normally one large or two small pieces of toast only (with spreads) and coffee. Fruit also to be enjoyed. Porridge as an occasional treat.

   Normally one cooked meal a day. No beef or pork if there is a parallel choice. Second helpings to be considered a treat, i.e. when guests are invited.

   Occasionally, as outside commitments allow, a day at home without eating any solid food until supper; i.e. an approximately twenty-four hour fast from solids.

2. Drink. Alcoholic drinks to be normally confined to holidays, celebrations and when guests are invited. No purchase of wines or spirits. Not more than four cups of tea or coffee a day. Normally drink water with meals other than breakfast.

3. Clothes. Not more on average than one new suit every three years. Other purchases of clothes as may be necessary.

4. Transport. For short journeys walk. For long journeys by myself take the train.

5. Household services. Only use lights as may be necessary. Use the hours of daylight to the full. Only switch on gas fire if room temperature is below 60°F. Write letters when it is cheaper than telephoning. Use telephone sparingly.

6. Purchase of goods. Avoid the purchase of souvenirs, extra toiletries, records, accessories, etc., etc., for myself but be free to buy them for others. Use only book tokens received to buy books for myself, except for any book which seems at the time to be essential for my work.

7. Be personally content with inexpensive holidays.

8. Giving money away. Budget each year to spend not less than 10 per cent of net disposable income on missions and charities, hospitality, gifts and allowable 'expenses of office'. Make such allocations a first charge on income.

9. Do not parade this Life Style but live it in such a way as to inconvenience others as little as possible.

The decision to make public even so bare an outline has not been an easy one. In any case I have found it impossible to maintain even so modest a limitation on my self-indulgence. But then 'Life Style' is about 'guidelines rather than rules' and defeats its own object if it becomes oppressive. For any reader who has not already done so to commit your own guidelines to paper as I have done might well be a helpful challenge. But in the end the 'right' Life Style is different for each one of us. Indeed for each one of us it has to be dynamic, constantly changing. In Calcutta I accepted with considerable diffidence an invitation to speak about the Life Style Movement to a group of theological students from Bishop's College. As is often the case (and quite right too) one question was about what difference the Movement had made to my own style of life. By way of specific example I mentioned that Life Style had helped me to decide that it was quite unnecessary for me to buy a new overcoat since the one that I had had for about twenty years remained entirely adequate for my needs. 'And how many pairs of socks do you have?' asked the meeting's chairman, my friend Canon Subir

Biswas, with appropriate irony. Another commitment which the attentive reader would reasonably expect of me is to a refusal to buy a car of more than, say, 1200cc capacity. I am also committed to make any car that I do purchase last as long as is prudent. I also refuse on principle to borrow money on a credit card.

4. *If we do learn to consume less, are we not just playing games, avoiding the real tough economic and political issues?*
This question has been challengingly put in a communication from the Alliance of Radical Methodists:

> We have read the 'Life Style' literature . . . and we agree with many of the sentiments expressed; but we believe that these publications and others like them do not go far enough . . . Most of the Life Style literature is too personal, too individualistic; such problems cannot be solved by personal action alone, but demand far-reaching transformations of the nature of the society in which we live . . . Personal life style without political commitment is ineffective in its impact, but political commitment without personal life style lacks credibility.

The anonymous writer goes on to say more positive things about our Life Style Movement, acknowledging in effect, though not explicitly, that we too 'pledge our active support to such political action and to such economic policies as tend to conserve, develop and redistribute the Earth's resources for the benefit of the whole Human Family'. It cannot have escaped your attention, that Life Style radically questions a whole range of the basic assumptions of capitalists and socialists alike; the former, I suppose, more than the latter. If Life Style were taken seriously and widely adopted, the foundations would be laid for a far more just and equitable society. All labels are libels. But if we must label, then Life Style is a radical rather than a revolutionary Movement, seeking to facilitate radical changes in the structure of society by persuasion rather than by violence.

We have now, however, to put some flesh on the bones of this generalization by identifying certain major political and economic issues at home and abroad, and briefly examining the effect that a substantial adoption of Life Style principles and practice might have on them. Only thus can we clear ourselves of the accusation that we are 'just playing games'.

First and foremost must come the issue of international peace, followed closely by the related issue of world hunger. The conservation of the Earth's resources for our own and for future generations must rate as a third issue of major political and economic importance. Only slightly less 'global' and certainly vital to citizens of the United Kingdom is, fourthly, our role in the European Economic Community.

To these four great international issues I would add four vital domestic ones, recognizing of course their international implications: inflation; incomes policy (or lack of it); health and education services; and unemployment; this last already partly covered in previous discussion. Indeed much of what I would wish to say on several of these issues has already found its way into these pages.

Four Global Issues
A basic ingredient in war and in large-scale violence has often been, and usually is today, the existence, side by side and in competition for the same resources, of an identifiably richer and an identifiably poorer community. This factor was a major cause of the French, the Russian and the Chinese revolutions and their accompanying cruelty and bloodshed. It was present in Vietnam as it is a major factor in the racial conflicts in Southern Africa, the guerilla warfare in South and Central America and the long-standing conflict between Israel and her Arab neighbours. Even the Israeli-Egyptian peace treaty does not seem to have brought any nearer the cessation of violence between the comparatively wealthy Israelis and the dispossessed and impoverished Palestinian refugees. This factor is even present in Northern Ireland where the Roman Catholic community remains in fact identifiably less affluent than the Protestants.

To make this observation is not necessarily to make a judgement on the rights and wrongs of any particular conflict. But it stands to reason that if we could somehow substantially reduce the inordinate over-consumption of scarce resources by the more wealthy community in any particular conflict, we would reduce at a stroke the temptation to violence both for those who are determined to hold what they have and for those who are equally determined to gain what they have not. Since this temptation is bound to increase as non-renewable resources become more scarce and as the gap between the richer and the poorer community inexorably widens, Life Style and similar movements which lead to a decline in the ostentatious consumption of resources by the rich are bound to become more and more significant in the quest for international, inter-racial and inter-cultural peace. In particular a substantial reduction in our consumption of oil would reduce international tension at its most dangerous point.

On the related issue of world hunger it may only be necessary to repeat what is axiomatic to the whole purpose of this book. If the copious yet limited resources of available food and other necessities, and of the land, labour and capital required to produce these necessities, are relieved of the strain imposed on them by the luxurious over-consumption of the rich, then more would inevitably be available to feed, clothe and house the hungry.

Similar considerations apply to the third major issue, the conservation of the Earth's resources. The evidence piles up from a surprising variety of sources. On 1 June 1979 it was reported that the Saudi Oil Minister, Sheikh Yamani, had said that he expected a recession, even a deep depression, if the West failed to cut oil consumption. He told French Television: 'I do not think you will avoid it, unless you change your life style.'[10]

His prophecy is being swiftly realized. Consumer restraint, both voluntary and imposed by law, preferably by international law, is in fact the only solution to this urgent political and economic problem. At a different level and by way of specific example, I have already referred to the predicament of that beautiful, gentle and intelligent creature, the whale. How obscene it would be if the whale were exterminated in order to provide our generation with cosmetics, pet food and other luxuries. How vital it is to reach more and more stringent international agreements to ban the use of the products of his inoffensive bulk or at least to confine that use to the human consumption of his meat, if and where that remains a necessity or near necessity. Remove the inordinate desire for luxury products he supplies and the danger progressively, indeed dramatically, disappears.

The fourth and last primarily international issue under review concerns Britain's role in the European Economic Community. Some are inclined to magnify our influence, others to deprecate our weakness. But on any showing we cannot be other than a major partner. Our imperial past is of progressively less significance. But taken together with our continuing global contacts by means of trade, culture, language, political institutions and so on, it should equip us today with a profound understanding of the aspirations of the peoples of Asia and Africa. I do not think that we are at present displaying such an understanding. But we are offered, if we choose to take it, a genuine vocation to work for the liberalization of the trade and aid policies of the EEC, particularly towards the peoples of the Indian sub-continent. So many members of the Human Family live there. Their need of human dignity and of economic liberation is so urgent. Under former EEC policies they have had, broadly speaking, a particularly hard deal as compared with many African countries. Perhaps our four year sojourn in India makes me prone to special pleading, but I do believe that this is both a moral issue and also a matter of enlightened self interest. More liberal policies become progressively easier to pursue wholeheartedly and without fear of possible conse-quences for ourselves, only as and when we learn to demand for ourselves a smaller share of the global economic cake.

Four Domestic Issues

As we turn now to our homeland, major issues crowd upon us for attention. At the time of writing inflation continues to cause grievous harm to all of us but particularly to the most vulner-able. Of the great German inflation between the wars, Stefan Zweig wrote: 'Standards and values disappeared during the melting evaporation of money; there was but one merit; to be clever, shrewd, unscrupulous and to mount the racing horse rather than be trampled by it.'[11] I have already quoted Dr Schumacher's diagnosis of the cause of inflation. In brief, 'prices are put up . . . by those who have the power to do so and can get away with it.'[12]

Against such price increases the powerless have but one weapon. Refuse to buy what you need not. Then either the price will come down or the productive capacity will be channelled into making something more socially useful. But why do the powerful want to increase their economic power anyway? Included among many complex factors is the desire to consume and to be seen to consume more and more than one's share of goods and services. If we can only remove or at least diminish this inordinate desire for over-consumption by the promotion of a more honourable and indeed a more satisfying life style, we shall begin also to remove the threat and the actuality of inflation. Another way of defining the cause of inflation is to say that we consume more than we produce. We have therefore either to produce more or to consume less or to do both. To consume less is even more necessary than to produce more. It is also easier.

Similar considerations apply to our second domestic question: the question of incomes policies, or sadly the lack of them. It is precisely the general desire to consume more goods and services than the next man that makes it so difficult to work out an equitable incomes policy. At the time of writing some Members of Parliament were complaining bitterly about a pay rise which amounted to more than my total salary. Diminish that desire by a combination of personal restraint and legal constraint and you have a greater room for manoeuvre, a greater opportunity to realize the slogan, 'from each according to his ability; to each according to his need'. When I was a missionary of the Church Missionary Society in the 1950s we were all paid the same basic wage, irrespective of status or experience. I expect that this practice remains in force. Allowances were added according to need; for children, for school fees at schools where English was the medium of instruction, for medical services as necessary; sometimes an expensive station allowance; a car allowance for a bishop and, I daresay, an entertainment allowance as well; and so on. Of course that was a small group with a high motivation. And it has to be added that in those days we were paid substantially more than our national colleagues doing the same work. So it was not ideal. But it was on the right lines; a life style for today.

In all this there is nothing new.

> The people asked him [John the Baptist], 'Then what are we to do? He replied, 'The man with two shirts must share with him who has none, and anyone who has food must do the same.' Among those who came to be baptised were tax-gatherers, and they said to him, 'Master, what are we to do?' He told them, 'Exact no more than the assessment.' Soldiers on service also asked him, 'And what of us?' To them he said, 'No bullying; no blackmail; make do with your pay!'[13]

Our third major domestic political and economic issue concerns the development of the hard-won achievements of the Welfare State, particularly in the fields of health and of education. The complaint appears to be justified that in Britain, as in other developed countries, Denmark for instance, the production base for all the goods and services we expect is too slender to bear the great edifice of demand that is placed upon it. So severe cuts are ordained in our public services. But of course if we would learn to limit our obsessive demand for goods, especially for goods which we do not really want or need but which we acquire usually on credit, then more productive capacity would become available for hospitals and clinics, schools and colleges and their staff. This kind of argument was of course brilliantly sustained by Professor J. K. Galbraith in his best-selling *The Affluent Society*.[14]

Of the fourth and last domestic issue, the vital issue of unemployment, I have already written in this chapter. I only wish to add that a shift of the overall pattern of consumption from the present inequitable distribution of goods and services to a massive satisfaction of the basic needs of the majority of the Human Family would provide, as had already been suggested, a much more stable and secure pattern of employment. Such needs are with us for the foreseeable future. The opportunities for the production of a great variety of goods and services are boundless.

If we do learn to consume less are we just playing games, avoiding the real hard economic and political issues? Of course not. It is those who imagine that we can go on consuming inordinately who are living in a world of fantasy—but not for long. If, which God forbid, we drift into nuclear war, the most probable cause will have been the Western world's inordinate consumption of oil.

CHAPTER NINE

A PARABLE OF SHARING

'He spoke to them in parables.'[1]
I see the Life Style Movement as a 'Parable of Sharing'. This word 'parable' is forever associated with the teaching of Jesus of Nazareth. The Greek word it translates means basically 'a placing beside, juxtaposition, comparing, comparison,'[2] thence 'a comparison, illustration, analogy.' The lexicographers Liddell and Scott go on to distinguish the New Testament usage as 'a fictitious narrative by which some religious or moral lesson is conveyed'.

I have elsewhere developed the definition further with specific reference to Jesus' own parables:

> Of the two terms of the parabolic comparison the first is fixed, the second variable. This latter is some person, thing, action or event within the experience of his hearers. The fixed term, the kingdom of heaven, exactly fitted contemporary interests and aspirations. It might seem that he could as well have said, 'the glory of God is like' or 'the love of God' is like. But to a people in bondage both to the Law on the one hand and to the Roman power on the other, it was God's kingdom, his sovereignty, which needed above all to be proclaimed and interpreted. We may take it with all reverence that the term was chosen not without much prayerful consideration of contemporary needs.[3]

When Jesus taught in parables, 'the mass of the people listened eagerly'.[4] His parables spoke to their condition. And many of those stories were, among other things, 'parables of sharing'. Only the tradition of centuries of spiritualizing these dense and complex, yet paradoxically clear and simple stories can obscure from us the call to share which is so common a feature. The

Good Samaritan for example, hero of the best known of them all, shared with the victim his time, his money, his donkey, his wine, his oil. He even risked his life. For, then as now, the injured decoy is an old trick of robbers and dacoits.[5] The great parable of the Father and the Two Sons, sometimes inadequately known as 'The Prodigal Son', is also a story about sharing. The Father in the story whom we rightly interpret as representative of God Himself, is the archetypal 'sharer': 'The younger said to his father, "Father, give me my share of the property." So he divided his estate between them.'[6] When the prodigal returned, the father's 'heart went out to him. He ran to meet him, flung his arms round him, and kissed him.'[7] To his elder son, this father is equally generous. 'My boy, you are always with me, and everything I have is yours.'[8] This elder brother is brilliantly portrayed in a few words as an unsympathetic figure who yet commands a grudging pity. He is characterized by an unwillingness to share.

The rich man at whose gate the beggar Lazarus lay,[9] is not in fact represented as a villain. Under circumstances which would have engendered in most of us a total self regard, he has the loyalty and the decency to remember his five brothers and try, though in vain, to do what he can for them. His only fault is that he is unwilling to share with his brother, Lazarus; or more probably does not in practice notice him. He looks most uncomfortably like a type of Western man, of you and me, today. The Rich Fool presents us with another portrait of Western capitalist man. A born entrepreneur, he takes the risk of financing a massive property development. 'But God said to him, "You fool, this very night you must surrender your life; you have made your money—who will get it now?"'[10]

This straightforward story always went down well with the villagers to whom, with the help of pictures, I used to try to tell it in halting Tamil, as a member of the Evangelistic Band of staff and students from St John's College, Palayamkottai, South India. I fear that they often delighted to identify the Rich Fool with their own village landlord!

All these examples so far are taken from St Luke's Gospel. And indeed Luke, an ardent champion of the poor, did specialize in recording such parables of sharing. But St Matthew's Gospel is by no means lacking. O. R. Jewiss[11] in the report already quoted reminds us that 'the Parable of the Sower illustrates the danger of riches: the seed that fell among thorn bushes is likened to those who hear the message, but the worries about this life and the love for riches choke the message, so that those who hear do not bear fruit.' (Matthew 13:22)[12]

Is this true for us as members of an affluent society? This parable is of course only a 'parable of sharing' by implication; the same might be said of the Parable of the Trusty Servant or Faithful Steward.[13] And both of these are found in Luke as well. Peculiar to Matthew and, in my opinion, highly characteristic of his writing is the great set piece of the Last Judgement and the criteria there to be applied. 'When the Son of Man comes in his glory and all the angels with him, he will sit in state on his throne, with all the nations gathered before him.'[14] This famous story is addressed to 'all the nations', the whole Human Family. The criterion of final righteousness is the criterion of sharing; sharing food with the hungry, drink with the thirsty, shelter with the stranger, clothes with the naked and friendship with those who are ill or in prison. Such sharing is accorded ultimate, eternal and decisive significance.

At a recent session of our monthly Bible Study Group at Bristol Cathedral, our leader chose from St Matthew's Gospel the Parable of the Labourers in the Vineyard.[15] We began by reading this story of a village landowner who hired day labourers to work in his vineyard, a familiar enough transaction, repeated thousands of times daily from that day to this. Every three hours he returned to the market place to recruit more men. At the end of the day he paid them all the same generally accepted subsistence wage. Those who had worked the whole day complained at this lack of differential. But he reminded them that he had fulfilled his contract with them. If he wished to be generous to the others that was his affair and not theirs.

Our leader asked each of us to identify with someone in the story; the owner of the vineyard perhaps; the men who had worked all day; or the men who worked for only one hour or a little more. One member at once identified with the men who had worked all day. To a chorus of murmured assent from others in the group who had similarly identified, he admitted that technically the owner had played fair. He had fulfilled his contract. But his method of paying out first those who had worked least—a detail in the story that had not escaped his notice—looked like deliberate provocation. Of course the hardest workers complained. He would have done the same. 'I suppose there must be more to it than that,' he concluded loyally but ruefully.

No one was keen to identify with the landowner. Perhaps a delicacy of feeling whereby we vaguely identified his role with that of God Himself held us back. At last someone said that, though a trifle eccentric, he must have been basically a good and fair-minded man. After all that was how parents should treat their children, not favouring those who worked hard at school for example, as against the slackers; but loving them all alike. That also drew a general murmur of assent.

As the only clergyman present I had managed to hold back so far. But as no one else seemed willing to identify with the late comers to the vineyard, I had a try. I did my best to set the scene. The landless day labourers assemble ever hopefully in the cool of the morning; perhaps before sunrise so as not to miss the chance of employment. The landowner comes to the market place after his bath and his breakfast. Probably he has known them all all their lives. He knows who is young and strong, who is a good worker, who has malaria or some other disability, who is getting old. It is natural enough for him to pick out the best workers and to contract with them for the usual daily wage; a miserable pittance by our standards, but enough to buy food for the family.

I imagined the unsuccessful in this process of selection hanging about hopefully. Something might turn up and save their children from going hungry to bed that night. As the hours pass, some give up and return home to the anger or the despair of their wives. Others are so keen to work that they stick it out and are rewarded at last for their persistence. The just and merciful owner of the vineyard (yes, we were right, he does to some extent represent God) comes back again and again to those who are so utterly dependent upon him. There is now no need to strike a bargain. They are eager enough to accept whatever he offers them, both because they trust him and because as permanently under-employed they have no option. I was able to point out that 'argous', the Greek word that is translated 'idle' in the older versions, simply means 'without work', that is unemployed.

So, I concluded, granted the feudal style of society that still operates in many thousands of villages throughout the world, the owner of the vineyard was the best kind of employer. He shared out the money that was considered to be a fair wage, making sure that everyone received roughly according to his need and gave according to his ability. By choosing to pay the last first, he made his purpose and policy doubly clear. God must be like that man.

The Greatest Parable of Sharing of Them All

The prophet Jeremiah once took a cooking pot to one of the city gates and invited some priests and elders to join him. A crowd gathered wondering what this strange man might do or say next. He dashed the pot to the ground, warning them that God would surely do the same to Jerusalem. Jeremiah was flogged for his pains and put in the stocks. The authorities were so angry, I think, because they believed that Jeremiah's acted parable might prove even more powerful than his prophetic words in bringing about what he proclaimed. In their minds there was a sense that the pot really was Jerusalem in the breaking, certainly an effective sign of the destruction of the city of God. So they hated him and tried in vain to silence him.

I have long been convinced that Jesus was in this same tradition of acted parables when He took bread the night before He died and broke it and gave it to His friends to eat; when He blessed the cup of wine which He had poured out for them to drink. The breaking of the bread was and is the effective, sacramental sign of the breaking of His body on the Cross. The pouring out of the wine was and is the effective, sacramental sign of the pouring out of His lifeblood in death. His distribution of the life-sustaining bread and wine for all of them to eat and to drink was and is the effective, sacramental sign of the new life which He shared with them, and through them with the whole Human Family in His rising again from death. 'Drink from it, all of you,'[17] He said. 'Take this and share it among yourselves.' 'And they all drank from it.'[18]

I have deliberately conflated quotations from each of the first three Gospels, not because this is a scholarly thing to do (it is not), but to convey the impression, which I believe to be correct, that what He did there, He did for the whole Human Family, all of us. The Eucharist is in fact, amongst other things, the sacrament of the more equitable distribution of the Earth's resources among us all—Bread for the World, a true parable of sharing.

A Cross of Nails and a Branch of Olive

> Share everything with your brother. Do not say, 'It is private property.' If you share what is everlasting, you should be that much more willing to share things which do not last . . . On the Lord's day, gather in community to break bread and offer thanks. But confess your sins first, so that your sacrifice may be a pure one. No one who has a quarrel with his brother may join your gathering, not until they are reconciled . . .

These words from that ancient book of Christian instruction, the *Didache*,[19] or *The Teaching of the Lord, through the Twelve Apostles, to the Gentiles*, may serve to introduce a contemporary series of 'parables of sharing', the Coventry Crosses of Nails. As I mentioned at the beginning of this book, these Crosses of Nails are signs of that self-same ministry of reconciliation and of sharing to which the writer of the Didache refers.

Two months before I took a Cross of Nails to the Corrymeela Community I had taken another to the Taizé Community in France. The presentation at Taizé took place on the Feast of the Transfiguration 1971, the feast of the Dedication of the Taizé Brothers' Community Church. Some fifteen hundred young people from many nations were there and some older people too. Such assemblies occur daily throughout the summer at Taizé, a tiny hamlet in Burgundy. One Easter some seven thousand young people had turned up to celebrate the Risen Christ and the springtime of the Church; and the Community had taken the decision, both practical and symbolic, to tear down a section of the wall of the church for the occasion and place up against it a great marquee to accommodate all the worshippers.

When, the evening before, I had shown the Cross of Nails to the Prior, Brother Roger, he had spontaneously grasped it and pressed it to his lips. We had met in the chapel for the Orthodox in the undercroft of the church. He also seized a lighted candle and gave it to me. After some use in our home at Christmas and for other celebrations, I gave it in turn to the Cross of Nails Centre at Holland Hostel in Kowloon, Hong Kong. In the bowl of Taizé ware in which it stood, now stands the Fitzharding Candle in Bristol Cathedral. But these are other stories.

Brother Roger accepted the Cross of Nails in the Community Church with some generous yet perceptive words. He went on to speak of another gift recently received: a sprig of olive, sent by a young Portuguese on compulsory military service in southern Africa, a cog in the ramshackle machine of his country's remnant of Empire. Brother Roger read from the accompanying letter (which I quote only from a memory somewhat clouded by the emotional impact of the event): 'I am a poor labourer whose job is to look after the olive trees. But they took me away from my trees and put a gun in my hands. What have I to do with a gun? I send you, my brother, this sign of love and of peace and ask you to pray that whatever happens I may live and act in the spirit of the olive branch.'

In the complete stillness of the darkening, close-packed church, we experienced together a 'parable of sharing'. The gleaming Cross of Nails, the grey green olive branch glowing in our imaginations, the lighted candle plucked from the Orthodox altar all were effective, quasi-sacramental signs of a profound sharing in the life of the Spirit.

It is in fact to the Taizé Community in the first place that I personally owe the notion of a 'parable of sharing'. In the 'Second Letter to the People of God'[20] we read:

As a contribution to another future for all, the People of God has one possibility all its own: spread across the entire world, it can build up a parable of sharing in the human family. Such a parable will have force enough to propagate itself, shaking even the most immovable systems and creating communion throughout the whole human family.

To lead the People of God into this radicalism of the Gospel you, now reading this letter, whether you be young or old, begin at once to make your own life a parable of sharing, by accomplishing concrete acts whatever the cost . . . The creation with others of a parable of sharing is first and foremost a question of material possessions. It begins with a transformation of the way you live . . . In transforming your life, nobody is asking you to opt for stark austerity without any beauty or joy.

Share everything you have and freedom will be yours.

Resist the urge to consume—the more you buy the more you need. The accumulation of reserves, for yourself or for your children, is the beginning of injustice . . . It is not possible to change living-standards overnight. So we call upon families, Christian communities and Church leaders, to establish a plan covering seven years, enabling them to give up, in successive stages, everything that is not absolutely in-

dispensable, beginning with what is spent on prestige . . .
Sharing is also going to mean changes in where you live. Turn
your home into a place of constant welcome, a house of peace
and forgiveness.

Simplify where you live, but without demanding the same
of older people whose homes are filled with memories . . . The
parable of sharing also concerns your working life . . . Work
to earn what you need, never to accumulate more.

Sharing involves the human family as a whole. It is essential to struggle together for the goods of the earth to be rightly
shared. A redistribution of wealth requires the industrialized
nations to do more than just give away their surplus. The
system underlying international injustice must be changed at
all costs.

If the Church gives up all that is not absolutely essential . . .
she will begin a hope which has no end.

That Second Letter to the People of God was written in
Calcutta in 1976, some four years after our Life Style Movement
saw the light of day. It has so much in common with our
Movement's aspirations but looks like stronger meat. It has
proved more effective, being rooted in the struggle and in the
contemplation of a Community who are practising what they
preach; the contemplation of God's sharing with us no less than
His Only Beloved Son, and the struggle that 'man be no longer
the victim of man'. 'The rediscovery of the necessary unity
between contemplation and resistance, the mystical and the
prophetic,' writes Kenneth Leech, 'is perhaps the central need of
modern Christianity.'[21] And he quotes Daniel Berrigan: 'The
time will shortly be upon us, if it is not already here, when the
pursuit of contemplation becomes a strictly subversive activity
. . . I am convinced that contemplation, including the common
worship of the believing, is a political act of the highest value,
implying the riskiest of consequences to those taking part.'[22]

In a 'Parable of Sharing' such as I hope and pray the Life Style
Movement might increasingly become, struggle and contemplation come together. Eva-Maria Antz, inspired by Taizé, writes:

A parable is a certain way of expressing something, an anticipation. Living a parable means making a thought or a word
come alive. Living a parable in the Church means making
visible, here and now, something of the Kingdom of God. It is
always just a few, a small number who follow this road. But

do not they become the seed which grows in the love of God
and bears fruit a hundredfold? And is not this very question
the hope which keeps us moving forward?[23]

'Good Luck, Old Man'

The Community Church at Taizé is a modern building designed
for a religious Community within the Reformed tradition. It was
built with the help of members of 'Aktion Suhnezeichen' (Action
for Reparation, now renamed Service for Peace), the continuing
group of young Germans who are committed to build both
materially and spiritually in places where their fathers were
agents of destruction. By contrast the church of St Paul's
Outside the Walls in Rome, to which I took a Coventry Cross of
Nails six months later, is one of the great patriarchal basilicas of
Western Christendom. According to a tradition, supported by
such archaeological evidence as is available, it houses the tomb
of St Paul himself. By an imperial rescript of A.D. 386, orders
were given to replace the previous church by a magnificent
basilica with five aisles and eighty columns. The present
building, which can accommodate a congregation of some
twelve thousand people, replaces the one which was partially
destroyed by fire in 1823. By contrast with the burning of
Coventry Cathedral in the course of the most universal public
quarrel in human history, St Paul's roof was set on fire by a
private quarrel of deafening insignificance. A workman on the
roof threw the contents of a burning brazier at another who, as I
was told, was taunting him for his inadequacy as a husband.
Some glowing coals rolled unheeded into the gullies.

On the Sunday before Christmas 1971 some twelve hundred
people had assembled at midday, as was their custom, for the
weekly 'Youth Mass' under the gorgeous mosaic roof of the
great apse. In this mosaic Pope Honorious III, who in A.D. 1226
restored the ancient work, had had himself portrayed in full
eucharistic vestments as a small beetle at the feet of the ascended
Lord. Every Sunday morning the Benedictine Community to
whom this partiarchal church had been entrusted for a thousand
years and more, celebrated the Mass in full traditional
Gregorian style at half past ten. Then at the 'Youth Mass' at
noon a choir with guitars would take over the leading of the
music. Boys and girls read the scriptures, friends and strangers
held hands during the Lord's Prayer. During the communion of
the people, the congregation sang Italian versions of such songs

as 'We shall overcome', 'The Saints come marching home' and 'Were you there when they crucified my Lord?'.

When I rose at sermon time during the Mass to make the presentation, the retired Italian bishop sitting next to me behind the altar, whom I had supposed to be innocent of English, leaned over and whispered in a faultless Oxbridge accent, 'Good luck, old man!'. Equally delightful was the 'peace', shared as it now is again throughout the world before the Eucharistic prayer. Husbands and wives, boyfriends and girlfriends hugged each other. Some thirty members of the congregation crowded the sanctuary to shake our small party warmly by the hand and welcome us in English, French or Italian as they were able. At Bristol Cathedral by the way, our sharing of the 'peace' is more restrained, adjusted to the temperament of the English middle-aged and the mores of the English middle class. 'What happens on Match of the Day after a goal has been scored won't do for us,' a friend had duly warned me when I was about to introduce the practice.

'The Mass is ended. Go in peace.' At once a hundred people surged forward, crowding the Cross of Nails now placed on the altar, shaking our hands, asking a stream of questions. Three old ladies in black kissed the Cross with transparent devotion as Brother Roger had done. Then we all went off to lunch, enjoying 'recreation' afterwards with the monks in the room in which good Pope John in the presence of his cardinals had formally announced the Second Vatican Council. Benedictine hospitality, by the way, is in itself a 'parable of sharing'. Nearly two years later I also took a Cross of Nails to the Abbey Church of St Miniato al Monte, on the outskirts of Florence. We presented the Cross during the Good Friday ceremonies. The next day, Eric Buchan, the other priest in our party, and I were invited to lunch with the brothers. After the lengthy Latin prayers which precede lunch, Father Abbot announced in English that 'because of the presence of our beloved English guests we have advanced the feast of Easter in all things other than liturgical by twenty-four hours!' Broad smiles wreathed the faces of the expectant monks and we all sat down to a splendid feast with excellent wines!

But let us return to St Paul's Outside the Walls. In the spirit of that Second Vatican Council and under the exuberant leadership of Abbot Franzoni, St Paul's had become in itself an effective 'parable of sharing', a 'voice for the voiceless',[24] expressed in deeds as well as in words. When the workers in two industries, believing themselves to have been victimized by being 'locked out', had retaliated by occupying their factories, St Paul's had judged it right to help them financially to feed and clothe their families. Neo-Fascist demonstrations followed. I was told that the guitars of some of the youth choir were broken over their heads in church by invading rowdies. At a more personal level of ministry some church members had taken into their own homes mentally disturbed adolescents whose own parents had found them to be too violent to be received back home during or after treatment.

This particular 'parable of sharing' extended far beyond such concern for the 'exclusi', the 'dropped out'—a more accurate description than our 'drop outs'—of their own city. As the crisis mounted which led to war in Bangladesh, the Abbot called the community and the congregation to a fortnight of fasting and prayer. In the light of this commitment and of the reflections and insights it produced, he sent a considered appeal for certain specific action to the Indian, the Pakistani and his own Italian governments. One of the monks told me that from time immemorial the Abbot of St Paul's had been consecrated bishop on his appointment, *honoris causa* and to give him dignity, precedence and status. But Abbot Franzoni had caused many a raised eyebrow in the Vatican establishment by refusing this honour on the proper ground that it was a bishop's job to be the chief pastor of his diocesan flock and that it would be quite improper to use this holy office as a means of conferring status or prestige. It is indeed sad to record that, for what precise reasons I never heard, Father Franzoni was suspended from priestly duties in 1974. I wrote to him assuring him of my prayers and support. His reply began: 'I thank you with all my heart for your words. I hope in God for better times.' 'Parables of sharing' can be people as well as things, actions as well as words.

We Must Sing to Them

There is a Coventry Cross of Nails at St Paul's Cathedral, Calcutta. I have already referred to the visit which Canon Subir Biswas arranged for our ecumenical choir to Prem Dan, one of the homes for the destitute and ill which are run by Mother Teresa's Missionaries of Charity. Let Dr Suranjan Bhattacharji, a young doctor from Vellore describe the scene at Prem Dan, the name which means 'Gift of Love'.

Started only a few years ago, it is housed in the huge ICI building off Park Circus. Across the road are numerous tanneries—and so, when the wind is right, the whole of Premdan is suffused with an 'exotic' smell! I've been told that the odour is good for Tuberculosis patients and it may well be! One can only sympathize with the AFB (Acid fast bacillus —TB germ) which stage a walk-out under the circumstances . . . Outside the walls of Premdan is a high pile of tender coconut shells. They are collected from the streets all over the city, wherever they are strewn by thirsty Calcuttans. At Premdan the fibres they yield are used to make ropes and doormats. While the mothers are thus occupied, the children attend a school run by the Sisters.

Both outpatient and inpatient facilities are available in Premdan . . . the daily general dispensary . . . free Homoeo-pathic, Opthalmic and Dental clinics. There are two large 'general' wards (so called because they contain non-TB patients) . . . At the back of the main building there is a ward for women psychiatric patients. Upstairs there is a forty-bed children's ward, mainly admitting malnourished patients . . . Sister Albertina 'mothers' the children . . .[25]

Mother Teresa was away from Calcutta when we visited Prem Dan but Sister Albert, as she introduced herself to us, soon made us welcome. First we visited the children's ward which is her special responsibility. To see the more recent arrivals, destitute and abandoned children brought in from the streets by the police or by well-wishers, was a shock even to the three of us in the party who had lived in India before. But Sister Albert cheerfully assured us that, given good food and above all love, all of them had a good hope of recovering their health before too long.

We then moved to the women's psychiatric ward. Sister Albert told us that many of the women had come to Calcutta from the surrounding villages, looking for their husbands who had preceded them, seeking work, and had simply disappeared. She told us what a joy it was when a woman recovered suffic-iently to be returned to her village, her family and friends; a joy of course tinged with a great grief if the husband were still missing. Meanwhile some of the women paced up and down. Others sat still and listless. Others swayed to and fro. I shall never forget their misery.

Someone said: 'We must sing to them.' The choir lined up. They sang the Twenty-third Psalm. The effect was miraculous. The moaning and the listless wandering stopped. All attention was riveted on the singers. There were tears in the eyes of some, both singers and audience. At the end the women smiled and greeted us with the traditional Indian greeting of hands raised and joined in recognition of the divinity within the other. Then one woman came forward and began to sing; a prayer to the Lord Krishna, Sister Albert told us, that he would redeem her from her agony. Thus was enacted a small 'parable of sharing' within a greater one. The 'parable of sharing' wrought by Mother Teresa and her devoted sisters is rightly known throughout the world. At Prem Dan we were enabled to take part. What we had to offer was in worldly terms hopelessly unsuitable. It is probable that none of those women could understand a word of English. The Twenty-third Psalm was a closed book to them and the Western tradition of music was totally strange. But they sensed that these strangers were sharing what they could with them. So they responded with smiles and shared a moment of healing sanity.

We returned to the Children's Ward to sing madrigals. Some of the children beat time and grinned. We sang in the general wards, then passed the chapel's open door. This was a bare, square room, containing only a small wooden altar table, mats on the floor and on the wall a crucifix, flanked by the words in English, 'I thirst.' Such was the effect of our experiences that we filed silently into this holy place. Most of us were there for quarter of an hour on our knees; something that one member told me she had never done before.

Share Your Bread, Share Your Life
Chief Seattle's 'Lament' was delivered in 1854, the year before a treaty-making council was held in the North West between fourteen Indian tribes and the United States Government. It began as follows:

> The Great White Chief in Washington sends word that he wishes to buy our land. The Great Chief also sends us words of friendship and goodwill. This is kind of him, since we know he has little need of our friendship in return. But we will consider your offer. For we know that if we do not sell, the white man may come with guns and take our land.

How can you buy or sell the sky, the warmth of the land? The idea is strange to us.

If we do not own the freshness of the air and the sparkle of the water, how can you buy them? Every part of this earth is sacred to my people. Every shining pine needle, every sandy shore, every mist in the dark woods, every clearing, every humming insect is holy in the memory and experience of my people. The sap which courses through the trees carries the memories of the red man.

The white man's dead forget the country of their birth, when they go to walk among the stars. Our dead never forget this beautiful earth, for it is the mother of the red man. We are part of the earth and it is part of us. The perfumed flowers are our sisters; the deer, the horse, the great eagle, these are our brothers. The rocky crests, the juices in the meadows, the body heat of the pony, and man—all belong to the same family . . . This shining water that moves in the streams and rivers is not just water but the blood of our ancestors . . . The rivers are our brothers, they quench our thirst . . . carry our canoes and feed our children.[26]

There is poetry in the 'parable of sharing', whether written or spoken, embodied in a person or acted out in a Movement of those who 'propose to live more simply that all of us may simply live'. There is poetry and there is song:

Share your bread. Share your life. Share your joys. Share your sorrows.
  Share, always share.
  Whatever happens on your way, Sun or clouds, Mud or flowers. Share, always share.
  Whatever happens in your life, Songs and dances, Hope or even fear. Share, always share.
  To the end of your road, To the end of your journey.
  Without waiting for tomorrow, Give your heart and your hand.[27]

This may not be great poetry, but it is good to sing particularly in the original French and in the company of pilgrims. Which of my readers would like to put to music these words from the 'Declaration of Conscience'[28] written in prison by the Korean Christian, Kim Chi Ha?

As you cannot go to heaven alone,
Food is to be shared . . .
As all share the sight of the heavenly stars,
So food is something that must be shared . . .
Ah! food is something that must be shared.

NOTES

Chapter One
[1] From 'The Commitment of Each Member of the Corrymeela Community'.
[2] The phrase 'a parable of sharing' which forms part of the title of this book has come to me from the Taizé Community. See Chapter Nine.
[3] André Frossard, *God exists. I have met Him* (Collins, 1970).
[4] Both Einstein (1919) and Rutherford (1932) are quoted by Kenneth Vicary. 'The nutritional improvement of life', *Health and Hygiene*, vol. 1, no. 1.
[5] Translated by Norman Kemp, III, 2, 2, p. 635, as quoted by D. L. Edwards *Ian Ramsey, Bishop of Durham. A Memoir* (Oxford, 1973).
[6] Hans Kung, *On Being a Christian*, p. 70 (Collins, 1974).

Chapter Two
[1] Paulo Freire quoted in War on Want Pamphlet no. 77.
[2] Darryl D'Monte, *Guardian*, 27 June 1975.
[3] Kevin Rafferty, *Guardian*, 9 October 1978.
[4] Rosamund Essex, *Church Times*, 2 September 1978.
[5] F. J. Glendenning. 'The Servant of the Servant Church'. For a similar 'parable' compare 'The Height of Absurdity', *New Internationalist*, no. 39, May 1976.
[6] Altaf Gauhar, *Guardian*, 11 September 1978.
[7] Simon Winchester, *Guardian*, 9 June 1978.
[8] Jill Tweedie, *Guardian*, 11 November 1974.
[9] Paulo Freire. See note 1 above.
[10] The title theme of *New Internationalist* no. 56, October 1977. This section owes much to this issue of an impressive monthly. See also *Guardian* article, 'The Farmer is a Wife', 4 April 1978

and Jenny Rathbone, 'The Meek Who Inherit Nothing', *Guardian*, 9 October 1978.

[11] This reference is not dated in my source—an information sheet prepared for a conference on 'What about tomorrow?' at Guildford, October 1976.

[12] *Epworth Review*, September 1975.

[13] John 4:1-42.

[14] Stephen F. Bayne Jr., *Caring for God's World*.

[15] *New Internationalist*, no. 32, October 1975.

[16] John Donne (1572-1631), Dean of St Paul's.

[17] From a study document entitled 'World poverty and our responsibility'.

[18] In *Population and Social Organization*, edited by Moni Nag and summarized in *New Internationalist*, no. 52, June 1977. A 'Population Special' issue.

[19] Richard Norton Taylor, *Guardian*, 14 January 1977.

[20] Barbara Ward and René Dubos. *Only One Earth*, p. 176.

[21] Edward Goldsmith. 'This Very Dangerous Illusion of a Third World Problem', *Guardian*, 25 April 1979.

[22] Bill Penney, '1975 and Beyond', Kent Industrial Chaplaincy, Study Paper.

[23] Adrienne Keith Cohen, *Guardian*, 22 April 1978.

[24] Otto Koenigsberger, in a paper written for the 1976 International Habitat Conference.

[25] Barbara Ward, 'A New Creation', quoted by Ian Breach, *Guardian*, 29 November 1976.

[26] Roger H. Charlier, 'Death of the Great Lakes?', *New Scientist*, 18 December 1969.

[27] Anthony Tucker, *Guardian*. My cutting does not bear the date.

[28] Anthony Tucker, *Guardian*, 20 June 1977.

[29] Evelyn Wroe in a leaflet published by the Church Missionary Society.

[30] *Sunday Times Magazine*, 18 November 1973.

[31] From Soren Kierkegaard, *The Gospel of Suffering*, p. 123. Translated by David and Lillian Svenson (Augsburg Publishing House). Quoted by Vernard Eller, *The Simple Life*, p. 12 (Hodder and Stoughton, 1973).

[32] Barbara Ward and René Dubos, *Only One Earth*, pp. 45, 46.

[33] From information accompanying the Grimes Graves (East Anglian prehistoric flint mines) exhibition in the British Museum 1975.

[34] Klaus Bockmuhl, 'Conservation and Life Style', quoting W. L. Oltmans *Die Grenzen des Wachstums, Pro und Contra*, English translation Grove booklets (1977).

[35] Richard Leakey and Roger Lewin, *Origins*, reviewed in *The Guardian*, 19 November 1977.

[36] From 'Life style, Ecology and Christian Responsibility', a lecture I gave at Valparaiso University, Indiana, USA, March 1975.

[37] See particularly Lester R. Brown, *The Twenty-ninth Day* (Norton, 1978).

[38] Fawley lecture 1978, 'A Second Look at Doom'.

[39] *Guardian*, 10 September 1975. The car is British Leyland's Jaguar XJS.

[40] E.g. Peter Preston, *Guardian*, 31 January 1973; Richard Boston. *Guardian*, 9 October 1976; Dennis Barker, *Guardian*, 7 July 1979.

[41] Quoted by Simon Barrington Ward, *CMS Newsletter*, April 1975.

[42] Orwell Park (Preparatory school) Magazine, 1978.

[43] *Guardian*, 17 October 1972.

[44] Catalogue supplied by Bourne and Hollingsworth.

[45] 'Economies That Go Up In Smoke', *Guardian*, 6 June 1978. See also Richard Norton Taylor, 'Big Seven Pass Round a Packet', *Guardian*, 13 November 1978.

[46] Mike Miller, Published by War on Want.

[47] *Guardian*, 22 January 1976.

[48] *Guardian*, ibid.

[49] Richard Boston, 'Holy Write-off in the Sky', *Guardian* article. My cutting is undated.

[50] 'Britain's Flying Overdraft', *Guardian*. My cutting does not bear the date.

[51] *Guardian*, ibid.

[52] Gerald Leach and Andrew Wilson in *The Observer*: 'New Jets Could Bring a World Oil Shortage'. My cutting does not bear the date.

[53] *Guardian*, 15 December 1977: 'Travels with an Airbus'.

[54] United Nations Publications, Sales no. E72, ix 16.

[55] Ibid, p. 36.

[56] United Nations Document A/32/88. Prepared 1976-77.

[57] Bertrand Russell, 'Has Man a Future?' Quoted in *New Internationalist*, no. 51, May 1977.

[58] Philippa Pullar, *The Times*, 28 April 1976.

[59] Anne Karpf, 'Eating Can Damage Your Health', *Guardian*, 18 June 1979, Reviewing *Food and profit—it makes you sick* (Politics of Health Group).

[60] 'One for Christian Renewal' folder, January 1978.

[61] Lester R. Brown, *The Twenty-ninth Day*.

[62] 'A Matter of Justice. Janata Colony's Fight for Life', Australian Council of Churches.

[63] Australian Council of Churches, 199 Clarence Street, Sydney, NSW.

[64] Published by War on Want, 467 Caledonian Road, London, N7 9BE.

[65] Harford Thomas, 'Closing the World Energy Gap', *Guardian*, 30 July 1976.

Chapter Three

[1] I John 1:6.

[2] From Helmut Thielicke, *The Waiting Father*: 'A prayer for use by those in doubt'.

[3] Matthew 4:4. cf. Luke 4:4, quoting Deuteronomy 8:3.

[4] 'A Litany of the Disciples of the Servant'.

[5] 'The Litany of Reconciliation', Coventry Cathedral.

[6] Y. T. Yevtushenko, *A Precocious Autobiography*.

[7] *Christian Aid News*. My cutting does not carry the date.

[8] Hymn by Brian Wren. From 'Growing Joy', an order of service for Christian Aid Week 1978.

[9] John V. Taylor, *Enough is Enough* (SCM Press).

[10] Numbers 11:29.

[11] Quoted in the programme for a conference on 'Communicating Survival. Teaching for a Sustainable Future'. Friends House, Euston Road. 29 October 1973.

[12] From Geoffrey Parrinder. *The Wisdom of the Forest*, quoting Brihad-Aranyaka.

[13] 'Poverty as a World Problem'. War on Want article published by 'One for Christian Renewal'.

[14] H. W. Montefiore, 'Doom or Deliverance'. The Rutherford Lecture delivered on 19 November 1971 (Manchester University Press).

[15] E. F. Schumacher, Address to the Catholic Institute for International Relations, 13 June 1975.

[16] H. W. Montefiore, from an article in *The Observer* based on the 1971 Rutherford Lecture (Manchester University Press).

[17] *Guardian*, February 1976.

[18] *Guardian*, 3 July 1978.

[19] *Guardian*, 18 April 1979. cf. Peter Jenkins, *Guardian*, 10 April 1979.

[20] *Guardian*, 1 February 1979, 'After the Answers, What Else?'.

[21] Published in *Three Crowns*, Bristol Diocesan News, September 1978, and reprinted in the *Bristol Evening Post*. Out of the candidates for the Bristol constituencies one Conservative and one Ecology Party candidate published their answers to this catechism in the Bristol Evening Post.

[22] Published in *The Guardian*, 2 May 1977.

[23] *Guardian*. My cutting does not bear the date.

[24] *Guardian*, 21 June 1977.

[25] *Guardian*, 25 June 1977.

[26] *The Australian*, 4 August 1978.

[27] 'Don't Leave It All To The Experts. The Citizen's Role In Environmental Decision Making', published by the US Environmental Protection Agency, Office of Public Affairs (Washington DC 20460).

[28] Ibid.

[29] The (Anglican) Australian Prayer Book. Holy Communion. Second order, p. 141.

[30] Nick Downie, *Guardian*, 14 May 1979.

[31] Published by Foodshare, Bedford Chambers, Covent Garden, London WC2. Undated.

[32] As reported by Albert Tévoédiré. *Poverty; Wealth of Mankind* (Pergamon). Reviewed in *New Internationalist*, No. 76, June 1979, p. 30.

[33] Hamish McRae, *Guardian*, 24 October 1977.

[34] *Washington Post*. My copy is undated.

[35] *Hamlet*, III, 2:255.

[36] From a *Guardian* article written in the early seventies. I have taken the liberty of doubling the figure of £50,000 which occurred in Davis' text, as some adjustment to inflation.

[37] Victor Keegan, *Guardian*, 8 February 1978.

[38] *Guardian*, 24 January 1978. Review of *Britain 1978* (Stationery Office).

[39] 'Household Readership, Income and Consumption'. A summary report issued by Mirror Group Newspapers Ltd. Reviewed in *The Guardian*. My copy does not bear the date.

[40] John Davis, *Guardian*, 'Phoney figures in the Price Index'. My cutting does not bear the date.

[41] John Madeley, *Church Times*, 6 January 1978.

[42] Ibid.

[43] From *Glencoe* by John Prebble (Penguin).

[44] James 2:17.

[45] Habakkuk 2:4, cf. Romans 3:28 etc.

Chapter Four

[1] Exodus 3:13.

[2] John 7 and John 8.

[3] Isaiah 49:16.

[4] *Guardian*. My cutting does not bear the date.

[5] Pierre Gaxotte, *Mon village et Moi*, pp. 266, 267. My translation.

[6] Ibid.

[7] Robert Pirsig, *Zen and the Art of Motorcycle Maintenance* (Corgi, 1976).

[8] Subir Biswas interviewed in the Christian Aid film, 'The Living City'.

[9] Chateaubriand. Quoted in 'Back to the Trees' Development Forum, April 1976.

[10] *Guardian*, 7 April 1972. 'The Greening of the Sahara'. Wendy Campbell Purdie talks to Ruth Adam.

[11] Sir Kenneth Clark, *Civilization*, pp. 229, 230 (BBC—John Murray, 1969).

[12] *A Blueprint for Survival* (Penguin).

[13] United Nations Association News and Notes, April 1978.

[14] The Population Reference Bureau, Washington USA. Quoted in *The Guardian*, 19 April 1978.

[15] Report of the United Nations Fund for Population Activities. Reviewed by Anthony Tucker in *The Guardian*, 18 June 1979.

[16] From a Calcutta daily newspaper, 12 March 1976.

[17] Quoted by Denzil Peiris, *Guardian*, 2 July 1979.

[18] Ibid. This article is acidly entitled: 'Britain's Aid to India, a Drop in a Leaking Bucket'.

[19] E. F. Schumacher. *The Age of Plenty. A Christian View*, pp. 4, 5 (St Andrew Press, 1974).

[20] Ibid.

[21] Quoted by Dr Don Warren, *New Villages Association Newsletter*, 10, Spring 1978.

[22] Romans 8:31-39.

[23] Hebrews 11:1ff.

[24] Obtainable from the Faith and Order Commission, World Council of Churches.

[25] I Peter 3:15.
[26] Romans 8:25.
[27] *A Common Account of Hope.*
[28] Ibid.
[29] Ibid.
[30] Jurgen Moltmann, *A Theology of Hope*, pp. 25, 34, (SCM).
[31] Ibid, p. 324.
[32] Ibid, p. 166, c.f.p. 182.
[33] Rabindranath Tagore. *The Hidden God*, quoted by Tissa Balasuriya, *The Eucharist and Human Liberation*, p. 165.
[34] Charles Wesley, 'Come O Thou Traveller Unknown', Methodist Hymn Book, No. 449.
[35] Jorgen Lissner. See 'Ten Reasons for Choosing a Simpler Life Style', quoted above.

Chapter Five

[1] Published by One for Christian Renewal as a Broadside, 1979.
[2] I John 1:1.
[3] *Unity Begins at Home* (SCM, 1964).
[4] Quoted in E. Milner White and G. W. Briggs, *Daily Prayer* (OUP) p. 173.
[5] From a paper I read to the first International Conference of the Community of the Cross of Nails at Ottobeuren Abbey, April 1972.
[6] From the cover of David L. Edwards, *The British Churches Turn to the Future* (SCM, 1973).
[7] Ibid, p. 73.
[8] Ibid. At about this time One for Christian Renewal published an excellent Group Study Kit entitled 'Can Man Survive?'.
[9] Ibid, p. 75.
[10] Christopher Hall, 'Face to Faith'. *Guardian*, 21 April 1979.
[11] 'Letter from Taizé', no. 27, September 1976.
[12] Fully reported in Eloise E. Lester, *Ecology and Christian Responsibility*, published by the Community of the Cross of Nails, Coventry Cathedral 1976.
[13] *Crusade* Magazine, 19 Draycott Place, London SW3 2SJ.
[14] John W. Taylor, *Enough is Enough* (SCM, 1975), p. 109. Edward Patey, *Christian Life Style* (Mowbrays, 1976), p. 69. Patrick Rivers, *Living Better on Less* (Turnstone Press, 1977), pp. 40-3.
[15] Christian Aid annual report. Postscript 1975.
[16] Ibid.

[17] Quoted from 'Our Daily Bread. A Policy for the Diocese of Bristol 1975' obtainable from Church House, 23 Great George Street, Bristol 1.

[18] *Church Times*, 18 November 1977.

[19] Oxfam, Ref. S 189/75.

[20] Aide Mémoire of the Commission on the Churches' Participation in Development Core Group Meeting on New Life Styles. Geneva, 28 November 1977.

[21] Charles Foubert, 'Analysis of the Contents of IDOC Documentation on New Life Styles', undated. IDOC means International Documentation and Communication Centre.

[22] Hans Opschoor, *A Case Study. The New Life Styles Movement in the Dutch Churches 1975-1977*. With grateful acknowledgement to this the main source for this section.

[23] Statistics obtained from Ronald J. Sider, *Rich Christians in an Age of Hunger*, pp. 44, 45.

[24] Fremtiden I Vare Hender, Postgiro 22319000 Postboks 5304, Majorstua, Oslo 3.

[25] Quoted in *Christian Aid News*. My cutting does not carry the date.

[26] 'In Search of the New', Folder 11. Documents published by the Commission on the Churches' Participation in Development.

[27] Ibid. Manfred Linz. 'It Can Be Done, If We Make a Beginning'.

[28] Ibid.

[29] *A Case Study*. See note 22 above.

[30] 'Alternatives', *Guardian*, 8 March 1978.

[31] Brad Knickerbocker, *Christian Science Monitor*, 18 July 1977.

[32] Reproduced by Food Conspiracy', 412 N Fourth Avenue, Tucson, USA.

[33] *The Futurist*, vol. XI, no. 4, August 1977. World Future Society, 4916 S Elmo Ave, Washington DC 20014, USA.

[34] Quoted by S. Barrington Ward, *CMS Newsletter*, April 1975.

[35] CMS Magazine *Yes*. Interview entitled 'Life Style Indian Style'. My cutting does not carry the date.

[36] *New Internationalist*, May 1978.

[37] *Guardian*, 28 April 1978.

[38] Joseph Kraft. 'A Talk with Trudeau', *Washington Post*, 17 May 1977. Quoted by Lester R. Brown, *The Twenty-ninth Day*, p. 260.

Chapter Six

[1] David Sheppard, *Built as a City* (Hodder and Stoughton, 1974).

[2] Ibid.

[3] Council for Education in World Citizenship, Broadsheet, May/June 1977.

[4] Charles Elliott 'The Issues and Opportunities Facing the Church in Serving the Whole Man', Lutheran World Federation Consultation, Nairobi, October 1974.

[5] A. de Tocqueville, *Democracy in America*, II, Book IV, ch. 6 (World's Classics edition), p. 579. Quoted by J. Moltmann *Theology of Hope*, p. 319.

[6] *New Internationalist*, No. 63, May 1978.

[7] Jackie Gillott in *The Guardian*, 'The Era of Greed'. My cutting does not bear the date.

[8] *Guardian*, 2 January 1979.

[9] Ivan Illich, *Celebration of Awareness* (Calder and Boyers, 1971). Also in Penguin (1976).

[10] Matthew 7:5.

[11] *The Ice Age* (Weidenfeld and Nicolson, 1977) p. 128.

[12] CMS Magazine *Yes*, July/September 1975.

[13] Matthew 8:11.

[14] *Guardian*, 10 October 1967.

[15] See chapter V, note 34. S. Barrington Ward, *CMS Newsletter*, April 1975.

[16] Reported by Stuart Wavell, 'Jungle Warfare', *Guardian*, 21 May 1975.

[17] Johann Gaultung is Professor of Conflict and Peace Research, University of Oslo.

[18] John Lickorish, 'The Psychology of Inflation', *Guardian*, 15 July 1974.

[19] From *God on Monday* (Hodder and Stoughton, 1966).

[20] Sixth edition, 1979.

[21] SLIM, 27 Blackfriars Road, London SE1 8NY.

[22] *Bristol University Newsletter*, 27 April 1978.

[23] Oswald Barraclough *To Morrow: a Conservationist's View of the Future* (Conservation Society, 1977).

[24] Quoted in 'A Giant upon the Earth', an act of worship for European Christians.

[25] *Guardian*, 11 April 1972.

[26] *Guardian* article, 'Third World to the Rescue'. My cutting is undated.

[27] *Guardian*, 19 May 1972.

[28] *Three Crowns*, Bristol Diocesan News, June 1978.

[29] *Guardian*, 3 October 1975. Harford Thomas reviews *The*

Roots of Inflation by a symposium of eight American economists (Wilton House Publications).

[30] Hugh Hebert, 'The Price of Getting the Cans in the Can', *Guardian*, 28 February 1979.

[31] *Guardian*, 14 May 1979.

[32] Ibid.

[33] Sushma Kumar, 'The Poor Consumer', *New Internationalist*, no. 37, March 1976.

[34] *New Internationalist*, e.g. August 1973 and April 1977.

[35] *Guardian*, 25 January 1979. Richard Norton Taylor reviews *Insult to Injury*, Charles Medawar (Social Audit Ltd).

[36] Ibid.

[37] *Guardian*. 'Buyers' Guide to Economic Power'. My cutting carries no date.

[38] 33 Saddler Street, Durham. See the *Northern Echo*, 13 February 1978.

[39] John V. Taylor, *CMS Newsletter*, no. 363, September 1972: 'Enough is enough' Dr Taylor has of course developed this theme in his well-known book of the same title (SCM Press, 1975).

[40] I Timothy 6:9, 10, NEB.

[41] Thucydides, *History of the Peloponnesian War*, II 6.40 (Everyman Library translation).

Chapter Seven

[1] These figures come from an excellent but undated study guide on 'Money' published by the Servants of Christ the King, 29 Southwood Ave., London N6.

[2] See Colin Tudge, *The Famine Business* (Faber and Faber). Also Susan George, *How the Other Half Dies* (Pelican, 1976).

[3] J. V. Taylor, *Enough is Enough* (SCM, 1975). Compare also Klaus Bockmuhl, *Conservation and Lifestyle*, English translation Grove Booklets (1977).

[4] June 1977. I do not know where this 'monthly group' operates.

[5] II Corinthians 8:9.

[6] Book of Common Prayer, quoting Luke 1:52, 53.

[7] Quoted, along with other relevant authorities by T. Balasuriya, *The Eucharist and Human Liberation* (SCM Press, 1979), p. 26. I was fortunate enough to be reading this book while writing this section and so have brought it under contribution.

[8] *The Spiritual Exercises*. Quoted by E. F. Schumacher, *The*

Age of Plenty, a Christian View (St Andrew Press, 1974).

[9] Hans Kung, *On Being a Christian* (Collins, 1974), pp. 595-7.

[10] Ecumenical Press Service, No. 33, 7 December 1978.

[11] Study Encounter, No. 39, 1975. Another publication of the World Council of Churches.

[12] Mark 10:22.

[13] I have been unable to verify this reference.

[14] Quoted in the Bristol University Catholic Chaplaincy News Sheet, Autumn Term 1976, No. 5.

[15] This particular version of an increasingly popular prayer is taken from the Royal Tudor Ware plate made by Barker Brothers, Stoke-on-Trent.

[16] *The Eucharist and Human Liberation*, p. 117. See note 10.

[17] *The Observer*, 19 December 1971.

[18] *The Universe*, 19 April 1974.

[19] *The Eucharist and Human Liberation*, p. 145. See note 10.

Chapter Eight

[1] Acts 19:23-41 (NEB).

[2] Victor Hugo quoted by Robert Kemble. 'A Church without the Church'. One for Christian Renewal, Autumn 1979.

[3] Charles Elliott, article on 'Priorities in Education for Development', 19 October 1976. See also Chapter Two, note 6.

[4] *Guardian*, 1 July 1977.

[5] Kenneth Adams, Keynote Address to the Church of England Men's Society National Conference, 24 September 1977. 'More Wealth Please'.

[6] Ibid.

[7] Quoted in Chapter Three.

[8] 'Cathedral Relief Service—Cathedral Social Service', a leaflet published in 1975.

[9] One for Christian Renewal Folder, December 1975.

[10] *Guardian*, 1 June 1979.

[11] Zweig, *The World of Yesterday*, quoted in 'Inflation, Incomes and the Churches' by 'Christian Fabian', One for Christian Renewal.

[12] Chapter Three, note 15.

[13] Luke 3:10-14.

[14] J. K. Galbraith, *The Affluent Society* (1970).

Chapter Nine

[1] Matthew 13:3, 34; 22:1; Mark 3:23; 4:2, 13, 33; 12:1.

[2] Liddell and Scott, *Greek-English Lexicon*.

[3] *Theology*, February 1954. 'The Power of Jesus is Like'. A somewhat fuller treatment of contemporary parables is attempted in my *A.D. 1980. A Study in Christian Unity, Mission and Renewal* (Lutterworth, 1966), p. 90ff.

[4] Mark 12:37 (NEB Alternative translation).

[5] Luke 10:29f.

[6] Luke 15:12.

[7] Luke 15:20.

[8] Luke 15:31.

[9] Luke 16:19ff.

[10] Luke 12:20.

[11] See Chapter Seven, note 4.

[12] See also Luke 8:14. This interpretation is also found at Mark 4:18.

[13] Matthew 24:45ff; Luke 12:42ff.

[14] Matthew 25:31.

[15] Matthew 20:1-16.

[16] Jeremiah 19:1ff.

[17] Matthew 26:28.

[18] Luke 22:17; Mark 14:23.

[19] Didache IV. 8; XIV. 1, 2. Translation by T. Balasuriya, *The Eucharist and Human Liberation*. See also Chapter Seven, note 10.

[20] Quoted here from 'Taizé and the Council of Youth', July/August 1979.

[21] 'Contemplation and Resistance', A Jubilee Group Paper published by the Church Literature Association, 7 Tufton Street, London SW1.

[22] *America is Hard to Find*, pp. 77, 78, 1973.

[23] Eva-Maria Antz quoted in 'Letter from Taizé', May 1978.

[24] 'To me the Church has no reason to exist but to give a voice to the voiceless.' Albert van den Heuvel, 'Cathedrals as places of Learning and Influence in the Community' (1966), published by Coventry Cathedral.

[25] *Vellore Newsletter*, no. 69, November 1977.

[26] 'Testimony Chief Seattle'. Resource Pack published by the United Society for the Propagation of the Gospel.

[27] Words and music by Raymond Fau.

[28] Quoted by T. Balasuriya, *The Eucharist and Human Liberation*, p. 71.